BALI

Suzanne Charlé

Suzanne Charlé first visited Bali in 1978, when only the top hotels had electricity, and coconut groves and cow pastures separated Kuta and Legian, while Nusa Dua was just the dream of some World Bank planner. 'It's great,' old hands told her, 'but you should have been here ten years ago.' In 1986, she returned to Bali for a year's study, under the auspices of Dr Mochtar Kusuma-Atmadja, the then foreign minister of Indonesia, and the Nusantara Java Foundation. Since then, Ms Charlé has divided her time between Bali and New York, where she has worked as an editor for the *New York Times*, the *Herald Tribune* and the *London Times*, as well as for various magazines, including *Connoisseur* and *Travel & Leisure*. She is co-author, with Detlef Shrobane, of *The New Art of Indonesian Cooking* (Singapore: Times Editions, 1988). Now, when Suzanne's friends come to visit Bali, she too, says: 'You should have been here ten years ago. But it's fascinating now!'

Collins Illustrated Guide to

BALI

Suzanne Charlé

Photography by R Ian Lloyd

COLLINS
8 Grafton Street, London W1
1990

Author's Preface

When I first came to Bali in late November 1978, the island was still pretty much off the beaten track. Only a few hotels and offices in Sanur, Kuta and Denpasar had electricity. Kuta was basically a crossroads, dotted with a few shops and losmen. There was no beach road, no bypass, no fast-food joints—save the ever-present kaki-lima food carts. One-lane roads wound out to the cow pastures and palm plantations of Legian and Seminyak or up through the rice fields of Celuk and Mas. To get to Ubud was quite a trek. It was easy to meet the Balinese then—there just weren't many other Westerners around—time and again, I was greeted with kindness and humour. And time and again, I renewed my week-long visa.

Still when I left just over a month later, portents of the island's future were already in the air, as the first 707 landed at the tiny Ngurah Rai Airport.

A decade later, still larger jets are queuing up to land on the long runway of the international airport. Bali is no longer an out-of-the-way spot, but a major, world-class resort. The governor of Bali talks about the island welcoming 2,000,000, even 3,000,000 visitors annually in the near future.

This means many things: more hotels, more restaurants, easier access, better communications; also more traffic jams and modern-day hassles. It also means that it is harder for the visitor to meet the Balinese—there are just so many tourists. Consequently, most visitors only see the Balinese at work in hotels, shops or restaurants, or dressed up at some incredibly ornate ceremony.

By including the profiles in the book, I hope to introduce the reader to just a few individual Balinese and, in doing so, give a sense of what it's like to be Balinese today. Yes, some of them are directly influenced by tourism. But all are still tied up in the intense religious life of the island, following rites that date back millennia, yet very much part of the 20th century. Theirs is a world of fax machines and frangipani, rock'n'roll stars and demons of the dark, motorcycles and multi-tiered cremation towers.

The tourist coming to Bali to find the perfect paradise may be disappointed. The visitor coming to witness a unique and dynamic culture, that is trying to cope with many of the same problems of development found elsewhere, should be—as I certainly am—intrigued.

William Collins Sons & Co. Ltd
London • Glasgow • Sydney • Auckland
Toronto • Johannesburg

Whilst every care is taken in compiling the text, neither the Publisher
nor the Author or their respective agents shall be responsible for any
loss or damage occasioned by any error or misleading information
contained therein or any omission therefrom.

British Library Cataloguing in Publication Data
Collins Illustrated Guide to Bali
1. Indonesia. Bali—Visitors' Guides
915.98'6
ISBN 0-00-215229-0

First published in Great Britain 1990
© The Guidebook Company Ltd 1990
and Suzanne Charlé

Series Editors: May Holdsworth and Ralph Kiggell
Editor: Lesley Clark
Picture Editor: Carolyn Watts
Map Artwork: Bai Yiliang
Illustrations: George Ngan

Photograph (page 94) by Suzanne Charlé

Balinese paintings (pages 9, 71, 108–9, 196–7) reproduced courtesy of Agung Rai
Gallery, Bali; photograph (page 151) reproduced courtesy of
Dr A A M Djelantik.

Printed in Hong Kong

Contents

Acknowledgements

To thank properly everyone who helped with this book would take a chapter
in itself, something I shall spare the reader. Instead, a general *terima kasih*
(thank you) to all the Balinese who spent hours, and sometimes days, talking
about their lives and the life of the island, especially the subjects of my
profiles. Gusti Ayu Puspawati, my patient language teacher, introduced me to
a number of the Balinese who appear in these pages, as did Anak Agung Rai.
The dalang Wayan Wija often tried to help clear up questions about the
religion, as well as about wayang kulit.

Rai Girigunadhi of the Badung Government Tourism Office helped with
travel arrangements, as did Garuda Indonesia Airlines and the Nusantara Jaya
Foundation.

Others in Bali generously shared their time and knowledge including
Albert Beaucourt, Micki Altiveros and Ken Chomitz, Hildred Geertz, Rio and
Ela Helmi, Brent Hesselyn and Nancy Macy, Jean Lane, Nigel Geary and
Caroline McKinnell, Peter and Made Steenberger, Kristina Melcher, Sarita
Newson, Ketut Sarniati, Pat and Joel Siger, Wayan Sukra, Soosan and Wana
Suryawan, and Andy Toth.

Finally, thanks to Judy Warner and Max Berley who did much of the research, to my editors, and to Doc Jarden, my favourite travelling companion.

Bali, Island of Grace: an Introduction

Ever since 1902, when an outrigger pulled up on the beach at Labuan Bay and the first tourist arrived in Bali, people have come to this small island in search of paradise. Their conclusions: paradise found.

As early as the 1930s, Bali's development was a source of concern for visitors such as Margaret Mead, the anthropologist, and artist Miguel Corvarrubias. Over the years, their concerns were echoed by others. Today, inevitably, the first-time visitor is told, 'Sure, Bali's good now, but you should have been here in 19. . .', the year varying according to the date of the speaker's first visa.

They are right on both counts—the island of Bali is a jewel, with its volcanoes and undersea coral gardens, its rice terraces and sun-bleached beaches, its countless temples and above all, its unique culture and generous people.

But equally so, it has changed. In 1930, about 1,200 foreigners visited the island; in 1979, 119,272 passed through immigration; a decade later, there were over 700,000. Today, the tropical landscape is dotted with accoutrements of latter-day 20th-century life: computer clubs and a department store in the capital city and Burger King, Kentucky Fried Chicken and a Swensen's ice-cream shop in the resorts of Kuta and Sanur. 'It's not Bali,' some tourists complain, fresh off a jumbo jet, sipping their rum-and-cokes at a poolside bar. 'Yes it is,' the Balinese gently reply, 'it's just that Bali's not a museum.'

And for this we can thank the gods. If Bali were a museum, its temples would be dead, its dancers sitting on the sidelines, its musicians silent and its gods forgotten. Other sites of 'ancient' civilizations are testament to death by museumification. But Bali's gods are very much alive and a central part of the island's intense ritual life. Every temple has its day, as does just about everything else: scholars, puppets, animals, trees, even cars.

The gods' insatiable appetite for ceremony, coupled with the Balinese delight in pleasing them, has kept the arts of Bali alive. Entire villages of dancers, musicians, carvers, painters and weavers devote their work to the gods. When they're finished, they turn their thoughts back to everyday, 20th-century life.

These arts are not practised in a void. Bali is a dynamic culture and the Balinese have always been keen on new things. Centuries ago, they welcomed Hindu priests and princes and made the new gods and culture their own. Today, ideas come via television, film, radio, video as well as from tourists. Watch—on the beach, a young boy combines the fierce gestures of an ancient warrior dance with the sly moves of breakdancing; outside a trendy shop, a salesgirl in stone-washed jeans wraps a sash around her waist and makes her evening offering to the gods.

Madonna is popular now among young Balinese, right up there with *gong kebyar*, the 'heavy metal' of Bali, an incredible jazzy music played on

instruments forged by village smiths. Telephones are used to dial London and New York direct, but the *kulkul*—a split log drum—is used even in the resorts, to call neighbours together to work, to meet and to help one another.

The religion and arts remain intact largely because of the Balinese belief that the island is the property of the gods and that human inhabitants are simply privileged caretakers. The word for tourist in Bali is *tamu* (guest), a privileged and welcome visitor, deserving of hospitality and obligated to show respect and kindness to the hosts—the island's people and its gods.

Discover this paradise island for yourself. Get off the bus, walk off the beach, leave the hotel lobby. Walk through the fields at sunrise and watch young boys herding their ducks; wander country lanes in the afternoons as villagers bathe their cows, their cars and themselves in quick streams. Stroll along the beach at low tide, while women search the reef for seaweed; in the evening drop by the village *bale banjar* (meeting hall), where the local *gamelan*, or orchestra, plays and later visit a temple festival or just watch the moon rise and turn the palms to silver.

Leave behind the camera, the list of places to go, things to do and stuff to buy. Put down this book. Walk down a dirt path where fishermen nod and call out: '*Mau ke mana?*' 'Where are you going?' Answer simply: '*Jalan-jalan*', 'Just walking'. Pass women in bright sarongs carrying tall offerings of fruit and flowers atop their heads to temple. Walk slowly, slowly enough to hear the wind in the bamboo, the wings of a dragon fly, and the soft footfalls of grace.

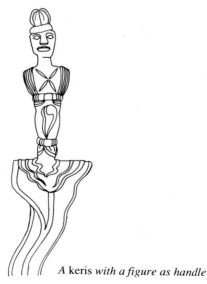

A keris with a figure as handle

Facts for the Traveller

Getting There

Visas

Citizens of the United Kingdom, United States and Australia planning a visit to Bali of two months or less do not need to obtain a visa prior to coming. They must, however, have a passport valid for six months after the date of arrival in Indonesia, plus proof of onward passage: a return airline ticket will suffice. Failure to produce the ticket at immigration may result in a quick, obligatory purchase of a full-fare (expensive) ticket at the airport. Visitors without passports valid for at least six months are simply not allowed into the country. The same rules apply to travellers holding passports from: Austria, Belgium, Brunei, Canada, Denmark, Finland, France, Greece, Iceland, Ireland, Italy, Japan, Liechtenstein, Luxemburg, Malaysia, the Netherlands, New Zealand, Norway, the Philippines, Singapore, South Korea, Spain, Sweden, Switzerland, Thailand and West Germany. Business visas for up to five weeks are available, if applications are approved by the immigration authorities. Check with local consulates for specific information.

Airport Tax

All departing travellers are required to pay an airport tax of just over $5. Lower taxes are levied for domestic travel.

Air Access

Only Garuda, the national airline, flies directly from London and Amsterdam to Bali via Jakarta and from Los Angeles via Honolulu and Biak. Additional stops must be arranged at the time of ticketing. Qantas Airways offers direct flights between Bali and Darwin, Port Hedland, Perth, Melbourne and Sydney. Continental flies from London, Sydney, Los Angeles and San Francisco, via Guam. Five other airlines fly to Jakarta where connections are made with Garuda flights. They are Thai Air, Cathay Pacific, Singapore Airlines, Malaysia Airlines System and KLM. All have offices in Bali.

Garuda Indonesia, Merpati Nusantara Airlines and BOURAQ Indonesia Airlines all offer regular inter-island flights throughout Indonesia. Garuda's flights are a little more expensive, but much more direct.

Over-booking often occurs on international flights during peak periods, such as July, August, Christmas and the Easter holidays. Travellers should reconfirm bookings 72 hours in advance and obtain a confirmation number and computer print out, if possible. Check-in time at the airport for international flights is two hours before flight time. Check in for internal flights is one hour before the scheduled flight; don't try to cut this close because flights often are taxiing on the runway at the departure time stated.

Getting Around

Transportation in Bali has a vocabulary and code of its own. It is also relatively inexpensive, fair and uncomplicated.

Public

Bemos, miniature vans, cover set routes of short distances and will stop at any point. See what other passengers offer for comparable trips before paying (it is usually about 20 cents for short hops) otherwise the driver may quote a higher price.

Inexpensive, albeit slow, **local buses** service most parts of the island and can be stopped anywhere en route. They depart from two main bus stations in Denpasar: Kreneng for east Bali; Ubung for north and west Bali. **Local minibuses** depart from the Tegal bus station in Denpasar for Kuta, Legian, Nusa Dua and Tuban.

Night buses, known as *bis malam*, leave Denpasar each night for Java. A ticket to Jakarta is less than a fifth of the price of flying. The journey, however, takes at least 26 hours and is hair raising and not particularly comfortable. Air conditioning usually means open windows.

Taxis

Airport taxis from Ngurah Rai International Airport are dispatched from a central desk outside the arrival area. Flat rates are charged to locations around Bali and fares are paid in advance at the desk. Private taxis can be called from hotels or found on street corners in the resorts. They are unmetered and prices must be negotiated beforehand.

Dokars

These tiny horse and buggies are the old-fashioned way to travel in Denpasar, Klungkung, Singaraja and Gilimanuk. There are even a few in Kuta and Legian. Fares must be negotiated with the driver.

Car and Driver

Chartering a private car with a driver as a guide is one of the best ways of seeing Bali and usually costs about $25–45 per day. Rates are significantly higher with guides. Bemos, mentioned earlier, can be chartered by the hour or by the day for even lower rates; a cheap alternative to driving on one's own and a good way to avoid frayed tempers that arise due to the poor condition of the roads, the erratic driving habits of the Balinese, and the problems of driving in a country where one doesn't understand the road signs. Negotiations must be made with the driver beforehand and passengers usually pay for the driver's meals, which cost about $2 a day.

Rental Cars and Motorbikes

Car rentals are approximately $20 per day, but weekly discounts can often be arranged. Motorbike rentals average about $7 per day, and are highly negotiable. Helmets are compulsory for drivers and passengers. Foreign drivers in Bali must carry a valid International Driver's Licence, available only in one's own country. A separate International Driver's Licence for motorcycles is also required. Visitors without such a licence must pass a difficult, frustrating test for a temporary driver's licence, given for a fee at the Traffic Police Department, Jalan Seruni, Denpasar (tel. 23199).

Driving in Bali is harrowing, at best. Trucks, buses, cars, cows, dogs, motorcycles, bikes, pedestrians and chickens all vie for their share of roads that, for the most part, started out as cow paths. Although the law is to drive on the left, most truck and bus drivers seem to believe the centre of the road is theirs and flash their lights at oncoming traffic to prove it. Smaller vehicles are frequently forced off the road, if they're lucky. Traffic accidents (particularly involving motorcycles) which were virtually unheard of a decade ago, are now a major cause of death. Even the most accomplished cyclist, after some time in Bali, will be involved in one when a stray dog runs across the road, or a car turns without signalling. Drive extra cautiously.

Ferries

A regular ferry service is available from Bali to Lombok or Java (see pages 133, 171).

Time

Indonesia is divided into three time zones with Bali on Central Indonesia Standard Time, which is Greenwich Mean Time plus eight hours.

Climate

Bali, only 8° south of the equator, enjoys a relatively mild tropical climate. On the southern coast, humidity averages about 75 percent; most days reach 30°C (86°F) and drop to 24°C (75°F) in the evening, while average daily temperatures vary no more than 6°C (10°F) from one season to the next. Mountain regions may be as much as 6°C (10°F) cooler than the coastal areas. Bali is subject to seasonal monsoons, with winds from the southeast during the dry season of April–September and from the southwest during the rainy season of October–March. July and August, *musin dingin* (the cold season), are the most pleasant, partly because of the lower temperatures and slightly lower humidity, but primarily because of the constant trade winds. Even in the rainiest months of January and February, the sun comes out on most days. Perhaps the least comfortable months are April and November, when the winds die. Because Bali is so close to the equator, days and nights are almost uniformly long with 12 hours of daylight and 12 hours of darkness. The island's proximity to the equator also spares it from typhoons and cyclones, which gain force only as they move away from the equator.

Health

Health risks tend to be greatly exaggerated by well-meaning people at home. The vast majority of visitors to Bali have no health problems. However, before travelling visitors should contact their doctors, or official vaccine centres for requirements and recommendations for inoculations and malaria prophylactics. Only a few cases of malaria have been reported in recent years. Still, the most certain way to avoid it is not to get bitten so bring mosquito repellent along and use it just before sundown.

As for eating, pity the poor tourist who comes and dines on nothing but meals out of tins and bottled water. A few simple precautions should suffice. Don't drink water out of the tap or a stream, no matter how clear it looks, stick to bottled water or water that has been boiled for ten minutes. There is no need to avoid iced drinks, as all ice vendors are government monitored.

Clothing

Save for a few old *ibu-ibu* (women), the days of the bare-breasted Balinese woman are gone. Though dress in Bali is mostly informal, rules of Western propriety apply, especially in government offices. T-shirts, skimpy tops, shorts and bathing suits are considered acceptable only for children, or adults in resort areas and on the beach. Taking cues from the Balinese hosts women should wear simple cotton skirts, dresses, or trousers and short-sleeved tops; while light-weight trousers or jeans and short-sleeved shirts are ideal for men. At night, a cotton sweater and trousers may be useful in the mountains or to attend an evening-long shadow-puppet play. Many visitors bring virtually empty suitcases and do all their shopping in Kuta and Sanur where there is plenty of stylish, inexpensive clothing.

Money

The Indonesian currency is the rupiah. Currently $1 equals about 1,800 rupiah, so 1,000 rupiah equals about 60 cents. (All prices in the book are given in US dollars.) The rupiah floats, or sinks, against the dollar and so the figure above is only approximate. The Indonesian Government has devalued the rupiah against the dollar several times in the past decade, so the rate may change dramatically, sometimes 30 percent or more, without warning. Paper currency is issued in 100, 500, 1,000, 5,000 and 10,000 rupiah denominations and there are 5, 10, 25, 50 and 100 rupiah coins.

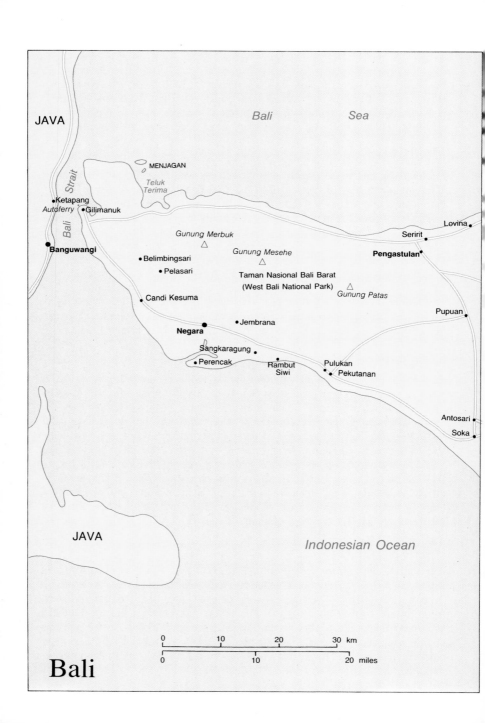

JAVA

Bali   Sea

MENJAGAN

Teluk
Terima

Strait

•Ketapang
Autoferry •Gilimanuk

Bali

Banguwangi

Gunung Merbuk
△

Lovina•

Seririt•

Gunung Mesehe
△

Pengastulan•

•Belimbingsari

• Pelasari

Taman Nasional Bali Barat
(West Bali National Park)   △
Gunung Patas

Pupuan
•

•Candi Kesuma

Negara ●   •Jembrana

Sangkaragung •

•Perencak

Rambut
Siwi

Pulukan
•
• Pekutanan

Antosari •

Soka •

JAVA

Indonesian Ocean

| 0 | 10 | 20 | 30 km |

| 0 | 10 | 20 miles |

Bali

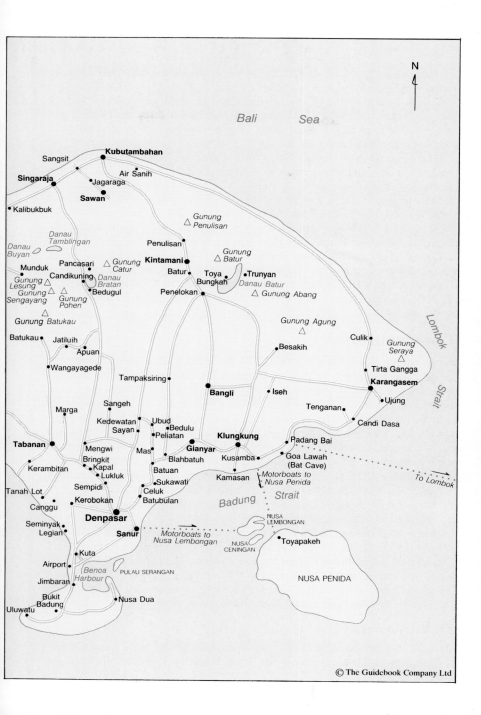

Money changers have offices in all resorts. Banks are located in Denpasar, with branches in large hotels. Banking hours are from 8 am–noon, Monday to Friday; 8–11 am, Saturday. It is advisable to change money before leaving the larger tourist areas as money changers and banks can be hard to find in more remote parts of the island. Also, keep a supply of the smallest bills as shopkeepers almost never have change.

The easiest way to transfer funds from abroad is by credit card. Present your credit card and a passport at a credit card office, and a personal cheque can be cashed against your bank account. Credit card offices also handle refunds of lost or stolen travellers cheques and emergency card replacements. American Express is at P T Pacto Ltd., Hotel Bali Beach, Sanur (tel. 88449, 88511 ext.783). It is open from 8 am–4 pm, Monday to Friday; 8 am–noon, Saturday. Visa is at Bank Duta, Jalan Hayam Wuruk 165, Tanjung Bungkak—between Sanur and Denpasar (tel. 31481). Mastercard is to be found at Bank Central Asia, Jalan Cokroaminoto 39, Denpasar (tel. 35799). Diners Club is at Nitour Travel Agency, Jalan Veteran 5, Denpasar (tel. 22791). It is open from 8 am–5.15 pm, Monday to Friday; 8–11 am, Saturday.

Communications

When calling Bali from abroad dial 62—the country code, and 361—the island code, before the local phone number. The cheapest, and sometimes the quickest, way to make international phone calls in Bali is through the *kantor telepon* (telephone office) found in all major resorts, towns and cities in Bali. Offices are open 8 am–6 pm. They are closed on Sunday. Telegrams may also be sent from phone offices. Once off the tourist trail there are no phones.

International telephone calls can be made from almost any major hotel, but there is usually a steep surcharge. Many of these hotels have International Direct Dialling (IDD), which speeds up the process enormously. Sometimes, however, even IDD is slow because the number of callers exceeds the number of lines. A call might take a few minutes, two hours or, after heavy rains and winds have put lines out of service, days.

Many large hotels and some offices are now equipped with facsimile machines as well. In Sanur, you can send and receive facsimiles and telexes at Darma Sari International Cargo, Ngurah Rai Bypass, near Jalan Segara. In Kuta, you can phone abroad or send or receive a telex at Bali Government Tourist Office, Jalan Bakung Sari. Also for telexes, faxes and IDD telephone calls try KCB Tours and Travel, Jalan Raya, Kuta.

Postal Services

Post offices, located in all major towns, are open from 8 am–2 pm, Monday to Thursday; 8–11 am, Friday; 8 am–1 pm, Saturday. Poste restante services are available.

Office Hours

Most businesses are open from 8 am–4 pm or 9 am–5 pm, Monday to Friday though some shops in Denpasar may close for a siesta from 1–5 pm and reopen for evening hours. Some businesses are open on Saturday morning. Government offices are open from 8 am–3 pm, Monday to Thursday; 8 am–1.30 pm, Friday; 8 am–2 pm, Saturday. Shops in resort areas have longer hours, usually from 8 am–8 pm, Monday to Saturday; often on Sunday.

Courtesy

The Balinese, like other Indonesians, are typically polite to guests, which is how they refer to tourists and is indicative of their attitude to visitors. They are also generally accepting of others' ways. Nonetheless, there are a few general rules one might bear in mind while travelling through the island. Contrary to the impression given by tour agents' posters, funerals and other ceremonies are religious and personal affairs and temples are holy places. Visitors are welcome, but only if they dress and behave respectfully. Men, in trousers, and women, in skirts, should carry temple sashes to wear around their waists whenever they enter a temple. Sarongs and dress shirts (*kebayas* for the women) are appreciated at holy occasions as well, if they're properly worn. Smaller ceremonies in the home are private and should be attended by invitation only.

Some customs and attitudes in Indonesia differ from those in the West, so there will be some misunderstanding and frustration. Whatever happens, try not to get angry; the Balinese call angry people 'hot', which is exactly how one feels when one loses one's temper in this climate. It is much better to try to work things out gently. A smile, here as elsewhere, tends to work better than a raised voice. Which leads to the notion of . . .

Rubber Time

With a few exceptions, most things in Bali and the rest of the Indonesian archipelago are ruled by *jam karet* (rubber time). Time simply isn't measured by seconds and minutes. Schedules are made, it seems, to be broken. The sacred dance that a Balinese friend says should start around 3 in the afternoon at the local temple festival may start at noon or at 5. A 'quick' sandwich may take an hour. There are pleasant aspects as well. A total stranger may walk kilometres out of his way to make sure one reaches one's destination.

Delays should be expected and, if possible, enjoyed. Balinese, who tend not to like to disappoint others, often make promises that cannot possibly be kept. Arrange to pick up commissions well in advance of departure or be prepared to have the goods shipped.

Bargaining

Bargaining is an island pastime. With few exceptions, prices can be reduced. But bargaining should be done with humour, grace and a sense of perspective. Don't pass up a beautiful painting for a few dollars, the difference will mean nothing back home.

Drugs

After 1830, a driving force in Bali's economy was opium. 'May you not fall into opium peddling' was a popular parental blessing, a blessing which apparently didn't stick. Though the Balinese put an end to opium addiction years ago in their own society, they had little effect on the waves of Western hippies who showed up on their shores in the late 1960s and 1970s, travelling the KKK (Kuta–Kabul–Kathmandu) circuit.

Any drug consumption among the Balinese is virtually unheard of; most Balinese shy away from alcoholic beverages for fear of becoming *pusing* (confused). Strict enforcement of Indonesia's drug laws has dissuaded most travellers from drug taking. Dealers can be sentenced to life imprisonment.

The Lay of the Land: Bali's Geography

Bali, for all its influence on art, myth and fantasy, is a relatively small island measuring 145 kilometres (90 miles) long and 80 kilometres (50 miles) wide. It lies 8° south of the equator, in the middle of the Indonesian archipelago. It is one of 13,676 islands that punctuate tropical seas from Sumatra in the northwest to Irian Jaya, which shares its border with Papua New Guinea in the east—a distance of about 6,400 kilometres (4,000 miles). The population of Indonesia, which inhabits about half the islands, is the fifth-largest in the world at 173 million. Hundreds of local dialects and languages are spoken, though the national language Bahasa Indonesia, a Malay-based lingua franca, is now taught in all schools and is known by most of the population. This national language policy has been a very effective nation-building device, it was decided upon by Sukarno and other nationalists in the 1920s.

Following Java, Bali is the second most densely populated of Indonesia's 27 provinces, with 2.7 million people. It has about 500 people per square kilometre (half a square mile).

Geologists believe that during the ice ages Bali was linked to Java to the west and to Lombok to the east; one theory suggests that shifting plates in the ocean floor split the islands apart. Balinese legend has it that Bali and Java were divided by the hand of a powerful Javanese priest who banished a recalcitrant son to Bali and then drew his finger across the sands which linked the islands. The shallow strait which separates Java and Bali would indicate the mythical father's reluctance to lose his son as it is less than three kilometres (two miles) at its widest point and 60 metres (200 feet) at its narrowest.

The 19th-century naturalist Alfred Russel Wallace, who spent years travelling through the archipelago, postulated in his book *The Malay Archipelago* that Bali was the easternmost Indonesian island with flora and fauna that could properly be classified with those of Asia. Drawing what came to be called the Wallace Line through the deep waters separating Bali from Lombok, he noted that the tropical jungles, monkeys and tigers of Asia ended in Bali, while the eucalypti, parrots and marsupials of Australia were first found in Lombok, then extended through the islands beyond. The narrow and treacherous Lombok Strait is one of the deepest in the world.

Though tigers no longer roam Bali's few remaining jungles, there is diversity in Bali's geography and climate. Its eight *kabupaten* (districts) include: Badung, in the south; Gianyar, Bangli, Klungkung and Karangasem in the east; Tabanan and Jembrana in the west and Buleleng in the north. They vary widely in elevation and vegetation: cacti spike the dry coast of Buleleng while tree ferns hug the misty slopes of Bangli. A range of volcanic mountains running east to west forms the island's jagged spine; it is the source of Bali's rich volcanic soil. The peaks trap clouds that drench the southern part of the island in rain—up to 1,725 millimetres (68 inches) a year. Rivers run down to the sea, irrigating the rice fields and carving deep gorges thick with tropical trees. Clifford Geertz suggests in his book *Negara: The Theater State in 19th Century Bali* that these very peaks and ravines encouraged the formation of the island's numerous kingdoms, the strongest of which eventually became regencies.

The richness of the land has boosted the island's wealth. Doe-like cows graze in pastures. High in the cool mountain regions, coffee, tobacco, citrus fruit, peanuts and, recently, vanilla are grown, while grapes and tropical fruit lace the coastal plains. And almost everywhere are fields of rice.

Bali's volcanoes are all less than 10,000 years old, dating from the Recent, or Holocene period. Only Gunung (Mount) Batur, at 1,717 metres (5,633 feet), is still actively volcanic. Gunung Agung is Bali's highest volcanic mountain at 3,142 metres (10,308 feet). To the Balinese, it is a supremely holy place, a Mount Olympus where the gods alight when they visit the island. In 1953, a French film maker visiting Bali wrote that Gunung Agung was 'a benevolent volcano which need not be feared'. Only a decade later, the benevolent mountain erupted with a violence, blowing over 914 metres (3,002 feet) off its top, devastating villages and countryside. West of Gunung Agung is Gunung Abang, at 2,152 metres (7,060 feet). In Tabanan, Gunung Batukau dominates the landscape at 2,276 metres (7,467 feet).

These mountains, particularly Gunung Agung, are the spiritual and directional magnetic poles of the island. Direction is very important in Bali, where life is a realization of divine order. In this world of balance in which everything has its own place and boundary, the sacred direction, *kaja*, is mountainwards and *kelod*, towards the sea, is profane. *Kangin*, the east, where the sun rises symbolizing rebirth, is also holy. *Kauh*, the west, symbolizes death with its setting sun. Visitors asking directions will often find the Balinese response a full-blown chorus of kangin, kauh, kaja and kelod—all the more complex, as the latter two directions take on totally different points of the compass if the answer is given south or north of the mountains.

Traditionally, all family compounds are set up with the directions in mind. The house temple, the head of the compound, is closest to the mountains, as is the master bedroom. The rubbish dump and pig sties are the most profane places so they are found at the back of the house, towards the sea. The Balinese themselves seem to have internal compasses, once the external points are lost, though, they become confused and dizzy. On a visit to the United States, the Balinese painter Made Budi wanted to shift his bed to Kaja so that his head would point in the proper direction, towards Gunung.

'Contagion of Civilization': the Island's History

Discoveries in Central Java of the remains of an early species of Pithecan-thropus erectus, popularly known as Java Man, suggest that tribes had settled on some islands of the Indonesian archipelago by the Middle Pleistocene Age, around 400000–120000 BC. Scholars believe that the first bands of proto-Malays migrated from what is now southwestern China sometime around 3000 BC, followed by the deutero-Malays, who brought knowledge of wet-rice cultivation.

Few archaeological traces of Bali's earliest inhabitants have been found and whatever bits and pieces do remain are, no doubt, covered under ancient layers of lava and volcanic dust. Nonetheless, conjectures abound, and academics tell us that, even in prehistoric times, Bali was densely settled by a people who were socially stratified, used tools of stone and weapons of metal and worked in the rice fields. Even then, the Balinese were carving the mountainsides with picks and hoes into the web of terraces that cover the island today.

These early Balinese worshipped the goddess of the rice harvest and fertility. The *cili* (a small doll made of rice stalks or palm leaves pinched in the centre), believed to date back to these rice cults, was dedicated to the rice mother and later, after the coming of Hinduism, to the goddess Dewi Sri. Today, the cili—a symbol of wealth, fertility and luck—is found on every-thing from temple decorations to labels on bottles of *brem*, Bali's sweet rice wine.

Just how and when Hinduism reached Bali is unclear. Some academics suggest it came directly with Indian traders and priests, others argue that the religion followed a more indirect route, with Javanese Hindu and Buddhist holymen and artists acting as proselytes, travelling through Balinese courts and the countryside. Whatever the case, it is clear from early copperplate inscriptions that Hinduism was well established on Bali by the ninth century.

'The conversion of primitive Bali into a Hindu society was the result not of conquest and colonization, but rather of the contagion of civilization,' writes Willard Hanna in his excellent history, *Bali Profile*. 'The rulers found in Indian culture the religious and administrative practices which exactly served their purposes, and the people responded with . . . enthusiasm.'

One of the earliest events historians can trace from records was the birth of a son in AD 1001 to a Javanese queen, Mahendradatta, and her consort, Udayana—the Balinese king after whom Bali's premier university is named. According to legend, this queen was a sorceress who was banished to the woods where she became the much-feared witch, Rangda. To this day, the frightful figure is evoked in dances and carvings throughout the island.

The son, Airlangga, became one of the outstanding kings of east Java, extending his empire to Bali via the rule of a brother. For three centuries, Bali remained closely associated with Java, sometimes as an autonomous state, other times as part of the Javanese empire, as was the case in 1343, after the successful pacification of the island by the renowned general of the Majapahit kingdom in Java, Gajah Mada.

As Islamic influence spread throughout Java, the power of the Hindu Majapahit Empire, weakened by internal fighting among its princes, waned. One picturesque account describes how in 1478, after hearing a warning from a priest that Majapahit would fall in 40 days, the son of the last emperor fled Java for Bali, the last stronghold of Indic religion and culture in the archipelago. Followed by a procession of courtiers, priests, scholars and artists, the young prince crossed the narrow straits separating Java and Bali and declared himself Dewa Agung—the king of Bali.

About this time, the first Europeans started sailing these waters, lured by Marco Polo's tales of unimaginable riches, gold, jewels and spices. Portuguese and Spanish explorers passed by the island, but no one stopped. The Magellan expedition (1519–22) noted 'Java Minor', an island that appears to be Bali from the charts. Others, including Sir Francis Drake, wrote of an island variously called Boly, Bale and Bally.

Ironically, it seems the first Westerners to set foot on Bali were washed up on Nusa Dua, the island's newest resort area today. A Portuguese ship, sent in 1585 to establish a trading post, foundered on the coral reef off the Bukit and the five surviving crew members were pressed into the service of the Dewa Agung.

Some 12 years later, Cornelis de Houtman, the earliest of Dutch explorers in the East Indies, was reported to have been 'so moved by the beauty and wealth of the island' that he christened it Jonck Holland (Young Holland). Members of his crew were greeted at the huge palace by the Dewa Agung, described by one officer as 'a stout, vigorous man of 40, with 200 wives, 50 misshapen dwarves (their bodies deliberately deformed to resemble grotesque figures of keris [traditional sword] hilts).' Despite the sight, so taken were the Dutch sailors with Bali that some jumped ship.

By the 18th century, the island was divided into a dozen small states, none larger than 7,770 hectares (19,185 acres) and each headed by a raja who raised taxes and kept his palace guard busy warring with the other kings.

Joining this chaotic circus, in the early 19th century, was a parade of European traders and scholars, administrators and adventurers. By the 1830s, the island was a port for international traders and travellers, such as British and American whalers who made brief stops here to stock up with game, livestock, rice, fruit and vegetables.

But with few exceptions, the parade did not stop long. Unlike Sumatra with its pepper, Banda with its nutmeg and Ambon with its cloves, Bali offered little of interest to European markets. Nor was the topography welcoming. Treacherous coral reefs ringed the island and a harsh range of mountains hugged the arid north coast—a foreboding barrier to the merchant ships that plied the Java Sea, while the fertile south, facing the Indian Ocean, was well off the trading routes. Then there were the Balinese themselves, fierce and proudly independent.

Nevertheless, a few traders set up shop: Mads Lange of Denmark, a dashing young adventurer, built a factory in Kuta and involved himself in the politics of the island. Another European, a Dutchman, intent on winning the support of the Dewa Agung, promised the raja whatever gift he asked. Eventually, he managed to deliver the king's wish—a rhinoceros!

The Dutch East Indies Company, busily establishing control over the archipelago, was not content with such a free-form situation and appointed a special commissioner 'to bring the radjas . . . into such a relationship [with the Netherlands] that they will be removed from foreign influence.'

In 1841, a Dutch frigate ran into the Kuta reef and was plundered by local villagers. The commissioner required restitution. A quarrel over reef rights ensued. Djilantik, a young prince from Buleleng, the area surrounding Singaraja, rejected the Dutch right to rule over the island. 'Never while I live shall the state recognize the sovereignty of the Netherlands,' he declared. 'Not by a mere scrap of paper shall any man become master of another's land. Rather let the keris decide.'

And the Dutch did, responding with force. In the first of six military expeditions, the Dutch sent a fleet of two large frigates, four steamships, four brigs, 12 schooners and 40 small craft, with 1,700 soldiers and 230 pieces of field artillery. Buleleng was burned and the prince agreed to Dutch terms, only to ignore the agreement as soon as the fleet left.

Accordingly, in 1848, the Dutch sent a second fleet, the largest ever assembled against a native power. But after losing 264 men, they retreated, to return the following year with 100 ships and 5,000 troops. Against such odds, Prince Djilantik was helpless. Ambushed in the mountains, he took poison, while his wife, trapped in the palace at Jagara, proudly led the ladies of the court in a formal procession into the gunfire of the Dutch infantry. Hearing news of the slaughter, the raja of Karangasem led his children and wives in a *puputan*, or mass suicide.

By 1882, northern Bali was under the administration of the Dutch. The southern kingdoms, however, managed to maintain a haughty independence which rankled the Dutch, who by this time had most of the archipelago under their control. Determined to rule, the Dutch sent two more expeditions to try to pacify the south. It was not, however, until 27 May 1904 that the Dutch found sufficient cause to attack the southern palaces.

A Chinese trading ship foundered on the coral reef just off Sanur. The Balinese, who believed any such ship and its goods were fair game, despite agreements signed by the rajas to the contrary, fell to the business of plundering. The merchant demanded an outrageous sum in restitution, and the Dutch, eager for a chance to bring the southern Balinese to heel, sent letters requiring payment. The Balinese refused, and on 14 September 1906, Dutch troops landed in Sanur and proceeded to march to Badung (present-day Denpasar). As Dutch artillery and cavalry surrounded the palace, the doors opened and the raja walked out, followed by the men and women of the court, all dressed in white cremation gowns, all wearing kerises and their finest jewels, flowers decorating their dark hair. The Dutch watched in amazement as the raja gave a signal and the high priest plunged a keris into the king's breast. The Dutch fired, but not before many of the courtiers had killed themselves, the women throwing their jewels contemptuously at the soldiers before they died.

The Dutch Army marched west to Tabanan, where the raja and prince surrendered but, upon hearing the Dutch terms of exile, killed themselves. The ignominious campaign ended in 1908 in Klungkung, where, once again, the raja and his followers elected puputan rather than surrender. (By dying in battle, it was believed, the spirit could reach nirvana.) As Dutch troops marched to the palace gates, the raja led the great and tragic puputan. As he thrust his sacred keris into the ground, the raja was shot dead by the Dutch; six of his wives plunged keris blades into their own hearts and the rest of the palace—children, men, women—died either by their own hands or were killed by the Dutch. This was a turning point in Bali's history marking the end of resistance and feudalism. Remarkably Bali's culture survived.

There was peace, for a short time, on the sad island. Back in Europe, the Dutch public was horrified by the nightmarish puputans. In response, the colonial government sent officials who took an active interest in Balinese culture. In an attempt to 'Keep Bali Balinese', only a few missionaries were allowed on the island and no white man was allowed to own land. The Dutch stopped *suttee* (the burning of widows), abolished slavery and built roads, dams and bridges. They also established health clinics and restrained island courts from handing down barbarous punishments.

Still, Dutch rule damaged Balinese culture. By controlling the sale of opium, the Dutch profited handsomely. It has been estimated that in 1910 they took in one million florins, while expending less than 20,000 on education. Virtually every royal family was affected. Those who didn't buy their 'daily dose' from Dutch-sanctioned traders were fined, since it was presumed they were buying from illegal sources. More insidious, perhaps, was the erosion of the people's image of themselves; no longer were they a self-sufficient people controlling their own political and economic destiny.

This era of 'benevolent paternalism' came to an abrupt halt in February 1942 when the Japanese landed in Sanur. Although they occupied Bali until 1945, they intervened little in Balinese affairs, for the most part, and despite the economic hardships the Balinese suffered, they regained control of the administration of their island, as did Indonesians elsewhere.

After the end of the Second World War, the Dutch sought to pick up from where they had left off, but the Indonesians had other plans: *Merdeka*— Freedom. On 17 August 1945, the national leader Sukarno declared independence but war against the Dutch stretched out for years. In November 1946, Lieutenant Colonel Ngurah Rai of the Balinese defence force led a brave attempt to halt the Dutch in the hills of Tabanan. Woefully outnumbered and outarmed, Rai and his troops fought until every Balinese lay dead on the field—a modern-day puputan.

Though most of the battles were fought in Java and elsewhere, the Balinese were influential at the Round Table Conference held in The Hague in 1949 which resulted in Dutch recognition of Indonesian independence.

But the new republic was plagued with problems. The Dutch left little in the way of infrastructure: virtually no schools or hospitals, few roads, no civil-service system. Mills had been destroyed during the war, plantations left to ruin. Less than ten percent of the people were literate.

One hundred or more political parties proliferated, rebellions erupted in Sumatra, north Sulawesi and Ambon. The United States, unhappy with what it considered to be the left-leaning policies of President Sukarno, took advantage of the unrest, and the CIA supplied the rebels with arms and several paramilitary specialists; one American flier was shot down over Ambon in 1958, when he accidentally bombed a church on a Sunday morning.

Bali was one of the most neglected of the islands and the most exploited by the central government. As the economic situation deteriorated and inflation topped 600 percent, many Balinese turned to the Communist Party of Indonesia (PKI), which was then legal. The PKI promised land reform, a much-cherished notion on islands like Bali and Java where few farmers owned their own land. Quickly, it became the largest communist party outside the communist bloc.

Tension mounted as President Sukarno tried to balance the various demands made by the military, communists, Muslims and other groups. For reasons that continue to be debated by historians, on 1 October 1965 a small band of officers calling themselves the 30 September Movement kidnapped and killed six generals (a seventh escaped). Some PKI members seized the radio station in Jakarta and declared a coup d'etat. The Indonesian Army, led by a lieutenant-general named Suharto, immediately took control.

Though the coup lasted only 24 hours, six months of bloodshed followed as the country ran amok. Tens of thousands of PKI members and suspected members, their families and friends were thrown into prison without trial. Others were killed, some by the army, others by bands of students wielding knives and clubs. Many of those murdered were simple peasants who had merely followed the lead of their village chiefs. Others were victims of old jealousies and hates; in Bali, an entire community of Chinese Indonesians near Marga was forced from its home, the land taken away.

Estimates of the number killed vary. The Indonesian Government has suggested 80,000 but other sources give a figure closer to one million. Most families in Bali lost someone, though few Balinese want to or can bear to speak of those times, 'One doesn't dare,' said one young woman.

President Sukarno transferred much of his power to Suharto, who was named president in 1968. Since then, Suharto has been re-elected four times. There has never been any doubt of the election outcome; of the three legal parties, only Golkar, the government party controlling voter registration and supervising voting, is allowed to organize on a local level. The Communist Party of Indonesia, wiped out in 1965, is still illegal.

The New Order, as Suharto's government is called, has stabilized the economy and encouraged development; living standards in most areas have improved dramatically; life expectancy has increased by more than ten years; the number of people living in poverty has declined by more than 25 percent; new roads have been built and the number of schools has mushroomed.

Today, Bali is one of Indonesia's most prosperous islands. According to government officials, it is self-sufficient in rice production, almost all large villages have electricity, paved roads connect all the major towns and trade schools have opened to train young adults in fields linked with Bali's expanding tourist trade.

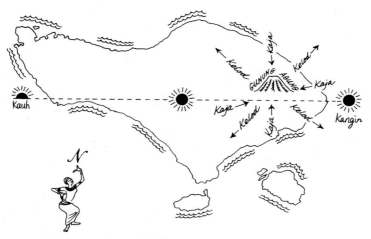

The spiritual and directional poles of Bali

Caretakers of the Island of the Gods: the People

When Majapahit priests, nobles and artisans left Java for Bali in the 15th century, they brought with them a caste system derived from that of Hindu India. Priests were *Brahmana*; the warrior-kings were *Ksatriya*; and the merchant class were *Wesya*. These three castes were known as the *Triwangsa*. All of the original Balinese, 90 percent of the population, belonged to the *Sudra*, 'outsiders' according to the Majapahit ruling classes.

Though there were no Balinese 'untouchables', the rules of feudal Bali were strict. The upper castes had divine rights and it was for the Sudra to support them economically and give deference. If a woman was so bold as to marry beneath her caste, she could be punished by death; a man would merely face disapproval.

Today, there is still a caste system in Bali but this is not to say that there is no social mobility. Many legislators and educators come from Sudra families and Brahmans and Ksatriya may be waiters or mechanics. Many social and religious customs remain, however, and an inherent respect is given to members of higher castes, even though much of their power is gone. This is evident in the complex, three-level Balinese language, still used in daily life. Irrespective of economic position, lower caste Balinese will speak polite or high Balinese, derived from Sanskrit, to a member of a higher caste, who may respond in common Balinese, a Malay–Polynesian dialect. Because of this, younger Balinese often prefer to speak Indonesian in business situations so that they don't have to worry about offending anyone and can be more direct while still being polite. Only the Brahmans may become *pedanda*, or high priests, and a Brahman woman who marries outside her caste is often shunned by her family and stripped of her Brahman duties.

For all that, there seems to be little 'social striving' in Bali. If anything, many see advantages to being part of the 90 percent Sudra caste. For example, a girl in a Brahman family may spend her entire day making offerings, while a Sudra girl would have a chance to work and make money. For their part, educated Brahman women often find their desires to fulfil familial duties in conflict with their professional interests.

What's in a Name?

Traditionally, there are no family names in Bali, though this is changing, especially among children of well-known Indonesians. Some names reflect caste, such as Ida Bagus and Ida Ayu for male and female Brahmans, and Anak Agung, Cokorda and Dewa for Ksatriyas. Names may also indicate birth order. For Sudra, for instance, Wayan is often the first child, Made the second, Nyoman the third and Ketut the fourth—hence the slogan for Bali's successful family-planning programme: 'No more Nyomans'. The families that have more than four children—most uncommon today—go back to Wayan for child five. Brahmans and Ksatriya may be called Putu, Raka or Kompiang, if they are the first child; Rai, if the second; Oka, if the third; and Alit, meaning small, if the fourth. Second names may describe a flower in bloom when the child was born or a physical object or sound resembling the child. Names often change throughout life, so that a man becomes known as 'Father of . . .', or 'Grandfather of . . . '

The Child Is Father to the Man

The custom of naming people after their children or grandchildren relates to the Balinese belief that children are celestial creatures. Traditionally, infants are not allowed to touch the ground until their *oton*, a celebration three or six months after birth, so that their tender spirits will not encounter the profane spirits lurking in the ground. The extended family makes this practice possible as father, mother, aunts, uncles, grandparents even older siblings, help care for a baby. A common sight in Bali is one tiny child carrying an even tinier child down a village path. 'How many children do you have?' is one of the first questions visitors are asked. Adults without children are pitied and men often take a second wife if their first is barren.

One rarely hears a Balinese child cry and there are few temper tantrums. Children, like all Balinese, know their place in society and they feel respected and loved. They're cared for, but they also feel self-sufficient from a very early age.

Part of this sense may come from the fact that even very young children are expected to do their part in the family. Little girls mimic their mothers and elder sisters, walking to temple with tiny offerings balanced on their heads, and boys, carrying long poles topped with flags, lead ducks in long lines to the rice fields.

A Family Affair

Although in the last few decades more and more Balinese have been lured to the city by the prospect of jobs, in villages it is still quite common to find several generations of a family living in the same compound. The group, rather than the individual, is stressed. Solitude is not valued by most Balinese and almost no one lives alone. To be left at home alone is an uncomfortable experience as a house left empty, even briefly, is believed to attract *leyaks*, witches who can transform their spirits into various creatures.

Traditionally, when a woman marries she goes to her husband's family home; if she later divorces him—a relatively rare phenomenon on the

island—she simply returns to her family's home, leaving the children with her husband. This notion that the married woman should go to the husband's home extends to immigration regulations. Foreign wives of Indonesian men have little trouble staying in Bali whereas foreign husbands of Indonesian women are constantly facing problems. This comes from the old idea that the woman should be in the man's home.

Despite this inequity, Balinese women are at the heart of the island's commerce. They watch over the family's finances and run the *warungs* (market stalls and food stands). Road crews are invariably made up of women, gracefully balancing heavy loads of cement and gravel on their heads, while the men supervise. At harvest time, the women can be found in the fields, or *sawah*, threshing grain. Recently, quite a few women have entered the professional ranks as doctors, dentists or lawyers.

It is the men who direct village life, primarily through the male-run *banjar* (neighbourhood association). The banjar is the social centre of the community. At midday, men snooze in the bale banjar before peddling off to sell mattresses or brooms; at night, they gather here to watch television or play music. It is also the production and communications centre for weddings, cremations and temple festivals where work schedules are planned and structures jointly built. *Gotong royong*, the Indonesian concept of mutual cooperation, has been deeply rooted for centuries in Bali's banjars.

These groups have also proven to be incredibly effective instruments of government policy. Bali's successful family-planning efforts have been credited largely to the banjars—the first, and possibly only, time that men's organizations were effectively used to promote the use of the Pill.

A Religion of Holy Water

Disembarking at Ngurah Rai Airport, the religious life of the island is immediately apparent: small offerings of flowers and rice sit on a ticket agent's computer or a taxi dashboard, while palm-leaf offerings hang on the grill of a police car. Such physical evidence of Bali's spiritual life is everywhere. In courtyards every morning and evening, the women of Bali, dressed in sarongs and sashes, place offerings in the temples of homes and hotels, at crossroads and in kitchens and pray briefly, sprinkling holy water and wafting incense heavenwards to attract the gods' attention. On narrow lanes, *pemangku* (temple priests), dressed in white, ride on old Dutch bikes to their temples; entire families—husband, wife and two children dressed in temple finery—whiz by on a single motorcycle, heading for some ceremony. Even the beaches are scenes of the islanders' intense beliefs: at Kuta and Sanur, the sombre tones of a gamelan wash over sunbathers as a priest and his followers observe the final rites, casting the ashes of a loved one into the sea.

Muslims, Buddhists and Christians account for about five percent of Bali's population. Everyone else is Bali Hindu. The religion, sometimes known as Tirta Agama (the Religion of Holy Water), Agama Hindu or simply Agama Bali, is not an easy one for Westerners to understand. An admixture of Hinduism and Buddhism, combined with the islanders' original worship of ancestors and nature, it is nonetheless under one god, Ida Sanghyang Wichi Wasa, according to modern-day theologians. This way, it adheres to one of the tenets of the national code of *Pancasila*: belief in one God.

In daily practice, however, the Balinese pray to a pantheon of gods, ranging from the highest triumvirate of Brahma (god of creation), Wisnu (the preserver) and Siwa (the destroyer) to hundreds of lesser deities: gods of the mountains and gods of the sea; gods of planting and gods of the harvest. Each village has its own gods, as does each family.

The basic tenet of Agama Bali is that *atma* (the soul) lives on and that, after death, there is *samsara* (rebirth). Often families take a newborn child to a *balian* (soothsayer) to find out which ancestor has returned to earth.

Whether one comes back as a human or some lower form of life is influenced by *karma pala* (personal deeds). Final beatitude is *moksa*.

The spirit world of the Balinese is rich and frightening. Man stands between the gods and the demons and constantly worships one and placates the other. Unlike Western religions, which look forward to the day good triumphs over evil. Agama Bali seeks to achieve balance between good and evil. Notice the statues, draped in black-and-white-checkered cloth, at bridges and crossroads. Local people have dressed these grotesque guards in sarongs that admit both darkness and light. Villages that have suffered bad luck have cleansing ceremonies, while those with too much good luck may have ceremonies to give strength to the forces of darkness. Without balance, the Balinese believe, there is chaos.

Celebrations

In such a world, it is not surprising to find the calendar filled with *tanggal merah* (holy days, literally translated as red-letter days). There are celebrations for the gods and for the ancestors, for the saints and founders of the religion and to keep evil spirits at bay. There are even special days devoted to animals, scholars and metal things (in the old days, the curve-bladed keris, nowadays including cars, refrigerators and even fax machines).

There are also island-wide celebrations. The night before Nyepi, the Balinese new year, the streets writhe with monsters, fantastical papier-mâché creatures, carried by bands of boys holding torches and beating gongs. The noise ceases the next day—Nyepi—when all talk is forbidden, travel (except for tourists) abandoned, streets empty, kitchen hearths cold and all televisions and radios switched off. On this day, people sit at home, neither eating nor drinking, passing the day in silence, hoping to fool any evil forces into thinking that the island is deserted.

The two holidays of Galungan and Kuningan (almost like Christmas and Thanksgiving) are more festive and, rolled into one, make a ten-day extravaganza. Gifts and thanks are exchanged as families come together and the gods come down to the villages to enjoy earthly delights. Streets are lined with *penjors*—great arcs of freshly cut bamboo with palm-leaf tassles and curlicues, and bouquets of leaves and coconuts. Temple courtyards are alive with dances, plays, processions and music. During the entire period, little 9-to-5 work gets done, but nobody minds. 'If Western societies have spent the last thousand years laboriously disentangling the secular from the religious,' observes J Stephen Lansing in *The Three Worlds of Bali*, 'the Balinese have spent the same period attempting to integrate them.'

The Balinese religion is essentially a public one. Rather than silent prayer and contemplation, the Balinese make superbly theatrical displays of belief. According to Clifford Geertz in his book *Negara: The Theater State in 19th Century Bali*, the Balinese state was always pointed 'toward spectacle, toward ceremony, toward the public dramatization of the ruling obsessions of Balinese culture: social inequality and status pride . . . It was a theater state in which the kings and princes were the impresarios, the priests the directors, and the peasants the supporting cast, stage crew, and audience. The stupendous cremations, tooth filings, temple dedications, pilgrimages and blood sacrifices, mobilizing hundreds and even thousands of people and great quantities of wealth, were not means to political ends: they were the ends themselves, they were what the state was for . . . Power served pomp, not pomp power.'

Tradition and Change
Ida Bagus Surya, Trainee Priest

For generations, people around Denpasar have looked to the Brahman priests for spiritual guidance. In the old days, these priests would have studied under an old priest, usually a father or grandfather or some other relative. Since the 1970s, however, the Department of Religion in Bali has set up classes of special study, so that religious training is more formal. One of the student priests there is Ida Bagus Surya.

Monday to Friday, this tall, handsome 30-year-old works for the Foster Parents organization, analyzing projects, but after work and at the weekends, when other young men would be relaxing, he studies with 25 other students at the Hinduism Institute, learning religion, culture and *adat* (traditional law). The class is open to men and women of all castes, although one has to be a Brahman to become a pedanda, or high priest. Unlike Westerners, Surya, like other Brahmans, probably will not become a priest until he is 60 years old or more.

This weekend he is drawing *kajang*, intricate holy figures, onto fine white cloth, in preparation for a family cremation. In fact, though none of his 50 relatives are priests, there are many occasions throughout the year—weddings, tooth filings, or cremations such as this—when the courtyard in which his family and other relatives live becomes a hive of activity, filled with offerings prepared by the women of the compound.

Surya became interested in the basis of his religion several years ago: 'When I was in college studying English, I met a lot of Westerners. They always asked me about our religion. I felt guilty, because I couldn't explain why things happened. One day five years ago, I read a saying in one of the holy books from Java: "How stupid is the frog living in the pond who can't smell or enjoy the lotus that grows there." The frog sits there, ignorant of the beauty. But the butterfly, like the Westerner, comes from far away to taste the nectar. I didn't want to be the frog.'

The students at the institute grapple with religious theory, until recently rarely attempted in Bali's ritually rich religion. How can, for example, Bali's many gods be one?

'We believe in many gods and one God. You can think of it as something like sunlight, which is made of many colours, but forms one white light,' says Surya, dressed in a white shirt and sarong in preparation for the cremation. 'Another way to think of it is that the same person can have many names, can be many things: father, husband, uncle, boss, and when he's abroad, tourist. He's still the same person.

'Ancestor worship is most common among Balinese because God is not clear for us. If God helps us, where is he? We don't know. But the ancestors, we know them. The old people tell stories, and so we know about the balian who healed people and the other who was a great dancer. We can follow them, and pray to them, but, of course, they are all a part of God.

'I think priests here are different from in the West. In Bali a priest is not allowed to walk through the street at night or to see movies; that would make life very dull when you're younger,' he says, smiling. 'Also, a priest isn't allowed to drive a car, because if he did and had an accident, the judge would have a hard time finding him guilty; the priest is a holy, holy man, and to bring him to court would not be polite—he just can't be arrested.'

Wooden ornament for offerings

Surya believes many of his religion's traditions are good: 'We worship in four ways: through studying and teaching; through love; through meditation and through work. This means everyone can worship, each in his own manner. Even people who can't read can worship the gods by making offerings.'

Still, he hopes to see changes between now and the time that he becomes a priest: 'I'd like to be a latter-day priest, someone people feel comfortable around and whom they come to with their problems, for advice, just talking casually in Indonesian . . . Traditionally, pedandas have been up on a pedestal; common people have to speak high Balinese to them—they are quite removed.'

But Surya believes such changes will come slowly. 'It's hard for the Balinese to give up old ways,' he says. Even for Surya, some things are hard to imagine: 'Just living outside the compound, I've always lived here, and I can't imagine what it would be like. And yet I know my wife would like to live outside. It is not easy for her, being a working woman and having to reconcile herself to the expectations of my family. And I think it would be refreshing, too. It's hard for Balinese to progress because of the pulls of adat. If someone doesn't go to the ceremonies, people talk and brand them "un-Balinese"; a woman can't marry below her caste. Here I have six aunties who never married. I'd like the religion to respond more to the people and their problems; a religion that worried less about form, and more about true devotion.'

Today the pomp continues. Indeed, the flood of tourist dollars has meant that the displays are even grander. Many Balinese half-heartedly complain that they are almost always broke as so much money is spent on so many ceremonies, then they go off to enjoy yet another festival!

Temple Festivals

One of the most impressive ceremonies is the *odalan*, which occurs in every temple once every 210 days—a single cycle of the Pawukon calendar, which determines the dates of most of Bali's religious ceremonies. Since most Balinese belong to five or six temples—three in the village, then the state temple, the agrarian temple and the family temple—so odalans take up a major part of Balinese life. As the island belongs to the gods, only through the gods' goodness are the harvests bountiful and the tourists plentiful. Illness, famine and bad business all indicate the gods' wrath.

In *Balinese Temple Festival*, Jane Belo beautifully describes a temple festival as a sort of birthday party celebrating the founding of the temple. Although preparations may go on for weeks, the celebration itself lasts only a few days. Carvers are called upon to repair the temple and create new statues. Women make palm-leaf containers for the offerings and men erect temporary bamboo constructions to carry priests and the hundreds of offerings to the temple. Once preparations begin, the temple is never left vacant for fear that evil spirits might contaminate the site, and men sit up all night, reading the *lontar* (scriptures written on lontar palm leaves).

A few days before the festival, men festoon the temple exterior with *lamaks* (brightly coloured palm-leaf patchworks), and frame the entrance with penjors, the evanescent green-bamboo banners. Meanwhile, a *tukang banten* (offerings specialist) directs the women who assemble the offerings. The final day before the odalan, women wrap platforms in long stretches of new cloth painted with golden flowers, while unmarried girls assemble a tower of flowers, the *canang rebeong*. Ceremonial umbrellas shield the seats of the gods and bales are strung with palm-leaf streamers, and peppered with flowers that trace breezes with their colour and scent.

Early on the morning of the odalan, the kulkul is sounded. Men assemble to kill a pig or turtle, the roast meat of which is chopped and mixed with diced coconut, spices and raw blood into a type of Balinese slaw called *lawar* and served at the temple feast.

In the temple, everyone, including the statues, dresses in their finest. The pemangku purifies himself with holy water and then, after making offerings in five directions, sanctifies the holy water. Chanting mantras in ancient Balinese and Javanese, the pemangku invites the gods and demons to come and eat and drink, and cautions the demons not to wreak havoc.

The odalan is essentially a family reunion of gods and ancestors and men and demons. Throughout the day and into the night, women, wearing their finest sarongs and *kebayas* (finely fitted blouses), enter the temple, balancing offerings on their heads—metre-high Carmen Miranda-style headpieces of fruit and cakes, eggs, chicken and flowers. (It is a sign of the Balinese love of pomp and practicality that once the gods have taken their fill of the essence of the food, humans may take the physical remains home to eat.) In the innermost courtyard, women kneel and men sit cross-legged, cleansed and blessed with *tirta amerta* (holy water), blossoms resting between their fingertips, to pray to the gods.

The rest of the day is devoted to the entertainment and adoration of the gods. Small wooden figures called *pratima*, the temporary homes of the gods' spirits, are brought out and escorted by a procession of worshippers and musicians to a holy spring. Close to midnight, the *mendet* may begin, a slow dance of women in pairs who carry water vessels and smoking braziers, their free hands gracefully wafting the fragrant smoke towards the gods.

At night, a mask dance or a *wayang kulit* (shadow-puppet play) may be performed. Teenage boys and girls line the stairs of the temple, chatting and laughing, their flirtatious glances lighting the night like fireflies, for the odalan is one of the few chances for boys and girls to meet.

On the final day, the priest leads a procession of temple members and *gamelan* (the village orchestra), bidding the gods to leave. The congregation shakes the posts of the temporary shrines, shouting all the while to persuade those lazy gods who might want to dawdle to return to their homes on the mountain tops. After kneeling before the wooden pratima and again being blessed with holy water, the people leave and the pemangku returns the carved figures to their resting place until the next odalan.

Cockfights

On the second or third afternoon of the odalan, men often stage a cockfight just outside the temple gates. This is a ritual affair, the spilling of blood a requirement to complete the rituals. The government has banned all cock-fights except those for religious purposes; in the past, men too often gambled away their life savings and, sometimes, their wives! But the ban has been as ineffective as Prohibition was in the US: bamboo cages—the daytime perches for fighting cocks—line the streets of every village and a man can lose a week's pay, or even his new Suzuki motorcycle, when his luck runs out.

A typical cockfight is an all-male event, which often takes place in the *wantilan*, a covered arena within the village. Men and boys squat in a circle, while owners of the roosters size up the opposition and set up matches. At the edge of the group, a few women sell coffee, smokes and sweets. As the afternoon sunlight slants through the palms, fights follow one after another.

Owners attach spurs to the birds' feet and prime the birds by ruffling their feathers and massaging their legs. Minutes before a contest, the air is heavy with the ancient mantra of bettors—'putih, putih, hitam, hitam, hitam' ('white, white, black, black, black'). The fight—blurred wings and beaks, sharp squawks, a flurry of feathers—is brief; the winner fondled, the bloody loser bundled off to the stew pot. Now and then a losing cock tries to escape but is inevitably dragged back to meet its fate.

Temples

The lush landscape of Bali is laced with temples, their outlines reminding the viewer that this land, for all the work man may have done, is ultimately the property of the gods. It has been estimated that there are 20,000 temples in Bali, but the figure may be double. Large numbers for such a small island but not unrealistic, considering that every village has at least three temples: the *pura puseh*, the origins, or Brahman temple; the *pura balai agung*, dedicated to Wisnu, the preserver; and the *pura dalem*, dedicated to Siwa, the destroyer. Then, there are regional temples and state temples, water temples and sea temples. Just as Bali's ancient kings built their own temples, so dominant forces—large companies, banks and colleges of the island—have theirs. Added to these are countless family temples, clusters of peak-roofed shrines within compound walls devoted to ancestral spirits.

The days of the temple festivals are blurs of activity. But on days on which it is not 'activated', it is empty of worshippers and gods, all save for the pemangku whose job it is to take care of the temple. On these days, the temple is just a shell, waiting to receive the spirits of the gods.

The Balinese temple is, nonetheless, a fascinating shell and looking at it carefully, you can develop an appreciation for the great artistry of the Balinese craftsmen who carved the statues and built the gates and shrines. You can often gain insights, too, into the daily life of the community. In the beach-side village of Sanur, for instance, many temple walls are made from coral taken from the reef a few hundred metres away; and in Batuan, statues pose in the movements of the renowned dance the *gambuh*. There are even bits of historical whimsy: at the pura dalem in Blahkiuh, Denpasar, a fighter plane bores into the ground; in Pura Medrwe Karang, in Kubutambahan, a bas-relief of a Dutchman riding a bicycle harks back to gentler days when W O J Nieuwenkamp, one of the first Westerners to study Bali, peddled through the island, following dirt paths to erudition.

Many of Bali's most ancient temples, dating back a thousand years and more, are composites of various building periods and styles, where old statues stand next to new, eyeball-to-eyeball, wing-to-fang. Some abstract-looking statues are simply unfinished. Indeed, work is never finished in a temple, for renewal is as constant as the daily offerings. And so the temple becomes a sort of gallery, a concrete record of artistic trends and developments.

There is no 'typical' Balinese temple. Some are just clearings in a field, marked by a giant banyan tree adorned with a few holy objects. Others, such as the great mother temple Besakih, are elaborate affairs with dozens of minor temples.

There are, however, certain common architectural features. Westerners first coming upon a Balinese temple will be struck by its openness. The pura is not so much a building as a space, open to the sky and the gods. Only bales and the shrines are protected from the elements. A pura is usually oriented towards holy Gunung Agung. It is often divided into three parts, the number three having mystical significance.

Towering high above the rice fields are the *candi bentar*, the split gates of the pura. These are huge, mirror-image works of brick and tuff that bracket the first entrance to the temple. Some are elegant in their stark simplicity, like those leading to Uluwatu, others are great flights of fantasy, writhing with grotesque figures of witches and goblins, such as Pura Beji in Sangsit.

It is just outside the candi bentar in the uncovered area called the *jaba* that the secular events of an odalan take place. Here makeshift stalls cater to temple-goers, men play games of chance and children race about with toy guns and horns as hawkers' calls drown out the loud chorus of frogs and crickets.

Inside the gates is an antechamber, the *jaba tengah* (half outside), the preparation site for the odalan. Here is the kulkul, used to call people to work. Here, too, is a bale where women prepare food for offerings; another bale that acts as a bandstand for the gamelan and a third that acts as the rest area for worshippers. Midway, between the profane and sacred places, the jaba tengah is the site for entertainments that engage both men and gods: dances, shadow-puppet plays, and the reading of ancient texts by poetry clubs.

An arched gate, the *kori agung*, grander than the first, leads to the inner courtyard. Often it is flanked by two fierce stone *raksasas* (giants), who guard the temple's inner sanctum, and is topped by the wild-eyed face of Bhoma, the son of earth, who frightens evil spirits away. Beyond the narrow wooden door of the gate is a wall called the *aling-aling*. Often elaborately carved with demons, it is meant to stop any evil spirits from entering the inner sanctum—it seems demons have a hard time negotiating corners.

The inner sanctum, or *jeroan*, is a small village of *palinggih*—the altars where the gods sit when they visit. The holiest is devoted to the ancestor founder of the village. The altar is usually to the east and mountainwards, and is a brick shrine filled with relics and heirlooms of stone, gold and bronze. Shrines dedicated to Gunung Agung and Gunung Batur consist of a stone throne on top of a turtle-shaped platform wreathed with two stone

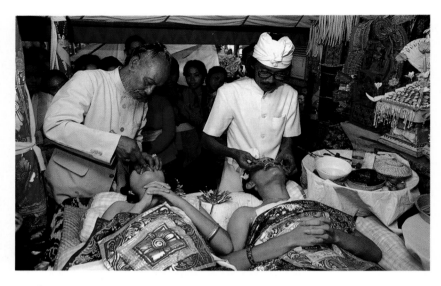

serpents and with small peaked roofs. This is the seat for Surya, the sun god. Elsewhere a small stone niche is the resting place for Taksu, 'the interpreter of the deities', who enters the bodies of worshippers when they go into trances. Towering above all are the *merus*, wooden pagodas with black, sugar-palm fibre roofs receding heavenwards. These are the towering seats of the high Hindu gods; how high depends on the always uneven number of roofs.

Life Ceremonies

In addition to festivals for the gods, there are rites-of-passage ceremonies, leading the Balinese from birth to death. There is a ceremony to commit afterbirth to the ground and the oton, when the baby is 210 days old and allowed to touch the ground for the first time. *Potong gigit*, the tooth-filing ceremony, celebrates the passage into adulthood. For this people often wait until they are in their 20s or even 30s and have a group ceremony which cuts the cost. A priest files the sharp points of the canine teeth, paring away the animal-like look and with it the base instinct of greed.

Weddings can be quiet gatherings or grand affairs, held at the family temple with the bride and groom in ancient dress. A favourite form of marriage today is 'kidnapping', in which the groom carries off his intended, usually on a motorcycle, to a third person's home. The young woman's family, who often knows of the kidnapping well in advance, pretends to be angry and, all in all, the expense of a large wedding is avoided!

Cremations

One of the most important rituals in Bali is the cremation known as *ngaben*, filled with music, offerings and processions. Such exuberant behaviour is surprising to Westerners, who expect funerals to be quiet, mournful occasions. But the Balinese, who grieve for a loved one just as others do, are following rites prescribed in ancient lontars, scripts with strict outlines for such ceremonies as this. According to Balinese belief, the body is an unclean, temporary resting spot for the pure soul. It must be returned to the elements of nature, so that the soul may return to its rightful place with the gods and, later, to life on Bali. This must be done through cremation, in a manner that the Balinese refer to as *panca–maha–bhuta* —exuberant, noisy and colourful.

Balinese carry out these edicts with as much great fervour as other rituals. Months are devoted to preparations, no expense is spared. (The cremation of the last raja of Badung in 1986 cost tens of thousands of dollars.) Any deviation, any mistake may mean that the spirit will wander the earth, wreaking havoc on those relatives who failed to act in accordance with custom.

The great expense means the body can be buried for years while the family raises an often ruinous sum of cash for a proper cremation. Poorer Balinese may cremate their family members in the same yard and at the same time as a wealthy nobleman or priest, thus sharing the reflected glory and cutting expenses. Recently, some villages have shared the expense with group cremations in which everybody pitches in to help build the altars, the funeral towers and the cremation animals.

Before work for a cremation begins, a propitious time is established by consulting the Balinese calendar and local priests. Sometimes, the ancestors themselves 'confirm' the date through a balian. On occasion, mass cremations are held to make the island clean. Late in 1988, thousands of cremations took place all over Bali, in preparation for a celebration at Besakih that occurs once every ten years. In the village of Sukawati, more than 250 bodies were burned on one day!

Once the date is set, the body is purified with holy water and ornamented: mirrors are put on the eyes, flowers in the nose, a gold ring on the tongue. Personal treasures and offerings ring the body in the death pavilion called the *bale bandung*. On the day of the cremation, the body, or sometimes an effigy of the body, is carried up a steep ramp of bamboo and placed into the *bade*, a multi-tiered, wedding-cake construction of wood and bamboo covered with white crepe paper, decked with mirrors and carvings of snakes, *garudas* (mythical birds) and glowering Bhomas.

With a great shout, as many as 100 men lift the funeral tower onto their shoulders and carry it through the streets, accompanied by priests, family members and gamelans. Sometimes, huge nightmare figures of papier-mâché

Evanescent Offerings
Ibu Aya Kompyang Putri, Offerings Maker

Every Balinese woman knows how to make *banten jotan*—small squares of banana leaf containing rice, flowers, perhaps coffee—which are prepared daily as offerings of thanks to god. They also know how to make the small woven trays for rice put out on the ground to placate evil spirits. Balinese women spend up to a third of their waking hours preparing offerings.

But important days require more elaborate offerings and families often turn to a *tukang banten*, literally an offerings worker.

One such tukang banten is Ibu Aya Kompyang Putri of the Geriya Kaliungu, a Brahman compound in Denpasar. A thin, middle-aged woman, Ibu Kompyang works, in her own words, 'from morning until night' making the delicate bantens that are part of the ritual of temple festivals, tooth filings, otons and the last rites of the dead. Sometimes, when there are many ceremonies, she doesn't get around to sleeping. 'I have to finish the bantens; there is no choice,' she says. 'But still I like it; I don't feel tired. Making bantens is like a medicine; if I'm sick, and someone comes to ask for help, I feel better.'

Ibu Kompyang has been making bantens since she was seven. After school, she and the other little girls helped the women of the compound make offerings out of banana leaves and flowers, coconuts and rice cookies. Her grandmother and great aunt were considered experts and slowly, the young girl learned the intricacies of the craft from them. 'There was no explanation of why things were made in one way or another, just "Do this, do that, this way, that way" ' she remembers. Only the pedanda knew the reasons behind the offerings and certainly a mere child would not dare ask him: 'The pedanda was the personification of Siwa and you couldn't ask a god "Why?" or you'd be punished for being too forward.'

By the time Ibu Kompyang was nine, she could make *canang*—small trays of young palm leaves put on the dashboards of cars, on top of tall offerings and on guardian statues. Then, as now, she had to include all the proper elements: *sirih* (areca palm nut), lime, golden bananas, sugar cane, little fried cakes, fragrant oils and pastes, beans, glutinous white and black rice and five coloured flowers—white frangipani, golden marigold, red bougainvillea or frangipani, black or green *bunga telung* and lotus.

Now she knows the designs of the 100 or more different offerings that are required in the rich ceremonial life of the Balinese. The most difficult of all, the *banten catur*, is a complex construction made into figures of people and birds and other animals, which can take three days of non-stop work. A few modern materials have crept into the tukang's supplies, food dyes have replaced colours given by herbs and grasses, and polystyrene now supports some of the more elaborate towers, instead of cork. But the methods employed by Ibu Kompyang and her assistants, who number as many as 20 for truly large celebrations, are the same as those used generations ago.

Offerings must be perfect, and while the untrained Western eye may not detect defects, the Balinese eye will. If something is missing, it must be made again. But some tukang banten are not as skilful as they should be and have been known to make the wrong banten for a ceremony. If this is the case: 'people—the tukang banten and the person who ordered the banten—become sick. If a whole village does it wrong, there can be disasters: an epidemic, many people may die. If the offerings are wrong, the gods let loose devils to wreak havoc.' Ibu Kompyang explains.

To make sure that she does nothing wrong, Ibu Kompyang often consults lontars, the ancient prescriptions listing how each offering should be made and how many offerings specific occasions require. This is somewhat unusual, since the reading of lontars traditionally has been left to the holy men. But Ibu Kompyang's grandfather taught and encouraged her rather than her brother, who was uninterested, how to read Kawi and she thus became his *pegandan*, his assistant.

For parishioners of the *geriya* (Brahman compound), people whose families have long attachments with the Brahman household, no payment is asked, but usually the supplicant knows the approximate cost of the materials and the time the workers spent and will try to leave that much or more. Sometimes families can't afford to pay the whole amount. 'They'll say, "I ask for your kindness, please make do with this." But it doesn't matter. I don't want too much money, I just like to help people, to make friends,' Ibu Kompyang says.

The reputation of a first-class tukang banten spreads by word of mouth, and often people outside the geriya's parish will ask for Ibu Kompyang's help. Recently, she oversaw the construction of two truckloads of offerings, costing almost $1,000.

It is hard for Westerners to understand how so much time, effort and money can be put into such evanescent beauty, yet Ibu Kompyang has no regrets that her sculptures do not last longer: 'As soon as the gods receive the offering, it really means nothing, they're spoiled. There is one type of banten, the *pedagin-gan*, which is made for the construction of a house temple. This contains gold and silver, rubies and fragrances, and is wrapped up and buried in the earth. Of course you can't see it, but it's there, I know it exists . . .'

'Besides,' Ibu Kompyang adds, 'the life of the banten is not just physical. The man sitting outside just now is building a new house. I will make the offering and he will tell his children about how beautiful it was. It will be remembered and perhaps the child will come and ask me to make bantens when he builds a new house.'

Perhaps. But what of future generations? Ibu Kompyang's daughter, in her 20s, does not make bantens but works in a government office. Even the tukang banten is not sure that, were she a young woman today, she would choose her profession again. 'Education makes a difference and because many women work in offices and either don't have the time for or the interest in making offerings, things may change in the future and, in that case, the religion will change, too. It will diminish. But I hope that will not happen. Certainly not in my lifetime. I am still strong.'

cavort in and out of the lines. The men crazily weave back and forth to confuse the spirit and prevent it from being tempted to return home.

The height of the tower depends on the caste of the dead: common people use a simple hip roof, but for others, the tower can go as high as 11 tiers and reach a height of 20 metres (66 feet). Because of telephone and electrical lines, many towers today have been built with a hinge midway up, so that the men can pull the top back, temporarily, to pass them successfully. In other cases, more drastic measures are taken. In 1986, during the cremation of the last raja of Badung, lines were taken down and a large part of the city went without electricity for three days.

At the cremation grounds, the body is carried down from the tower and placed into a cremation animal. These fantastical creatures, made of wood and papier-mâché, were once divided by caste: black bulls and white cows for male and female Brahmans; winged lions, deer and a curious creature that is a mixture of elephant and fish, for the Ksatriya and Wesya. Here, the Balinese show their humour and wit—male organs wiggle wickedly underneath the bull; a playful lion, covered in purple velvet fuzz, licks his white plastic teeth with a red towelling tongue.

All of this glorious artistry is not long for the world. A command is given and the animals are set aflame. Since wood is quite expensive and slow burning, more and more Balinese have taken to using blow torches.

The next day, the body ashes are committed to the ocean in a ceremony attended by family and gamelan, hence the odd spectacle of elegantly dressed mourners parading by skimpily clad tourists on Bali's resort beaches. Other ceremonies follow, until finally the spirit is freed and the family has fulfilled all obligations.

Luckily for women, some other cremation traditions have changed. In 1815, a British official, John Crawford, noted in *A History of the Indian Archipelago* (Vol II) that as many as 150 wives and concubines 'devote themselves to the flames' at a king's cremation. At one such suttee, he wrote that the three widows 'glanced towards one another to convince themselves that all was prepared, but it was not a glance of fear, but of impatience . . . When the door opened (they were on a high gilded platform above the flames) each took her place on the plank, made three *sembas* [reverences] by joining her hands above her head, and one of the bystanders placed a small dove upon her head. When the dove flies away the soul is considered to escape. They immediately leaped down. There was no cry in leaping, no cry from the fire . . . There was not one of the 50,000 Balinese present who did not show a merry face.'

The Arts

Invariably, two points are made about Bali's arts: that there is no word for art and that all Balinese are artists.

The first is true. No one word encompasses the music, dance, theatre, painting, carving and song that enrich and enliven the island's life. A dancer is simply known by the part he or she performs; a sculptor as a wood worker or a stone worker; a painter as a picture maker. The arts were practised for the beautification of the island, the delight of the gods, and for communal expression of religious devotion, rather than as acts of individual expression.

As for the notion that all Balinese are artists, many Balinese can neither sing nor dance, nor play an instrument, nor paint. However, the Balinese have always connected what the West calls art with worship and they have interwoven their worship with the coarser thread of everyday life. So it is not unusual for a rice farmer to be a painter, for a policeman to be a member of the local gamelan, for a cook to dance as Candra, or for a doctor to know the risqué movements of the flirtatious *joged* dance.

The myths that are at the heart of the religion are also at the heart of Bali's arts, so every boy and girl hears the various stories of the *Ramayana* and the *Mahabharata* again and again—at shadow-puppet plays, at temple festivals, and carved on temple walls. Even the least educated bemo driver knows these myths by heart and listens, not only with delight but with a critical ear, to the radio plays broadcast over Radio Republic Indonesia.

No, not every Balinese can claim to be an artist, but art, as a mainstay of the island's intense religious life, is vital to everyday Balinese life.

Music

It is almost impossible to visit Bali and not to hear its music. From the very basic tluk-tluk-tluk of the kulkul to the jazzy syncopation of the local banjar's *gong kebyar*, the air is alive with music. Every self-respecting village has at least one gamelan and in many villages there are several. Music is heard almost everywhere: at temple festivals; on streets as families walk in funeral processions; even in restaurants and hotel bars, where a handful of musicians play an endless loop of lilting 'cocktail' music on *tingkliks* (bamboo xylophones).

The ancestry of the gamelan can be traced back to the bronze kettledrums of Southeast Asia which date to the second century BC. The word 'gamelan' is derived from *pegamelan* (handler), for the musicians strike instruments, be they gongs, metalaphones or kettles, with hammers, or, in the case of drummers—the bands' leaders—their hands.

The music is captivating. 'For most Western ears Balinese gamelan is immediately attractive,' writes Mantle Hood, a pre-eminent ethnomusicologist, in *Indonesia*, edited by Ruth McVey, 'for the simple reason that it corresponds more closely to the Western ideal of dynamic contrasts, of sudden shifts from fast to slow and loud to soft. The most brilliant orchestral ensemble in the Orient, Balinese gamelan achieves its singular appeal . . . through an extraordinary precision in ensemble performance. Thirty to 50 players perform . . . to a standard of perfection expected in the West only from a string quartet.'

This standard of perfection is achieved by constant practice. Top gamelans meet almost every night, particularly before the annual island-wide contest sponsored by the governor. Little boys and, more recently, girls may be seen sitting on their father's lap at practice, learning the music even before they are large enough to hold the hammers by themselves.

In all, there are 16 different types of orchestra on the island, each played within its own context, using its own compositions. Some require only two musicians, others two score or more. Even among gamelans of the same style, each set of instruments has its own identity. When the instruments are forged, they are all tuned together as a set; consequently, no two gamelans have exactly the same pitch, nor can their instruments be mixed.

By far the most popular is the gong kebyar, the lightning 'speed metal' of Bali. At the last count, there were over 4,000 groups on the island. Gong kebyar, which means explosion or flash, is so jazzy, so syncopated that it has to be heard to be believed. Hood observed: 'Balinese musicians seem to operate on the principle that if two players play interlocking parts as fast as possible, that is to say, each player plays every other note but at his full capacity for speed, the result will be a performance twice as fast as either of them can play.' The principle works.

The gong kebyar is made up of 14 instruments: two rows of kettledrums, individual pots, hanging gongs, sometimes flutes, and two drums. Instruments are paired and tuned to a five-tone scale of the seven-tone *pelog* system, one purposely pitched slightly higher than its mate, so that as the corresponding keys of the pair are struck, the music attains a 'shimmering' quality.

Gong kebyar is a relative newcomer to Bali's music scene, and was first noted by a Dutch official in north Bali in 1915. It has even been suggested that some of the jazzy syncopation may have been an unintended cultural import of Westerners who travelled on the cruise ships that anchored at Buleleng. Whatever the original inspiration, the style spread quickly, since the Balinese love almost anything new.

Other, older-style gamelans, *gong selonding*, are rare. Today, only 12 selonding orchestras exist, one of which is in the Bali Aga village of Tenganan (see pages 136–40). This nine-instrument gamelan is mentioned in lontar manuscripts and has, as its core repertoire, sacred music that non-initiates are forbidden to hear. It is based on seven tones, a style of music considered esoteric by most Balinese but now enjoying a revival at Bali's arts university.

There is also the *gambang*, a quartet of unusual looking 'xylophones' with varying lengths of keys placed in seemingly erratic positions—three long, three short, three long again—which is played in octaves by musicians who strike with double-headed mallets. The result is some of the most complex interlocking riffs of music on the island, if not in the entire world. The music is primarily played in south Bali just before a cremation and in Karangasem at temple festivals.

Perhaps some of the most haunting music comes from west Bali, where giant bamboo is fashioned into huge instruments that make up the *jegog*, the deep tones echoing distant thunder.

For a time, there was concern that gamelan music was on the wane. During the Second World War, the occupying Japanese confiscated the bronze instruments and melted them down as part of their war effort. Decades later, gamelans were again confiscated during the political upheaval in 1965, and many musicians who had been members of the Communist Party of Indonesia, or simply members of a musical club whose leader was a suspected sympathizer, were jailed or killed in the months following the attempted coup.

Recent history is on a lighter note. During the past decade, more and more gamelans have been produced, and music, along with the other arts, has experienced a 'renaissance'—thanks in large part to the influx of money from tourists and the hard work of the professors and teachers at Bali's two performing arts schools: Konservatori Karawitan Indonesia (KOKAR), the Conservatory of Indonesia, and Sekolah Tinggih Seni Indonesia (STSI), which is the College of Indonesian Arts.

There are four ways for visitors to hear Balinese music. The best way is to attend a traditional ceremony, best because the music is being played for the gods as well as the people and the accompanying pageantry and dances are spectacular. However, as anyone who has attended a temple ceremony knows, there are no time schedules—rubber time applies—and when a temple-goer says that the dance will begin early in the evening, the actual time could be from 4 o'clock in the afternoon to midnight.

A second venue is the STSI on Jalan Nusa Indah, near the Art Centre in Denpasar. Between 7 o'clock in the morning and 1 o'clock in the afternoon every day but Sunday, students are practising gamelan and dance. They also give occasional performances on the campus or in the villages. Ask a Balinese friend to call for information (tel. 72316).

There are also special dances set up for tourists, usually cut to suit general foreign taste. Some of the orchestras are quite good and what is lost in brilliance and enthusiasm may be made up for by certainty: the shows are among the only things on the island not operating on rubber time. The Tandjung Sari Hotel regularly schedules dance evenings that are exceptionally good and the *kecak* and *legong* dances in Ubud and Peliatan are usually fine. The *barong* dances every morning in Batubulan are, at least, dependable. Government tourist offices will have a full list of dances (see page 219).

The third, and truly amazing, way to see and hear a group is to commission a performance. There are quite a number of groups, ranging from a pair of tingklik musicians to an entire gamelan with dancers. The cost, by Western standards, is ridiculously low, certainly no more than $150 for an entire gamelan and corps of dancers, including all food, coffee, smokes and transport. A private concert is not only a treat in these days of cassette tapes and audiodiscs but also may be considered an offering to Bali's gods, who enjoy a good performance as much as anyone. Contact Wayan Rai S, a professor at STSI in Denpasar, who is in touch with various gamelans (tel. 27316). Try Ketut Suwentra for the jegog (tel. 27330), or write to him at Jalan Sandat, Gang III–IV, Denpasar.

Dance

Mounting the steps of a Mercedes tourist bus after seeing one of the morning barong dances in Batubulan, it may be hard for the visitor to realize that the first Balinese dances, along with the music and dramas, were sacred: elaborate, glistening offerings created not for the sake of art but for the pleasure of the gods and, as a bonus, for the Balinese, the children of the gods. Only recently has the notion of 'professional' dancers and musicians and paying to see performances come into Balinese life and even now, the professionals tend to be teachers or university professors.

It should be no surprise that there are so many types of dances and dance-dramas—the repertoire at STSI includes hundreds—since the Balinese gods love variety and the Balinese people have an inveterate interest in all things new and different. *Kreasi baru* (new creations) attract eager audiences. Some are performed only once and fade, like a day's offering, others catch the imagination of the Balinese and become 'classics'.

One such classic, the kecak dance, a hauntingly powerful dance-chant with the look and feel of an ancient ritual, is, in fact, a 20th-century invention. Inspired by the chatter of men gathered in a circle at a cockfight and the chorus of a sacred trance dance, the German artist Walter Spies choreographed the 'Monkey Dance' in the 1930s for a film.

Despite its origins, the kecak dance, so named for the sound of the monkeys' chant—'chak-ke-chak-ke-chak'—is perhaps one of the most popular dances on the island, and is performed at temple festivals and tourist shows alike.

Balinese dances are highly stylized, with distinct character types: *keras* or rough characters, such as clowns, demons, evil kings, witches and animals; and *halus* or refined characters, such as righteous kings, virtuous princesses and gods. At most performances, the Balinese will know who the characters

Balinese Dances

It is impossible here to list all of the dances one might see in Bali, but some of the dances one is most likely to encounter follow.

The rejang Seen during odalans, including those at Sukawati, Tenganan, Bungaya and Asak. A procession of girls and women, dressed in temple dress and elaborate halo-like golden headdresses sprinkled with flowers, winds its way slowly through the inner temple.

The pendet A welcoming to the gods. It is performed by a group of girls (traditionally virgins) who carry offerings, and sprinkle flowers with their hands; a man may join in, offering burning incense. Almost every little girl in Bali learns at least the rudiments of the dance, which is often performed in cut-down versions as a welcoming dance for tourists and dignitaries.

The legong A traditional court dance considered to embody the quintessence of Balinese style and grace. Once believed to be danced by the heavenly nymphs, on earth it is meant to be performed by three pre-adolescent girls. Wrapped in golden costumes, crowns of frangipani shaking with their delicate movements, the two legong dancers and their *condong* (servant) perform a story of a king who captures a princess and, rather than let her go, fights her brother, despite the warning of a bird that he will die. The tale, a complex one to begin with, is made all the more confusing for visitors, since the male and female parts are all performed by the young girls.

The topeng A mask dance, one of the oldest styles of dance in Bali and one of its most challenging. Without the aid of facial expression, dancers must convey the personality and emotions of the character solely through movements. There are a whole host of characters: a king, a princess, an old man, a dog, the village idiot and a camera-clicking tourist. Each has specific steps and gestures. Performances can either be solo or with four or more actors. Various masks are donned and the stories of Bali's rajas are told, with plenty of slapstick comedy thrown in.

The arja Balinese opera is popular entertainment at temple festivals with women taking the leading roles as men. The singing style is not easily appreciated by the Western ear, as the singers are trained to originate the sound from their head, rather than their diaphragm.

The baris A warrior dance. There is the solo, described earlier, and also the *baris gede*, a company of older men usually carrying spears or kerises. There are as many types of this dance form as there are villages that dance it.

The sanghyang A diverse category of dances performed to protect people against black magic and to fight epidemics or cure the ills of a village: plagues, droughts, disease or, in recent times, crime waves. The popular fire dance, performed for tourists at Bone, is taken from the *sanghyang jaran*, in which a man dances across burning coals, 'riding' a cut-out horse.

The barong Another tourist favourite which is performed almost every morning of the year in the village of Blahbatuh. The barong is a mythical figure in Bali, a cousin of the dragons used to celebrate the Chinese New Year. In the dance, the barong inevitably meets up with Rangda, the witch and manifesta-

dance, the barong inevitably meets up with Rangda, the witch and manifestation of evil (the principal character in the *calonarang* dance-drama, now combined with the barong). Though the barong usually wins the battle, the war is never finished.

Almost every village has a barong, some resembling lions, others cows, elephants, tigers, wild-boars and dragons, each manned by two dancers. These fearsome-looking creatures, with great shaggy manes and extravagant tails, protect the villages from black magic, epidemics and demons, playing a saviour's role that extends back centuries. On the special day devoted to the blessing of the barongs, the roads and paths of Bali are filled with parades of beasts.

The calonarang This dance presents Rangda, the evil witch and former wife of King Airlangga who ruled Bali in the 11th century. Wild and crazed, the wicked queen, with great fangs and pendulous breasts, wanders the woods, accompanied by her beautiful daughter. No one will marry the daughter for fear of the witch and, in revenge, Rangda and her evil followers dance in the night, bringing pestilence to the kingdom. Eventually, the source of Rangda's powers is found and peace is temporarily restored.

The keris This often ends the calonarang. Men attempt to stab the witch but, because of her black magic, enter into trances and turn the swords upon themselves. The trances entered into by dancers who perform nightly at tourist shows are about as deep as the viewers' understanding of them, but at other odalans the spirit surges like an electrical charge as dozens of men, all at once, run amok until their friends can contain them and lead them to a priest who sprinkles holy water on them to purify them and chase away the invading spirit.

The kecak—the 'Monkey Dance' A small troupe of dancers enacts a shortened version of the *Ramayana*, surrounded by a chorus of as many as 100 men and boys, wearing only black-and-white-checkered loin cloths and flowers behind their ears.

The *Ramayana* ballet The adventures of Rama, Laksmana, Sita and Hanuman, the monkey general, have long been favourites of the Balinese (see page 99). *Ramayana* segments are presented in ballet form, originally in *wayang wongs*, epic masked dance-dramas occasionally mounted in villages.

The joged A flirtatious social dance, once banned by the Dutch who worried that it would corrupt morals. A young woman dances solo, then taps an onlooker to join her. Some partners are more eager than others, some more deft. All make good-natured passes at the dancer, who skilfully deflects their advances, then takes the 500-rupiah notes they hand her before returning to their seats. After three or four partners, the dancer leaves the stage to be replaced by another. Such dances can go on all evening in the villages; foreigners, male or female, are certain to be tapped. Jembrana and Luwus, between Mengwi and Bedugul, are well known for their joged dancers.

are by costume, movement and melody before the first word is uttered. Children watch the temple dances with great enthusiasm and often mimic the hilarious walk of Hanuman, the warrior monkey, in their play.

A few rudimentary guidelines may help determine who is noble and who is not. Movements of feet, arms and legs combine with the positioning of the head and the movement of eyes to define the character and the character's mood. A witch will gesture more violently than a princess; an evil king will walk with more sudden, large steps than a *manis* (sweet) lord.

Nowhere in all this drama is individual emotion shown; all actions are symbolic and stylized. It is as if the dancer were a medium; the dancing state is called 'other thought'. Audiences who witness a frenetic *baris* dance are surprised, once the performance is finished, to find that the ferocious warrior is only a shy little boy who slips into the crowd.

Dances are earth bound: there are none of the great leaps and extensions known in Western ballet. Legs tend to be bent with the knees outwards. Poses are often taken but quickly, and arms, hands and fingers are never at rest but always sharply articulated. Every part of the body is in complete control, with parts of the body used for a particular movement and the rest remaining almost inhumanly still. This creates the appearance of simple movement and gesture, but anyone who has tried to mimic the slow movements of the *topeng tua* (mask dance of the old man), for example, or who has been chosen as a partner by a flirtatious joged dancer knows many years of hard practice lie behind such 'easy' movements.

Unlike Western dancers whose days of performing end at midlife, Balinese dancers begin performing at ten or even younger and do not stop until life gives out. There are parts for all ages, starting, for the males, with the baris dance, which requires more stamina than finesse, ranging on to parts such as the topeng tua and the wise king, where the power and knowledge of the character are displayed with minimal physical gestures. This is also true for females. A little girl may dance the *rejang* in the inner sanctum at a temple festival; four score years may pass and find her an old woman, still dancing the rejang with a slow-moving elegance and assurance at festival time, and still making her offerings to the gods.

Wayang Kulit

It was almost nine o'clock in the evening in a small village on the east coast of Bali. Farmers, priests, shopkeepers, government officials, husbands and wives, grandparents and children sat in a large bale just outside the temple gates, chatting in the dark. In front of them, a white-cotton screen glowed from the light of a coconut-oil lamp; in the yard just beyond the bale, men gathered in circles to play games of chance, while women looked over the clothes and sarongs hanging in makeshift stalls, set up for the temple festival.

Suddenly, the bright sounds of *gender* (metalaphones) jolted through the night, joined quickly by the rest of the gamelan. The audience drew closer, most people sitting in front of the screen, others—some boys, young men and a few curious foreigners—disappearing behind it. A leaf-like shadow swirled onto the white cloth, as if caught up in some mystic wind. A solitary voice rose, reed-like, above the tune. The shadow play—the *wayang kulit*—had begun.

Wayang kulit is the oldest performing art form in Indonesia, its origins dating back more than a millennium to rites invoking the spirits of ancestors. Since the first play, the stories of the *Ramayana* and the *Mahabharata* have been playing to packed houses, their characters appearing as shades against a screen. Brightly painted puppets, carved of cowhide and laced with a thousand holes, dance on thin bone or horn handles. Lit from behind by a lamp, they cast the shadows of gods, courtiers, giants and clowns onto the screen in front.

Even in an age of television and video, the plays are an important part of Balinese life, keeping legends alive, passing on moral and philosophical lessons. Virtually any occasion, from conception to death, can be celebrated with a wayang. In Bali, these performances last anywhere from three to five hours; in Java the performances are night-long marathons which can last until dawn. The first act, for foreigners who neither know the language nor understand the tales, can be the most tedious. In it, two figures of gods or princes give a precis of the problem at hand.

The *dalang* (puppet master), sits cross-legged, just behind the lamp while assistants on either side of the screen hand him the puppets. Members of the gamelan sit at the rear of the stage, following directions the dalang clacks out with a small wood block grasped between his toes. This he knocks against the puppet box to indicate a change of scene or punctuate a statement.

Although everyone in the audience will immediately recognize the characters, few will understand the words, since the refined characters speak Kawi, the ancient Sanskrit-based Javanese language. Their dialogue is translated soon enough by servant clowns, Falstaffian figures given to pratfalls and flatulence.

As the evening progresses, characters flit through the shadowy world, some sharply defined, others just suggestions of figures. Children curl up in heaps like kittens as the nobles and gods discuss the finer points of philosophy. They awake quickly though, as the action reaches its peak when the forces of good collide with the forces of evil, the music thundering and the screen flickering with flying arrows and fighting warriors. Bodies of slain giants litter the battleground as the legions of righteousness win a battle, if only for the evening.

The impresario of this event, the playwright, director, choreographer, vocalist for the scores of parts and conductor for the musicians, is the dalang. Using scenes from one of the two epics, he (sometimes she) improvises subplots and themes, incorporating lines of philosophy and riffs of humour. An accomplished dalang may touch upon topics as diverse as moral obligation, infidelity, motorcycle maintenance and, ever so obliquely, politics, all in one evening.

In fact, wayang kulit has been connected with politics and power since the time of the early Javanese kings who studied with dalangs. More recently, modern politicians have adopted it to project their own images. President Suharto likes to compare himself to Semar, the semi-god clown figure in the *Mahabharata* who has a bowling ball of a belly and a mind that cuts through all fat: he always seems to know what to do and, by giving his master good advice in times of trouble, inevitably saves the day. Suharto's supporters and detractors alike compare him to a dalang, cleverly manipulating the affairs of state to his best advantage.

A puppeteer may have as many as 300 puppets to choose from, though many of the characters are repeated, changed only in age or mood, and the audience knows them all. If a puppet master does not play an individual character well, the crowd may jeer or simply walk away. And although physical comedy is part of the theatre, to be truly humorous a dalang must have an intimate knowledge of classical literature and use it.

But the dalang is not just an entertainer, he is a holy man, a religious bard. The wayang mirrors things that are happening in a community; the shadowy characters often wrestle with subjects that more substantial beings fear to touch. If, for example, family-planning goals are not being reached, there will

be a joke about overpopulation; elders in a village troubled with inter-family bickering will ask that the dalang touch on such tensions.

To get a taste of living theatre, the visitor to Bali should try once to see a full-length play in a village. This way, there is time to wander to the back of the stage to watch the dalang as he asks the gods to give him voice, then deftly wakes the puppets from their sleep in the box. You can witness the hilarity of the crowd as one of the young clowns suddenly breaks into rap, and watch in awe as the dalang, with god-like swiftness and clarity after hours of performing, brings all of the plots and subplots together.

Painting

Bali's oldest lontar tells of the origins of her arts. In the beginning, men and women wandered naked. They had no permanent homes, no fields, no manners; they were, in essence, little better than animals. The gods were so offended that they decided to teach humans the arts, each god according to his capabilities. Brahma taught men the art of forging iron to make weapons and tools. Mahadewa trained goldsmiths and silversmiths. Citra Kara introduced the art of painting and drawing, picking students who understood colour and line. These painters were called *sangging*.

The sangging, who lived in the banjar of the same name in the village of Kamasan, were commissioned by the early kings of Gelgel and Klungkung to work on cremation towers and to decorate a new wife's apartments.

Their style of painting, called 'Kamasan', had flat, two-dimensional characters reminiscent of those in the shadow plays. These highly stylized art works were early comic strips, serialized stories from the *Ramayana* or *Mahabharata* and old Javanese literature. These were morality tales, filled with the glory of rulers, the obligations of the ruled, the rewards of the righteous and hell's torments for the wicked. Bali's Hindu princes hung paintings at celebrations and festivals to make sure everyone understood the new order of the day, much as Indonesia's current leaders use state-owned television to promote their own policies. The Kamasan paintings even appeared on the ceiling of the courthouse at Klungkung (see pages 128–32), so judges could consult the visual codes for ways to sentence miscreants.

Today, more than 100 artists and 20 designers are at work in Kamasan village, most of them in the banjar Sangging, the original site given to painters in the 15th century by the court in Klungkung. Just as in the old days, a guild-type apprenticeship exists, with the eldest member of the family acting as a designer, making the initial drawing, overseeing corrections and finalizing the painting with fine lines of Chinese ink, while junior members of the family fill in the drawings with colour.

Although there were individual artists who broke the rules, most notably I Gusti Nyoman Lempad whose drawings elegantly delineated the life of the gods and everyday Bali in the early and mid-20th century, the Kamasan style dominated painting in Bali until the 1920s, when two Western artists, Walter Spies from Germany and Rudolf Bonnet from the Netherlands, took up residence in Ubud. Young painters from the region were quick to seize on new techniques demonstrated by the Westerners and were happy to accept the ready-made paints, brushes, paper and canvas that were offered. An artists' group was formed, called the Pita Maha, to promote the work of Balinese artists. Some painters, such as I Gusti Ketut Kobot, who still works from his home in Pengosekan, stuck with the traditional wayang stories, but extended the range of colour and worked with depth and perspective. Others, like

Sobrat from Padantegal, modelled their painting after Bonnet using scenes out of local life as their subjects, giving attention to semi-realistic colouring and depth and perspective.

In the 1960s, younger painters developed an off-shoot of this school, focusing on nature—or an idealized nature—populated with fanciful frogs, birds, insects and ducks with colours unbound by earthly limits and shapes which were inspired more by pleasure of form than the actual creature itself. I Dewa Nyoman Batuan and his Community of Artists in Pengosekan create endless worlds of such sweet creatures, more works of design than of art.

The Batuan style, named after the village where it developed, evolved in the 1930s. The painters here, many of whom were dancers and musicians, used their theatrical instincts for stories that came from Hindu myths and old Balinese tales and, more recently, personal fantasies and the odd comingling of traditional Balinese life with 20th-century tourism. As in traditional Kamasan paintings, the use of black Chinese ink and white paint, highlighted with rich greens, blues and reds, gives the scenes a dark, dream-like quality and creates a painted tapestry in which every inch of canvas is populated with figures and forms.

Another painting school, the Young Artists, creates naive paintings of village life in bright, clear colours. This group started when Arie Smit, a Dutch painter who came to live in Ubud in the late 1950s, took some young Penestan farm boys under his wing, giving them paints and brushes and some idea of how to use them. Today, these artists are not so young anymore and many churn out work that is as tired as two-decade-old wallpaper. But there are still some, such as Soki, Cakra, Gadot and Pugir, who create deceptively simple scenes of the complex life in Bali's temples and fields.

Diametrically opposed to this style is the Academic school: painters who have been trained in art schools in a traditional Western manner. Personal style of art is emphasized, which differs significantly from the communal approach so often taken in Balinese work. Some of these painters, such as Nyoman Gunarsa, still use traditional Balinese motifs (in Gunarsa's case, the wayang characters) but apply modern painting techniques to express highly individual visions.

The best places to see examples of these various schools are at the Neka Museum, just outside of Ubud; the Art Centre in Denpasar and some art galleries, most notably Agung Rai in Peliatan and Neka in Ubud. Once acquainted with the styles, one may visit artists in their villages, the names of which are usually written under the artists' names on the paintings. Visitors are usually welcome, though often the painter is off tending his fields; only a few painters are successful enough to live only on the sale of their paintings.

Widely divergent in styles, the paintings are bound by ties that make them 'Balinese'. Dr A A M Djelantik, in his book *Balinese Paintings*, suggests two common aspects: 'The artist's concept of values in relation to his work, and the technique or the method of painting itself'. Painters have traditionally considered their paintings works with a purpose: to tell a story during a religious occasion. Balinese painters were proud to have their work copied, as frequently occurred, since it meant that others admired their skill and careful technique.

Djelantik also writes: 'For the Balinese, life is the realization of a divine order . . . everything has its own place and boundary'. So paintings, too, must be ordered, pre-planned, with the boundaries stressed by line. This divine order is involved from the beginning. Kobot and Meja, two masters, begin paintings only on special days so that there will be energy and power in their work. In such cases, Kobot explained 'the hand just goes', and a drawing can be finished in a day, the 'harmonies of mind and fingers' as the dealer A A Rai explains it.

Carving in Wood and Stone

Anyone who has driven around Bali understands the close harmony between Bali's natural beauty and its art. The island's baroque landscape is laced with curlicues of vines and mountain streams and crosshatched by stands of bamboo and trunks and fronds of palms; even the air is carved into geometric shards by the paths of jewel-coloured butterflies. This lush natural landscape is mirrored in the island's arts. Carvings emerge over temple gates and hotel garages, at the top of bale posts and at the base of kulkul towers. No surface is left unadorned. It is as if the Balinese, framed by tall volcanoes, deep ravines, craggy coasts and ever-changing seas, cannot abide the boredom of blank space.

It seems as if the Balinese are always carving something new. No matter how old a temple, some stone dragon or garuda will still be unfinished. This is, in part, thanks to *paras*, the stone the Balinese use. Ranging in colours from light grey to tan to grey–pink, paras—a type of soapstone— is very soft, a ready-made plaster of Paris of volcanic ash that lends itself to the elaborate Hieronymus Bosch-like worlds of gods, demons and jungles that occupy temple walls and compound entrances. The soft paras requires constant restoration; exposed to the elements and daily wear, a stone railing may need to be totally reworked after only 30 years. Because of this, stonecarvers and sculptors are in constant demand. In Batubulan, dozens of men and boys work at making statues of every shape and size for house temples and hotels.

The Balinese take their everyday world and commit it, with artistic licence, and often humour, to stone. Bas-reliefs show men making their bets at a cockfight at Pura Dalem Purwa in Bangli; priests look out across the temple grounds, perched high atop the gate at Pura Taman Ayun in Mengwi; a young man makes love to a young woman while she bathes at Pura Me-duwekarang in Kubutambahan. Enlarged genitalia and sexual acts frequently

appear on temple wall reliefs, obscene symbols, it is said, which help protect the pura from the harm of evil spirits.

Wood is another favourite medium. Elaborately carved palace doors made to squeak so that no one could sneak in or out of the women's compound to which they once led, now lead to tourist bungalows and expat houses. Intricately carved posts and beams adorn palaces and temples, such as the Pura Desa at Sebatu with its colourfully painted bale posts. For centuries, master carvers have made masks for topeng, barong Rangda, and wayang wong dances, carving the power-charged masks out of lightweight *pule* wood.

Today, woodcarving is a major industry in Bali. Entire villages are devoted to chipping away at carvings of one sort or another. Wooden ducks abound in Kemenuh; cookie-cutter cats and lions in Mas; birds in Peliatan; frogs and fish in Nyuh Kuning; garudas in Pujung and Sebatu and banana trees in Teges Kawan. An entire generation of young boys taps out set patterns, time after time, to fill containers bound for the United States and Europe.

For all the repetition and commercial hustle, there are also sculptures of genius; some are found at the Art Centre in Denpasar, others in the gallery of Ida Bagus Tilem, master woodcarver and entrepreneur, at Mas. And in the villages, there are still master carvers, such as Wayan Tangguh of Singapadu, who makes masks for some of Bali's best dancers, colouring the wooden faces with traditional paints made of bone, soot and clay.

Bali's Arts Czar
Made Bandem, Director of STSI

Probably the best known figure in Bali's art world today is Made Bandem, the slight, energetic director of the College of Indonesian Arts, STSI. Through his intelligence, showmanship and political savvy, this son of a rice farmer has managed to initiate a master's programme in Balinese performing arts, set up an annual arts festival and prod the Balinese public into thinking about professional theatre—no mean accomplishments in a land where people associate performance solely with religion.

A man who can inspire admiration and, sometimes, jealousy among his colleagues, Made Bandem has revived ancient dramas and dances and provided valuable backing and encouragement to new compositions and dances. Bandem shrugs off doomsayers decrying the commercialization of Bali's arts, and declares that there is a renaissance of arts, that the government is putting up money to preserve the arts, and young artists are striving to push the boundaries. But to maintain the distinct identity of the Balinese arts created by these skilled workers, Bandem argues, there must be a group of professionals who will both perform and preserve.

Bandem started as a skilled, and very young, worker: 'I was taught by watching and imitating—my father was a master at arja and my mother was a dancer—so by the age of ten I was already performing the baris and the arja and *kebyar duduk*,' he says.

The young Bandem learned the kebyar duduk, a dance performed almost entirely in a sitting position, from its inventor, Mario of Tabanan, and went on to expand on the renowned dancer's techniques. He also became famous for his enactments of the character Hanuman, and brought a crisp intelligence to the exacting vocabulary of the character's eye and hand movements, while injecting a lively grace into the mythical monkey's antics.

After graduating from KOKAR, Bali's performing arts high school, in 1961 he studied at the then-new ASTI, Akademi Seri Tinggi Indonesia (predecessor to STSI). Bandem then became one of the island's first dancers to study in the United States. On his return, he became chairman of ASTI/STSI and immediately set about trying to preserve Bali's unique arts.

STSI has 30 masters, 475 students and employs 65 full-time faculty members, some of whom have studied under such prominent Western artists as Martha Graham.

A threat to the diversity of Bali's dance forms is television, but Bandem hopes that STSI will keep one form distinct from another. Here, students study with village masters, and are then sent out to the village to learn and to participate, particularly in the odalans. In this way there is a connection between education and the villages and the religion; Taksu, the traditional power, is not lost in the dance. 'I don't want the arts to become too intellectual, too Western,' Bandem insists. To this end, classes examine the roots of the arts. 'Students, whether they're Balinese or Muslims from Java or Christians from

Sumatra, have to be based in the Hindu religion,' explains Bandem. 'For some, it's deep; for others, it's technical. But the base has to be there.'

The arts of Bali are relatively conservative. Some of this stems from the master–apprentice method of learning, but, in Bandem's opinion, much is due to the Balinese audience: 'In Jakarta, there's a festival of young choreographers' and composers' new works, and it's almost always well received. But here in Bali, the audience is so deeply rooted in its own culture that big changes from outside are not so eagerly accepted.' Consequently, many new works in Bali still focus on the traditional characters from the *Panji* stories that come from ancient Java, or the Hindu epics, the *Ramayana* and *Mahabharata*. Movements tend to be low and close to the ground for traditionally dances were done in a small space in a temple courtyard. Dances are becoming gradually more expansive.

Indeed, the casual visitor may be amazed at the life of Bali's traditional arts. All over the island, dance classes are filled with little boys learning the baris and little girls learning the legong. Bandem estimates that about a quarter of Bali's children learn to dance. All three of his own children dance and have performed abroad, though the eldest daughter has decided to break with family tradition to become a doctor and the son is interested in computer science.

For all the interest in Bali's traditional arts, Bandem worries about the quality. 'One of the biggest challenges comes from audio tapes,' he says. 'New compositions are made to fit in to a time space of 30 or 60 minutes. Before, a dance could go on for three to six hours. Now, it's like a digest: you get the essence of the movement, but you lose the feeling in between.'

The worst offenders, he suggests, are the daily tourist performances delivered without energy: 'Balinese dance is like a flower, it needs time to grow. With no time to develop, the dance withers and dies.' Bandem, who is a member of the House Assembly in Jakarta and who works on issues of culture and education, is trying to convince the government that there should be a type of union system so that villages will not be forced to 'sell' the arts.

Still, Bandem understands the intricate steps of diplomacy and successful tourism, and has, at least in one instance, cut the bud of Balinese performance before it could flower. When President Reagan and his entourage came to Bali in 1986, Bandem scheduled a pendet as a welcoming dance. He cut the ten-minute dance down to seven and then, responding to requests from the White House, cut yet again. 'Eventually, it was about a two-minute dance,' he said, smiling shyly. 'Probably the fastest pendet ever. One blink, you'd miss it.'

Destinations

Almost every spot on the island can be reached in a day's drive, so many tourists choose to establish a beachhead in the southern resorts and make daytrips to the island's more famous sites. A more intriguing itinerary is to stay for a while in some of the smaller resorts and towns, taking time to explore a countryside that, in many ways, has changed very little for hundreds of years. In small villages all around the island, farmers plant according to millennium-old religious edicts and women take months to weave traditional sarongs, painters wait for propitious days to begin their work and fishermen make offerings for an abundant catch.

The South

Since the first Westerners were washed up on these shores in 1585, southern Bali has been a point of contact between the island and the outside world.

Denpasar

Unlike the international resorts to the south, Denpasar, Bali's capital, is as Asian a city as can be. Hawkers sell their wares on the streets, women carry their market purchases on their heads, and signs offer night buses to Java, Harry's Komputers, typing schools, Chinese herbs, Indonesian remedies called *jamu* and video cassettes.

What was once a small town is now a bustling city and, as Bali prospers, so does Denpasar. At the edge of town in **Renon**, in plots where rice once grew, huge government buildings spring up in fanciful, sometimes outrageous, Bali-*moderne* styles, all monuments to the island's thriving economy and dreams of a yet brighter future. City land is expensive, space at a premium and shrines of family temples poke up like miniature mountains on third- and fourth-storey roof tops, snuggled next to satellite dishes and TV antennae.

Motorcycles and bemos, horse-drawn carts and trucks—loaded with cows, field-hands, temple-goers and produce—fight for space in the narrow streets. Dust and diesel fumes, the honking of horns, the scream of brakes and overworked engines combine to make the hot air heavy and, at midday, oppressive.

But at dawn, the city is still cool. On **Jalan Sulawese**, the pastel walls of the old Dutch buildings are still in grey shadows and women in sarongs move quickly with their baskets down the long arcade to the central market, **Pasar Badung**. The huge parking area is crowded with trucks bringing chickens and fish, fruits, vegetables and every manner of spice to market. Calls from the saleswomen quicken the morning: 'Buy my avocados, my durian. These mangos are ripe, *sudah masak!*'

Denpasar means 'east market' and that is exactly what it is. At the **Pura Melanting**, in the centre of the bustle of Pasar Badung, the goddess of prosperity and saleswomen is honoured. On the opposite bank of the muddy river is **Kumbasari**, filled with clothing and souvenir shops, a beehive of activity and kitsch. Lurid banners hang from the railings, advertising the films now showing at the cinemas on top of the complex.

There are other morning markets: **Pasar Sanglah** in south Denpasar, **Pasar Kreneng**, which is also the major terminal for buses to central and east Bali, and countless tiny neighbourhood markets that disappear with the dew.

Morning is also the best time to visit **Pasar Burung** (the Bird Market) on Jalan Veteran at the entrance to **Puri Satria**. The market is a makeshift aviary of hornbills from Sumatra, cockatoos from Irian Jaya and, unhappily, some protected species of birds such as the *Leucospar rothschildi*, Bali's prized, and now almost extinct, white starling. So enamoured are the Balinese of song birds, especially the sweet-voiced *perkutut*, that competitions to judge the best singing bird are regularly held and cassettes with an hour's worth of the cooing winners from Bangkok, Jakarta, Surabaya and Cirebon are popular among cognoscenti.

Morning is also the time to visit **Museum Bali** on Jalan Mayor Wisnu, across from **Puputan Square**. Opening times are from 7.30 am–1.30 pm, Tuesday to Thursday; 7.30–11.30 am, Friday; 8 am–12.30 pm, Saturday. The entrance fee is about ten cents. Although the cases are often dusty and smudged with fingerprints, there are treasures here for those who take the time to look. Next door is **Pura Jagatnatha**, a recently erected state temple dedicated to Sanghyang Widi, the supreme god. Temple festivals here are crowded events, with announcements bellowing from loudspeakers, like at a county fair.

Another museum worth a visit, particularly for those interested in Balinese art and sculpture, is the **Werdhi Budaya Art Centre**, at the complex on Jalan Nusa Indah. The Art Centre, built in the 1970s, has permanent exhibits, as well as special performances. The most lively event is the Arts Festival in June and July, a four-week-long celebration of all Bali's performing arts. For a few days in February, the **Walter Spies Festival** stages a thought-provoking mixture of modern dance, music and traditional arts dating back centuries. The **Walter Spies Memorial Gallery** at the centre has a small, though useful, display of reproductions of some of the German artist's most famous paintings of Bali.

Nearby on Jalan Nusa Indah, one can watch Balinese dancers and musicians practise traditional and modern works at **STSI, the College of Indonesian Arts**. The best time to go is in the morning.

Shopping in Denpasar

Denpasar has always been a market town, not only for produce. One of Bali's most respected antique shops, the **Arts of Asia Gallery**, is hidden at the back of a shopping centre at 27–37 Jalan Thamrin, Block C5 (tel. 23350). Opening times are from 9 am–7 pm. It is closed on Sunday. Verra Darwiko, the shop's proprietor, travels the eastern islands in search of rare carvings, gold jewellery and ceramics. His wife has a particularly impressive collection of ikat (specially woven and dyed fabric) from the eastern islands.

Other, less exclusive, shops may be found on **Jalan Gatot Kaca** and **Jalan Arjuna**, just off Jalan Gajah Mada, but beware: a little paint, a few months in the ground and, *presto*, an 'ancient' Chinese water jug emerges.

To the east of the main market, on Jalan Sulawese, is Denpasar's **fabric market**. Among the best of the dozens of shops selling fabric are **Dua Lima** and **Toko Murah**. Prices, after bargaining, are reasonable and one can easily have a shirt or dress made up at one of Denpasar's many tailors, such as **Alus**, right around the corner at 77 Gajah Mada, which is quite good, though time should be left for a second fitting (tel. 24522).

Jalan Sulawese is also home to Bali's **gold market** and a large sprinkling of jewellery shops, most of which have rather indifferent designs. Here, as elsewhere in Indonesia, gold jewellery is sold by weight.

Across from Alus on Gajah Mada is Bali's best coffee store, **Bhineka Jaya**, which has been selling its own fine blend of *robusta* and *arabica*, grown in the mountains of Tabanan and Buleleng, for more than 60 years.

Bali is celebrated for its hand-woven *endek*—cloth produced from a complex weaving and dyeing process—(see page 143). **Pertenuan AAA**, at 9 Jalan Veteran, just north of Puputan Square, has a good selection of patterns in endek. For batiks, try **Winotosastro**, 102 Jalan Sanur, Tanjung Bungkak on the road to Sanur, east of the pertamina petrol station. Prices are 'fixed', but ask for a discount!

The evening, perhaps, is the best time to shop in Denpasar and to take a ride in one of the *dokars* (pony carts). Most shops are open and office workers and youths wander the streets, looking in the shop windows or taking in a movie, while Chinese and Indian shopkeepers gather in small groups to discuss the day's business or family affairs. All in all, the atmosphere is quite festive and the streets, though dirty and smelling of sewage, are quite safe.

One of the liveliest places is at the southern end of Kumbasari shopping centre. Just as the sun sets, women start selling from their booths at the **Pasar Malam** (Night Market).

Sanur

On a white sandy beach, beside a tranquil lagoon, is Sanur, Bali's first international resort—quite appropriate, really, considering the number of foreign landings made on this beach: the Dutch in 1906, the Japanese at the beginning of the Second World War, and the North Americans at the end.

In fact, the Hotel Bali Beach was built here in 1966 with Japanese war reparation funds. Construction of its nine-storey tower—a monument, in the eyes of then-President Sukarno, to modern Indonesia—eventually spurred passage of a law stipulating that no building on the island could be taller than the highest palm tree, about four storeys. The law still holds, though some greedy developers are constructing hotels that suggest palm trees are growing taller these days.

Sanur is Bali's most sedate resort, which is also apt, since the town itself is home to a surprising number of Brahman families. It also has some of Bali's most ancient temples: in the **Belanjong** section, just south of the Sanur Beach Hotel, is a pillar of paras topped by a lotus which, according to its inscription,

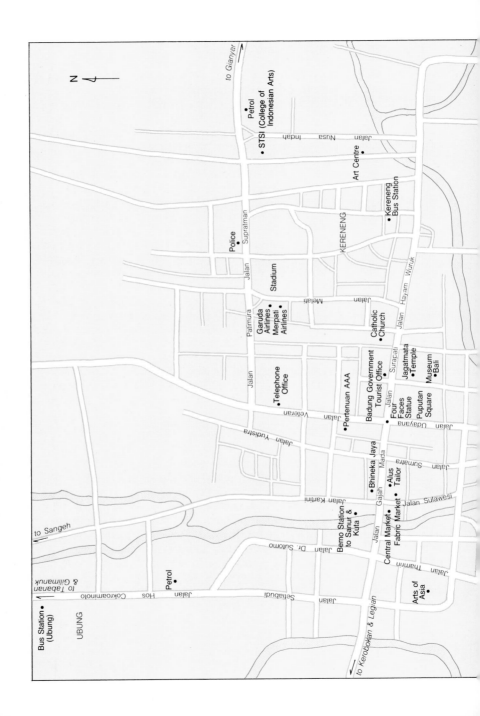

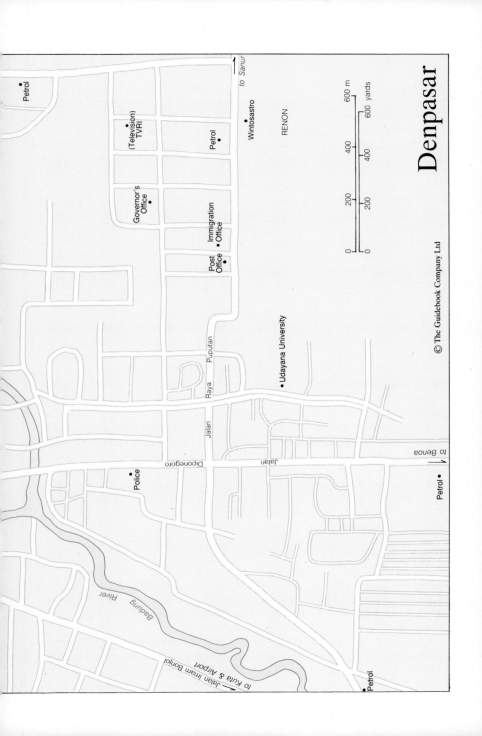

Denpasar

© The Guidebook Company Ltd

dates back to AD 914. At the end of Jalan Segara, in a small temple just before the beach, is one of several **coral pyramids** historians think may date to pre-Hindu times.

If visitors take the time, they can see shades of an earlier Bali, just by walking or jogging down the dirt paths that run off **Jalan Tandjung Sari** and the bypass. Here, Balinese farmers still walk along tending a few cows, sway-back pigs roll in the mud just beyond the family compound and old women wield long poles to pluck fragrant frangipani flowers. On the beach, at low tide, bands of women walk the flats to the reef, collecting coral and seaweed, while boys hunt for eels. At night, when the tide and moon are right, men fish by lantern light.

At odalans at the **pura dalem** many of Sanur's residents fall quickly into trances. There is a spiritually dark side to Sanur; it is a place known for its witches whose strong potions and spells are feared throughout the island so that those who do come here take extra precautions. One saleswoman never eats at her shop on the beach, otherwise some evil force 'jealous of my success, might put just a bit of potion in my food, and *pzzt*, it's over!'

Whenever there's wind, one is sure to see kites, some of them with tails of 20 metres (66 feet) or more that need six men to launch them and almost as many to hold the huge rope. In August, when the trade winds are blowing their hardest, an annual meet is held on the outskirts of Sanur when **kite-flying** teams compete against each other.

Also at Sanur is the rundown **Le Meyeur Museum**, the former home of Belgian painter A S Le Mayeur, who took up residence in the town in 1932 and painted warm-toned portraits of Balinese for the following 26 years. The small compound, which lies hidden behind the Hotel Bali Beach's sprawling grounds, on the beach just off Jalan Sanur, has been maintained as a museum since 1958 by his widow. The shutters of the house are carved with scenes from the *Ramayana*, while inside, walls are lined with Le Mayeur's paintings. The museum is open from 8 am–2 pm, Sunday, Tuesday, Wednesday, Thursday; 8–11 am, Friday; 8 am–12.30 pm, Saturday. It is closed on Monday. Admission is about ten cents.

Shopping in Sanur

Small stalls sell clothes, jewellery and art, most of which can be found elsewhere for less money. For books, however, **Sanur Bookstore**, just north of the Hyatt Hotel on Jalan Tandjung Sari, offers a wide selection of international periodicals, popular novels in English and books on Indonesia at prices considerably lower than those in large hotels.

Sari Bumi, on Jalan Tandjung Sari, is open from 8 am–8 pm, Monday to Saturday; 10 am–6 pm, Sunday. New Zealander Brent Hesselyn started one of Bali's first high-temperature kilns in the 1970s and since then he's made pottery for many of Bali's top hotels and restaurants. Here are plates, vases

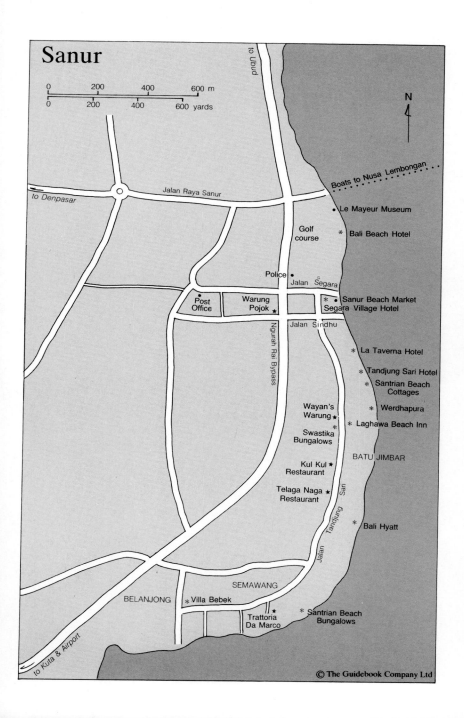

Sanur

0   200   400   600 m

0   200   400   600 yards

N

to Ubud

to Denpasar

Jalan Raya Sanur

Boats to Nusa Lembongan

• Le Mayeur Museum

Golf course

* Bali Beach Hotel

Police •

Jalan Segara

Post Office

Warung Pojok ★

* • Sanur Beach Market
Segara Village Hotel

Jalan Sindhu

Ngurah Rai Bypass

* La Taverna Hotel

* Tandjung Sari Hotel

* Santrian Beach Cottages

Wayan's Warung ★

* Werdhapura

* Laghawa Beach Inn

* Swastika Bungalows

Kul Kul ★ Restaurant

BATU JIMBAR

Telaga Naga ★ Restaurant

Jalan Tandjung Sari

* Bali Hyatt

SEMAWANG

BELANJONG

* Villa Bebek

★ Trattoria Da Marco

* Santrian Beach Bungalows

to Kuta & Airport

(Preceding pages) *The irrigation and harvesting of rice is managed by the* subak, *or rice cooperative*

and teapots in glazes of peacock blue, celadon, white and brown, as well as some huge handsome, unfired water jars from Lombok.

Linda Garland Designs, at 1001 Jalan Tandjung Sari (tel. 88765, 88557), sells home furnishings, encompassing 26 different crafts culled from seven islands, including batik quilts and oversized bamboo furniture. Quality is high, as are prices.

A bit further north, Lily Coskuner, a young Balinese who studied design in Germany, uses handwoven ikat for the stylish designer-look clothing that she makes and sells at **Nogo** on Jalan Tandjung Sari (tel. 88765, 88557). Rather than using the wildly mixed colours favoured by the Balinese, she has designed textiles that incorporate varying shades of one or two colours; because of the combinations, the handwoven cotton often takes on the lustre of silk. Customers may choose from styles on hand or have their own styles custom made for them in about four days. One can see lovely endek being woven in the shop.

A turn away from the beach at Jalan Pantai Sindhu leads to the **workshop of Pak Ferry**, who designs and makes rattan furniture.

On Ngurah Rai Bypass, at the corner of Jalan Bali Beach, Javanese gates and old Balinese tax-collector's trunks make a curious fortress around **Warung Sekar Tanjung**. The shop offers a wide selection of antique and re-production furniture. Prices are reasonable and the proprietor is quite helpful (tel. 88027).

Nusa Lembongan and Nusa Penida

Across the channel from Sanur are the dim outlines of two islands once used as penal colonies. Visitors can sail to Nusa Lembongan, the smaller of the two islands, which is part of the kabupaten of Klungkung. Hire one of the small motorized *prahus* (boats) that leave just after sunrise from the beach north of the Hotel Bali Beach. Prices depend on the number of people going, the speed of the current, the wind—which determines how much the skipper spends on gas—and one's skill at bargaining. Nusa Lembongan is known for its world-class surf and most Westerners heading over to the island are carrying a board. There is also a beautiful coral garden for snorkelling and diving that can be reached by chartering one of the small *jukungs* (fishing boats) on the island.

The island is only about two square kilometres (one square mile) and dry. Cacti grow under tall palms and most islanders make their living by harvesting seaweed at low tide. Sailboats wait offshore, to take bales of the stuff to Jakarta, where it is shipped to Japan and Japanese restaurants all over the world. There are a few cheap and basic *losmen* (family-run small hotels, like the British 'bed and breakfast' establishments) here, and a sprawling, sand-floored bamboo restaurant, where surfers hang out, talking about the day's rides.

The larger island, Nusa Penida, is the mythical home of the giant Jero Gede, an evil figure responsible for plagues and famine. The soil is too poor and dry for rice farming, and only cassava and corn can survive. There are few cars here, and foot and horse are the main methods of transport.

Serangan Island

Just a kilometre (half a mile) off the Sanur coast, Serangan Island can be reached by prahu from Sanur, or by a walk at low tide, starting from **Belanjong** in Sanur. It can also be reached from a road off the bypass, just to the south of Sanur. Serangan is called 'Turtle Island' after the giant sea turtles that come to lay eggs on its shores and that are subsequently caught and sold at market by villagers. Serangan is still home to some traditional boat builders and is also the site of **Pura Sakenan**, one of Bali's most sacred temples. During the two-day odalan here, the bay is so crowded with boats one could almost walk from one to the other to reach the island.

Between Sanur and Kuta, near the turn-off to Benoa Harbour, are mangrove swamps and mud flats used by residents to make salt from the sea. At present, **Benoa** is a sleepy little harbour with waters too shallow for most ocean-going vessels and an entrance that is equally dangerous. It was on these reefs that the Chinese ship foundered at the turn of the century, the plunder of which eventually led the Dutch to send their troops against the Balinese. There are a number of charter boats for hire (see pages 195–8), and more may be on the way, as the government plans to develop the harbour, complete with a water-ski-towing facility. So much for the sleepy harbour.

Kuta, Legian and Seminyak

Once upon a time, Kuta was a quiet little fishing village. Once upon a time. Today, there are more telephone poles than palm trees and the narrow streets and *gangs* (alleys) are honeycombed with shops and losmen. Tinselly, noisy, just a little naughty, Kuta is Bali's trendy resort town, catering for travellers on all budgets.

By day, **Jalan Legian**, Kuta's main drag, is hot and dusty and filled with roaring motorbikes and beeping bemos. Backpackers wander the alleys in search of a cheap night's lodging; Japanese surfers head for the beach, sporting all the right gear; shoppers stagger under bundles of baskets, wooden banana trees and micro-bikinis for the folks back home. Australians, most of them young, most of them swilling large bottles of Bintang Beer, are everywhere.

Armies of vendors showcase armloads of watches, boxes of silver bracelets and rings, portable chess sets and newspapers—today's, perhaps, or last week's. The onslaught is such that a best-selling T-shirt reads: 'No, I don't want a f—ing Bemo/postcard/massage'.

There are pubs and pizza joints and Mexican cafes; the roofs may be bamboo, the chairs and tables rattan, but the food is Western, the music is Western and the faces, for the most part, are Western.

But then there is the beach. Kuta's beach is wide, white and palm fringed. The surf rolls in from India in perfect crests, excellent for body surfing, boogey and surf boarding, and the cliffs of the Bukit rise up dark and dusty grey across Jimbaran Bay. On a clear day, turning away from the sea, one catches a glimpse of Gunung Batukau. Hawkers hover like flies over sun-bathers, offering some attractive services: a long massage in the shade of a palm tree; a pineapple sculpted like a child's top; plaited and beaded hair à la Bo Derek (remember?) and even a manicure for those into sand-buffed nails.

Everyone—tourists and Kuta residents alike—gravitates to the beach to watch the sunset. Little boys do handstands, their older brothers kick a ball around, Balinese fathers walk with their babies, while young Balinese women dip in the ocean fully clothed—more demure than their Australian counter-parts. The entire tableau is—briefly—backlit by a spectrum of gold, copper, pink, purple and cerise. Then darkness.

But only for a short time. Neon signs blink on: Manhattan, Casablanca, Waltzing Matilda. Blasts of rock and disco music boom out of competing bars with names like Cock 'N' Bull and Koala Blu. Contests—beer drinking, and wet T-shirt for the ladies—draw crowds of young Aussie students. After midnight, discos like **Peanuts**, primarily an Aussie hangout, the **Spotlight**, where Kuta cowboys ride a mechanical bull, the **Sari Club** and the **Connection** come to life.

There are still some drugs here, though dealers, as often as not, are undercover police and sentencing is severe. By and large, booze is the intoxicant and beer the drink of choice. On Tuesdays and Saturdays, as many as 200 partiers join the 'pub crawl', riding a bus on a jagged path to inebria-tion, via half-a-dozen watering holes—all that's needed is a few dollars and a hankering for a hangover.

A bit off the beaten track is Legian and its northern neighbour, **Seminyak**, where cars share the main road with old men selling *kue putih*, a sweet white rice concoction, from a steaming, singing pot. The beach is wide and for now, rice fields occupy the spaces between losmen.

The club scene north of Kuta is markedly different too. Two outdoor, beach-front discos, **Gado-Gado** and **Double 6's**, open on alternate nights. The collegiate gaiety lasts with the music, almost until sunrise. The crowd tends to be more international than that in Kuta—with young travellers who would be at home in the clubs in London, Paris, Berlin, New York or Rome. Many start their evenings at **Made's Warung**, a trendy cafe in Kuta that has become the social hub of expat life in Bali.

Despite the Western influence, the Balinese in Kuta, Legian and Seminyak still maintain their traditions. Just off Bemo Corner, gamelans practise in a

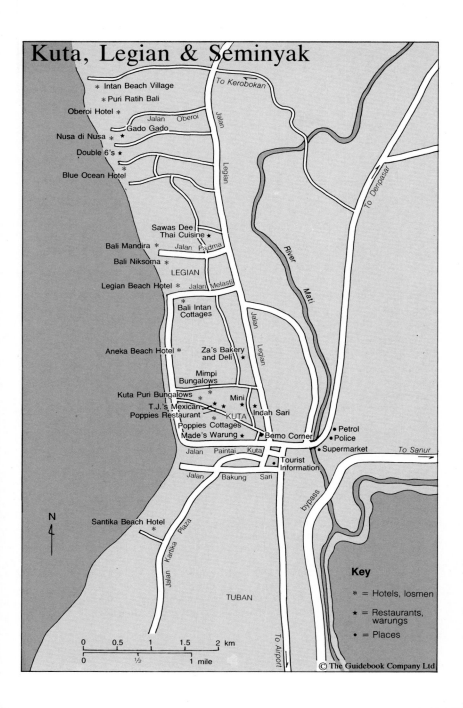

Kuta, Legian & Seminyak

* Intan Beach Village
* Puri Ratih Bali

Oberoi Hotel *

Jalan Oberoi

* Gado Gado

Nusa di Nusa * ★

Double 6's ★

*

Blue Ocean Hotel

To Kerobokan

Jalan Legian

To Denpasar

Sawas Dee
Thai Cuisine ★

Bali Mandira *

Jalan Padma

Bali Niksoma *

LEGIAN

Legian Beach Hotel *

Jalan Melasti

River Mati

*
Bali Intan
Cottages

Jalan Legian

Aneka Beach Hotel *

Za's Bakery
and Deli ★

Mimpi
Bungalows

Kuta Puri Bungalows

*
★

Mini
★

T.J.'s Mexican ★ ★

Poppies Restaurant ★

KUTA

Indah Sari

Poppies Cottages

Made's Warung ★

• Bemo Corner

• Petrol
• Police

Jalan Paintai Kuta

• Supermarket

To Sanur

Jalan Bakung Sari

•
Tourist
Information

bypass

N
↑

Santika Beach Hotel

*

Jalan Kartika Plaza

TUBAN

To Airport

Key

* = Hotels, losmen

★ = Restaurants,
warungs

• = Places

| 0 | 0.5 | 1 | 1.5 | 2 km |

| 0 | ½ | 1 mile |

© The Guidebook Company Ltd

New Perspectives

Ida Bagus Nyoman Rai, Painter

Though he is a member of Sanur's Brahman caste, Ida Bagus Nyoman Rai is most interested in the day-to-day aspects of the town's beach life. The painter started his career over 60 years ago with some sketches in the sand. 'There weren't many foreigners then,' he recalls. 'A few guests might wander by and look, but the winds always blew the pictures away.'

One day, the Swiss artist Theo Meier walked by and was impressed with what he saw. Meier offered the young Balinese some paper, ink and brushes. Since then, Rai has been recording the colourful life of Sanur in black and white, delineating the progression of a sleepy hamlet into an international resort. The paintings are peopled with Balinese working the fields and the seas and, more recently, tourists caught in luxuriant patterns of waves and vegetation.

Though he studies everyday life, Rai says he paints from his head. In a recent painting, for example, villagers surround a beached whale. 'Long ago when I was a child, the whales would often get caught inside the reef, when the tide went out, and die. The women would go and take oil from the dying animal and we would have light for our lamps for months.

'I like to paint the tourists, they're part of Sanur's life. But the tourists don't like to see themselves. They just want to see women harvesting the rice, men working in the fields, no cars—the way things used to be,' he says.

multi-storey banjar. A traffic jam may be caused by a procession of worshippers on the way to temple.

Shopping in Kuta

One does not go shopping in Kuta; shopping, to a large degree, *is* Kuta. Everywhere, one is greeted by calls of 'Hello! Come look here!' Art works, rolled in tubes, are peddled off motorcycles; shapeless cotton dresses hang on endless racks; surf shops sell bathing suits, surfer baggies and sleeveless T-shirts in colours as vibrant as the tropical sunsets. There's something for everyone: a cotton sundress for $6, a pair of shorts for $2, an elegant silk jacket for $150. At every level, prices are significantly lower than in stores back home and negotiable at all but the most exclusive shops—usually those with glass fronts, air conditioning and staff who are fluent in English, Italian, perhaps Japanese, as well as Balinese and Indonesian. Some shops add a six to eight percent surcharge for credit card purchases. This is the rate they are charged by the banks.

The following are a few select stores, most open daily from 9 am–9 pm. No credit cards are accepted, unless mentioned.

On Jalan Pantai Kuta, which runs from Bemo Corner to the beach, try: **Galang Dua Koleksi**, which has a small and unusual collection of antique-style clothes with handmade lace and delicate embroidery. **Mr T Shirt**, part of the three-store group that includes **Tops** at Bemo Corner and **E E Louisiana** on Jalan Legian, has very inexpensive men's batik shirts in many colours. **Mr Bali** was the first 'upmarket' store for men and sells shirts, jackets and pants. Two other Mr Bali shops are on the southern end of Jalan Legian and on Jalan Buni Sari. All major credit cards are accepted. **Kerta I Bookshop** has a useful selection of international periodicals and second-hand books.

North from Bemo Corner try **Hey** on Jalan Pantai Kuta. It has moderate to high-priced men's and women's cotton sports jackets, pants and printed T-shirts. **Indigo**, on Jalan Legian, sells a good selection of reasonably priced cotton batik shirts for men and women, as well as other styles. American Express cards are accepted. At **Baik Baik**, Asih Migliavacca, a young Balinese, designs the stylish men's and women's clothing, down to the fabrics and buttons. Some styles combine modern designs with antique batik chops from the court city of Solo in Java. Others, such as a print and sequined jacket, look as if they came straight out of *Vogue*. There is also a small, but interesting, collection of jewellery. Prices tend to be higher than in most other shops, but so is the quality. All major credit cards are accepted. Another upmarket shop, **Tao Galleries**, offers slightly more conservative women's clothing, again with specially designed fabrics. **Kekal**, across the way, is an appealing shop selling handmade lace-trimmed blouses, dresses and shirts, some highly detailed, some with pearl-drop buttons.

For home furnishings, **Ikat** sells sophisticated ikat and batik cushions, tablecloths, quilts and some furniture. Another Ikat store is on Jalan Pantai Kuta. American Express, Visa and Diners Club cards are accepted. In Legian, **Rumah Manis** displays tables, plates and lamps designed by a French woman who lives in Bali.

By far the best store for antiques in Kuta, and certainly the most charming, is **Polos**. No sign marks the entrance, just look for an arbour covered with vines on the ocean-side of Jalan Legian, south of Jalan Melasti. A courtyard and several rooms are filled with an impressive collection of masks and carvings from Java, Timor and Kalimantan; stonecarvings from Sumba and Savu; Chinese urns called *martavans* and reproductions of Dutch colonial furniture. An, the owner, got into the business by collecting masks and is gracious and helpful. Major credit cards are accepted.

For children, **Kuta Kidz** at Bemo Corner is a pint-sized store with pint-sized cotton tank-tops, bathing suits, skirts and shorts. **Bali Doll**, on Jalan Tanjung Mekar off Jalan Legian near Yanie's Cafe, is another minuscule shop with Balinese Cabbage Patch-style dolls.

Before the country signed the international copyright agreement, Indonesia was *the* spot for pirated tapes. Now the selection is more limited, but the prices are still low. **Mahogany**, once one of the best music stores to be found anywhere, thanks to the excellent and eclectic taste of the owner Wana, still has an intriguing selection of Indonesian and Western music. Wana is working on agreements with smaller record producers to bring the selection back to its days of glory. It is open until 11 pm. All major credit cards are accepted.

On Jalan Melasti, **Batik Banana's** has shorts, skirts and elastic-waisted pants in muted batiks of teal, rose and violet—a pleasant change from the primary colours elsewhere. Another Batik Banana's is in Seminyak.

Bukit Peninsula

The Balinese called this area *Bukit* (hill), the Dutch *Tafelhoek* (table land); tourists and travel agents, referring to the large enclave of international-standard hotels built on the southeast coast of the peninsula, call it **Nusa Dua**.

But the area they are all talking about is the high limestone plateau south of Kuta and Sanur, a 'hill' ringed with spindly skeletons of *kapok* trees and cacti and dotted with rocky fields of soybeans and cassava surrounded by fences of stunted trees and bushes.

Jimbaran

A few kilometres away from the turn-off to the airport, Jimbaran is a small seaside village of fishermen with one small hotel–restaurant overlooking the wide, arching beach. Though there are no waves here, it is much quieter than

Kuta and Legian beaches and a good place to windsurf during the rainy season when the winds blow from the west. This is also the Bali home of Fred Eiseman Jr, an American who has spent several decades here exploring the island to write *Bali Sekala and Niskala*. Several chapters are devoted to Jimbaran.

On the Road to Uluwatu

Narrow, twisting and potholed, the road climbs up sharply, close to the peninsula's highest point, **Gunung Ingas** at 202 metres (663 feet), just west of Bongol.

Hikers or picnickers looking for a quiet beach might consider **Palangan**. Just after the 'Y' in the road, a rocky dirt path, good only for motorcycles, four-wheel drive vehicles, or hikers, heads west. Three kilometres (two miles) away is **Cengiling**, a small village of fishermen and weavers. Beyond this, a trail down a cliff leads to **Pura Balangan**, a cave temple on a deserted, sandy beach.

Back on the road to Uluwatu, the rolling hills are covered with orchards of mandarin orange trees. Just before the parking lot for the temple of Uluwatu, a narrow trail cuts to the west to **Suluban**, Bali's most famous surfing beach. Marked by a sign, 'Berlilancar Pantai Suluban; Suluban Surfing Beach, 2 km.', the dirt path passes through small fields. A 15-minute walk leads to a small parking area for motorcycles. From here it is a few more minutes' walk to Suluban beach and the largest breakers in Bali which roll in from the Indian Ocean, uninterrupted for thousands of kilometres. During the dry season, when offshore winds make conditions ideal, surfers sit on their boards beyond the break, waiting for the perfect wave at high tide. But be careful; the beach is rocky and not for swimmers or novice surfers. A gaggle of small warungs at the edge of a steep cliff offers warm soft drinks (there is no electricity here), simple food and a spectacular view. And it's not just surfers who can enjoy this!

High atop a narrow promontory a ninth-century temple, **Pura Luhur Uluwatu**, is among the most important in Bali. It is also one of the most beautiful, with steep steps leading up a hill of frangipani and through elegantly simple split gates of limestone block and white coral. The Balinese call the temple style *bersayap* (winged), which describes it perfectly. Empu Kuturan, the Javanese priest who is credited with revitalizing religious customs and ceremonies in the tenth century, came to this spot and added shrines and merus to the temple. In the mid-16th century, the Siwaistic priest Danghyang Nirartha is said to have achieved nirvana here.

Pura Luhur Uluwatu means the 'Temple above the Final Stone', and so it is. Beyond the stark middle courtyard, past the guardian *ganeshas* is the tiny inner courtyard, precariously perched on cliffs so steep only swallows and a

Cili figure associated with the rice goddess

tribe of monkeys call them home. The sea crashes against giant boulders 50 metres (164 feet) below. Sunset is quite special, but be sure to leave enough time to get here.

Nusa Dua

For a vision of contemporary architectural styles on Bali, visit the huge hotel complex of Nusa Dua, started in 1970 with World Bank loans. On the site of a former palm plantation, this is a tourist ghetto, meant to keep the tourists and the dollars rolling in, without touching the local culture or, it seems, local life. Most of the hotels are owned by off-island interests, unlike the smaller hotels and losmen elsewhere. Some of the beaches are as good as Kuta's. A rock outcrop near the Nusa Dua Beach Hotel produces a fantastic water spout. Further south, out of the village of **Bualu**, a dirt road leads to a sandy beach, the centre of the area's seaweed-farming industry.

The *Ramayana* and *Mahabharata*

Two Indian epics, the *Ramayana* and the *Mahabharata*, lie at the base of many Indonesian arts. For centuries, Balinese kings and court choreographers found their casts of gods, kings, demons and clowns in these tales and those same characters are brought to life every night by Balinese dancers and puppet masters. Of course, it is impossible to tell such tales in one evening; instead small sections are told which emphasize some element that the village leaders hope will both inform and engage.

The *Ramayana* is an Indian epic of 24,000 verses that dates back to the first century BC. The epic poem was introduced to the Indonesian archipelago by Indian trader–sailors. Reliefs of the story can be seen on Prambanan, a ninth-century Hindu temple in central Java, and a Javanese translation dates back even further. Today, the story is retold in almost every style of performance in Bali and names of favourite characters are found on everything from fast-food restaurants to photocopy shops to beauty salons.

Briefly, the story is of Prince Rama, the reincarnation of the Hindu god Wisnu, and his beautiful wife Sita. Although the king intended to make his son Rama his heir, he is forced, through the treachery of his second wife, to banish Rama. Sita and one of Rama's brothers, Laksmana, follow him into the forest. There, the demon ruler Rawana tricks the two brothers into leaving Sita alone and kidnaps the princess. Realizing, too late, what has happened, the brothers follow the demon and, along the way, are helped by a magical bird, Jatayu, who dies attempting to rescue Sita. Eventually, the two princes join forces with the monkey king, Sugriwa, and his general, the white monkey Hanuman—a favourite among audiences. After yet more adventures, Rama and his forces win a final battle, with the prince killing the demon Rawana. In one ending, Sita jumps into a fire to prove her purity and is protected by the god of fire. The party returns to Rama's kingdom, where he assumes the throne.

The *Mahabharata*—one of the world's longest poems, with 90,000 stanzas—details the conflict of two related families, the Pandawas and their greedy cousins, the Korawas. Again, jealousy starts the action. When the eldest Pandawa is appointed king, the Korawas manage to steal the kingdom in a game with loaded dice. The five Pandawa brothers and their wife, Drupadi, are exiled for 12 years in the forest and, after countless adventures and a year of living among peasants, they return to claim their kingdom. The Korawas refuse to abdicate and a great war ensues. It is in this section that the *Bhagavad Gita*, the Celestial Song, is found, in which the Pandawas' ally Krishna, an incarnation of Wisnu, speaks to Arjuna of the virtues of obligation and duty. Ultimately, the Pandawas representing good, triumph over the Karawas representing evil, and balance is restored to the world.

The Hill Country

Here, in the hilly interior of Bali, is the heartland of many of the island's arts, with villages of craftsmen, dancers and artists, and vistas of terraces forged a millennium ago.

On the Road from Tohpati to Ubud

This road is a litmus test for the effects of tourism on the island. Previously a single-lane stretch of tarmac, it is now filled with heavy traffic. Shops and stores line the route, and villages, each known for a specific craft, follow in quick succession.

Batubulan

Batubulan means 'moonstone'. Here, stonemasons chisel many of the guardian statues that stand at intersections and bridges to frighten away the *bhuta kala*, ghosts who like to play in such spots. Made Sura, Wayan Mergog and half a dozen other carvers have set up shops where stone gods, demons and animals, fashioned from the soft paras rock, stand in disordered ranks along the roadside. Most business comes from local residents, but shops can also arrange to ship statues overseas. If there's time, one can have a statue custom made. The village is also known for its dance troupes, which perform the barong and keris dances daily.

Celuk

Just around a bend in the road, Celuk has grown prosperous from the sale of handcrafted silver jewellery. Several hundred silversmiths make their homes here and many of them have opened their own shops. Much of the jewellery is mass-produced, which in Bali means that one style is reproduced many times by several craftsmen, who make each piece by hand. One store that maintains a high level of craftsmanship is **Ketut Sunaka** at 28 Jalan Jagaraga just off the main road. Down a nearby alley is the young smith **Ketut Sudarsana's small shop in his family compound**. The selection is not as great, but the prices are slightly lower.

Sukawati

To see one of the island's most respected craftsmen at work, head up to Sukawati and visit **Nyoman Sadia's home and family workshop**, off the main road on a lane just north of the village's large temple. Each piece of jewellery is custom made here, some are traditional designs, others more whimsical—frogs clutching at pearls as earrings, a lotus encompassing a ruby as a ring. Wayang Wija, the island's most renowned shadow-puppet

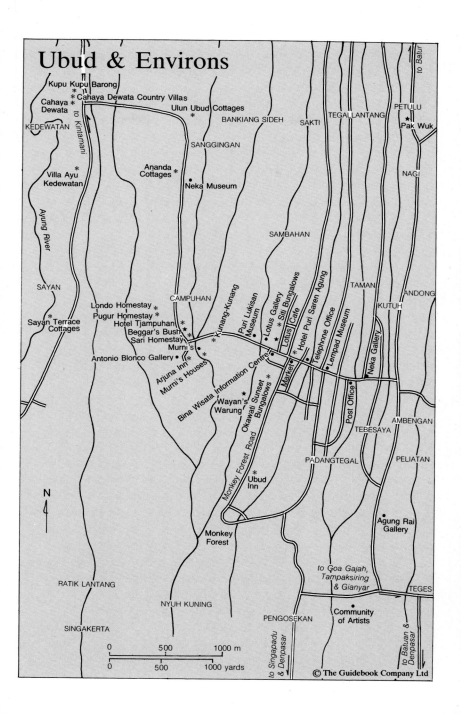

master, hails from here. Puppets may be bought at the **art market** or some-times at Wija's home which is just a block behind the morning market.

Batuan

For centuries, Batuan has been an artistic hub, home to dancers and musi-cians, carvers and painters, and scholars from abroad. The village temple, **Pura Desa Batuan**, is not only a product of these artisans, but a carved biography of village life, as resident Hildred Geertz notes. Sculpted gambuh figures dance at the east gate, much as the gambuh troupe of the village has performed for generations. Two of the **giant statues** standing guard on the road were built in the 1980s with money from one of the wealthy art-shop owners. (Professor Geertz is at work on a book on Batuan's village temple, which gives a fascinating tour of the temple and insights into the history and life of the village. Pick up a copy, if it is available; all profits go to maintain-ing the temple.) Local festivals are always enlivened with dances, such as gambuh, topeng and wayang wong. For those who feel inspired, a number of dance masters give lessons.

Batuan is perhaps best known for its artists. One of the most successful is I Made Budi, who does lively scenes of modern Bali, complete with tourists and buses and windsurfers. It is not hard to find his family compound on a narrow alley not far from the temple. He and his son, who paints scenes from the *Ramayana* and other myths, are quite willing to talk to visitors about their art and will point the way to other, respected painters in the village, including

Rajin, Togog, Bendi and Barak. Budi, who visited the United States and did a collection of lively paintings of Las Vegas there, has a small cottage overlooking a rice field, which he occasionally rents to visitors.

Mas

Mas, which means gold, is actually one of the centres for Bali's woodcarvers. The largest studio is that of Ida Bagus Tilem. Here the prices are high and so is the quality of carving. Tilem has put much of the money his shop makes back into the village; the temple has been refurbished with elaborate carvings, and at festival times, some of the best dances and most spectacular costumes can be seen here. Ida Bagus Gelodog and Ida Bagus Anom, among the island's most respected mask carvers, have studios here.

Peliatan

For generations, this small village has been famous for its legong dancers—one troupe appeared with Bob Hope, Bing Crosby and Dorothy Lamour in *On the Road to Bali*. **Tirta Sari**, a respected group which has toured in California and Tokyo, performs at 7.30 pm, Friday, at the **Puri Kaleran**. Those interested in taking **legong classes** may contact the group's leader, Anak Agung Gde Bagus, at Mandala Bungalows, a short distance south of Jalan Ubud's Apotik (Chemist), on Jalan Peliatan. His daughter, Raka Astuti, is a dancer and instructor for Tirta Sari and welcomes Westerners to her classes. Another young woman, Menuh, teaches legong to about 20 young girls every Saturday and Sunday. It was here also that Togog, a Peliatan craftsman, carved the first wooden banana tree, of which there are forests today.

One of the best places to get an overview of Balinese art is at **Agung Rai Gallery** on the main road. Agung Rai, the young owner, studied art, but in 1978 decided he would rather exhibit the work of others. The gallery/museum is a rambling collection of buildings on the family compound, where old women still cook at an open stove and chickens wander around the rice barn. Some paintings are for sale, others are part of the permanent collection. Classes are given for young boys of the village, and visitors are welcome to join in.

Pengosekan

One kilometre (half a mile) away from Peliatan is the **Pengosekan Community of Artists**. Started in the 1970s by I Dewa Nyoman Batuan, this group of painters creates Rousseau-like scenes in soft pastels of jungles, birds and animals, most of which have never existed in Bali but which fit tourists' ideas of a tropical paradise. Further along the road, past the Monkey Forest, the villagers of **Nyuh Kuning** are busy carving little animals dancing the pendet.

Ubud

Traditionally a centre for Balinese arts and crafts, Ubud has become the Asian equivalent of Saint Paul de Vence in France or Sausalito in California. Foreigners from around the world retreat here to get acquainted with the gentle pace of Balinese life. Some write books or paint landscapes of the hills, ravines and rice fields. Other Westerners, invariably wrapped in newly purchased sarongs and smoking *kretek* (clove cigarettes), talk about writing and painting. Here, it seems everyone, foreigners and Balinese alike, is an aspiring artist.

Information

To get one's bearings in Ubud, a quick visit to the well-informed, English-speaking young people at the **Bina Wisata tourist office** is in order. The office is in the centre of town on a road called Jalan Ubud, on the rare occasions it is called anything at all. Opening times are from 8.30 am–7.30 pm, Monday to Saturday. Bina Wisata offers free, detailed information about regularly scheduled and special cultural events. Staff can help arrange transportation to performances in nearby villages and can provide a complete list of hotels and homestays in the area. An invaluable map of Ubud and its environs is on sale here for about $1. It is designed by an Ubud resident, Silvio Santosa, and indicates bike and foot trails and selected points of interest. For about the same price, a companion booklet, *Bali Path Finder*, provides detailed descriptions of bike and walking excursions, a full schedule of dance and wayang kulit performances in the Ubud area, some herbal remedies and quirky stories about Westerners in 'Paradise'.

Communications

Tranquil and peaceful, until recently, Ubud seemed far away from it all. Now, thanks to communications gear that is said to have been left behind after then-president Reagan's visit to Bali, a number of hotels have direct lines, and some residents even have fax machines. It is now truly part of the global village. Long distance phone calls can be made and telexes sent from the phone office on the main road, just west of the market. Poste restante services are available at the post office, located about three-quarters of the way down Ubud's main road, going towards Peliatan.

The Arts

Ubud and the surrounding villages have always had thriving communities of sculptors, woodcarvers and painters working for Ubud's royal family and decorating local temples. It wasn't until the 1930s, however, with the arrival of Walter Spies and Rudolf Bonnet, that Ubud acquired its reputation abroad as a centre of the arts.

Spies and Bonnet began teaching Balinese artists Western conventions, such as the use of bold colours and perspective and employing scenes from everyday life, flowers and fauna as subject matter. (Up until then, Balinese painting had primarily been connected with religious ceremonies.) In 1936, local artists joined Pita Maha, a painter's cooperative aimed at encouraging the arts in Bali, established by the Cokorda Gede Agung Sukawati of Ubud, with the help of Bonnet and Spies.

Every Saturday night, the king held a reception in his palace, the Puri Saren Agung, and invited Westerners living or staying on the island to see the work of Ubud artists. These 'Bali nights' launched the careers of a number of Bali's better known artists, such as Ketut, Kobot, Sobrat and Meregeg.

Pita Maha survives today as the **Ratna Warta**, a group which organizes exhibitions of the work of local artists. And, across from the central market, the **Puri Saren Agung** is still active, with dance and gamelan performances. The **Lurah group** is considered one of Bali's top gong kebyar. Puri Saren Agung is the only palace that remains to the Ubud royal family. It is inhabited by the son of the last king of Ubud, and visitors are welcome to wander in its outer courtyards. The palace was built in the 17th century and has been renovated many times.

The **Museum Puri Lukisan** exhibits the work of Balinese painters. Opening times are from 8 am–4 pm. Admission is less than ten cents. The director, Tjokorda Gde Putra Sukawati, will help arrange group or individual lessons in painting, sculpture, music or dance. He can be contacted at Hotel Tjampuhan, just after the bridge (tel. 28871).

The **Neka Gallery** is a good spot to see and buy paintings. The **Neka Museum** is too, and traces the evolution of Balinese painting styles, with galleries devoted to Javanese and European painters in Bali as well. The museum is located on a ridge overlooking the Campuhan River, one kilometre (half a mile) north of the Hotel Tjampuhan. Opening times are from 8 am–5 pm. Admission is less than ten cents.

Shopping in Ubud

A few years back, the provincial government 'cleaned up' Ubud's **market** in the centre of town and erected a two-level concrete structure that has all the charm of a car park. Stalls are filled with more of what is found elsewhere: pretty baskets, cheap batiks, brightly painted wooden birds and banana plants.

Most interesting are the days when farmers come to sell their produce, on a three-day cycle between Ubud, Payangan and Tegalalang. Women whose earlobes have stretched wide around bullet-like gold earrings called *subeng* sell disk-shaped pink and beige rice cakes, and fruit and vegetables grown in the nearby mountains. If you miss the market in Ubud, consider driving or biking up to **Payangan**.

Two stores in Ubud are worth visiting for high-quality jewellery. **Lotus**

Ubud Hikes

Though Ubud's languorous beauty tends to lead most Western visitors to long days of faineantism, it would be a shame not to venture out into the hills and rice terraces which radiate out and away from the centre of the town. Mountain bikes are perfect for Ubud's hard climbs. They are, at this time, unavailable in the area. Those serious about biking should bring their own, or rent one in Sanur before heading out.

A most leisurely walk follows **Monkey Forest Road** into the sacred forest itself, with its noisy inhabitants. There is also the pura dalem, or temple of the dead, and a tall banyan tree, marking a gorge which leads to a swimming hole.

A favoured walk or bike ride begins at the **Campuhan Ridge** off the road at the Ubud side of the bridge crossing the Campuhan River. The entrance is to the right of two foodstalls. Take the middle of the three paths and follow it across the river. Continue up a hill and skirt the ridge which runs between two river tributaries. The path passes through the rice fields of Sebali and Keliki. Off the surface road in Keliki, a path leads to the left past a temple and down to a river. Cross here to reach **Payangan** and take a bemo back to Ubud.

If, instead of taking the path at Keliki, you continue 12 kilometres (seven miles) on the main road to Taro, you can find warungs, coffee plantations and family compounds that show no Western influence. A seven-hour walk ends at the village of **Batur**.

A less arduous trek starts with a right turn at the far end of **Keliki**, where a paved road leads to **Tegallalang** across a river valley. A small road leads back three kilometres (two miles) to Ubud through **Taman**.

The exceptionally steep flight of stairs which rises up on the left from the main street in **Campuhan**, just north from the Tjampuhan Inn, leads to a narrow path that winds up and down through the rice fields and past a small stream. Accompanied by well-behaved rows of ducks, you can walk west to Penestanan and come out at the road which runs along the Ayung River, at Sayan. Follow one of the paths to the steep, rocky climb down to the cool waters of the **Ayung River**. The views are well worth an hour's effort.

An arduous half-day hike starts in Ubud and leads across the river to the **monkey forest** at **Sangeh**. Cross the rice fields westwards from Campuhan, as described in the route to Penestanan, then walk north along the road from Sayan to Kedewatan. Take a path down to the river, wade to the other side, and climb to Bongkasa. Head west, via Taman, to **Sangeh** where bemos await.

Galleries on the main road next to the Cafe Lotus, features the work of Ela Helmi, an Australian designer who lives in Bali, along with designs of other artists. The quality of workmanship is quite high and so are the prices. **Kunang-Kunang/Murni's Collection**, a few doors down from Murni's Warung, has a tasteful, less expensive collection of jewellery, some casual clothing and household furnishings.

Campuhan

Just down the hill from Ubud, past cliffs of vines and ferns, and over a bridge where two rivers meet, is Campuhan, which means convergence. This has long been a favourite site of Westerners. Walter Spies built his home here, and the composer Colin McPhee lived just up the road in Sayan. Some long-term expatriates who came to Bali decades ago and married Balinese, still have studios here. Antonio Blanco, a Catalan humorist–painter has a gallery, studio and home at the bend in the road just past the old suspension bridge.

Penestanan

In the late 1950s, Dutch painter Arie Smit established himself in Ubud. In between painting his own portraits of village lives, Smit taught young boys to paint visions of their daily lives. These artists came to be known as the **Young Artists**. Although the adjective scarcely applies today, one can still stop in and see these painter–farmers at work in their home–studios and perhaps purchase their bright, naive paintings. Stone stairs across the road from the Tjampuhan Hotel lead to Penestanan, the centre for these artists. Pugur and Londo, two rice farmers, have their homestays just at the top of the stairs and will show visitors their paintings, as well as introduce them to other artists.

Sayan and Kedewatan

The road past Campuhan eventually meets the road which runs through Sayan and Kedewatan, two small villages that have some of Bali's most beautiful views. Just hidden from the road is the **Ayung River Valley**, a plunging gorge. Pause at one of the restaurants on the ridge for a look (see page 218).

The road north is a quiet, beautiful route to **Gunung Batur**; the road south, though riddled with potholes, passes through gorgeous countryside, eventually leading to **Batubulan**.

Petulu

On the road from Peliatan, north of Ubud, is the **Future Peace Art Gallery**, filled with the socially conscious art and writings of Made Kertonegoro. A bit further along on the left is the **shop and home of Pak Wuk**, one of the area's well-respected umbrella makers.

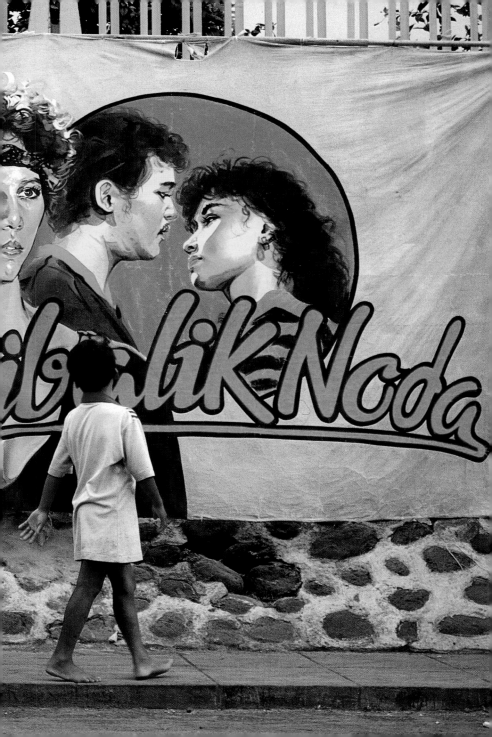

A Spirited Meeting

Ketut Rendo, Balian

Balinese from all walks of life consult balians, the island's shamans, who can offer special help and advice, where more mundane methods have failed. Recently, Puspa, a language teacher, went to the police in Denpasar to report that a thief had broken into her home and stolen her television and VCR. The officer told her to get a new lock—and to consult a balian.

There are two types of balians: *usada* and *ketaksan*. Usada spend years studying the lontar, learning the prescriptions to heal and ward off black magic; usually these balians follow a family tradition. Others, like ketaksan, gain their power from Taksu.

Ketut Rendo, the balian Puspa visited, is a ketaksan. The courtyard of her Denpasar home, scattered with children's bikes, birdcages, a Vespa, a British flag and a faded needlepoint of a dog, is almost always full of supplicants seeking the help and advice of the 52-year-old woman. While some balians stress the mystical side of their role, Ketut Rendo follows her 'calling', as she puts it, with an earthy practicality. She tries to get to the bottom of her visitors' problems—as if she were some sort of spiritual psychiatrist. 'Often, I ask the goddess not to make me go into trance,' she explains. 'It's tiring.'

The goddess, in this case, is the goddess of Batur, Ketut Rendo's patron. Sitting in a small bale, Ketut Rendo lights incense, pours some *arak* (a strong local alcohol) on the ground and then sprinkles holy water (kept in a small ketchup bottle), and flowers in five directions and on the visitor. With her eyes seeming to focus on infinity, she asks the goddess of Batur to come and give guidance. Then, listening to the complaints of her visitor, Ketut Rendo responds calmly with the information passed on to her by the spirits.

· 'Most people come because they are sick because of a spell, or to find out where something is that has disappeared, or because they got a message in a dream and they want to talk with an ancestor. Maybe they are having trouble conceiving,' she says. Some problems are easily solved by reminding the visitor to make the proper offerings in a timely manner at a family shrine. Others are more difficult. A group of engineers came once after a half-finished bridge collapsed for no apparent reason. The explanation Ketut received was that the gods would not allow the bridge to be built because there was an ancient shrine below. A new site was selected.

In Puspa's case, Ketut first described the layout of Puspa's living room, a room she had never seen. Then she described the thief. Puspa thought she knew the man and Ketut suggested she confronted him, when others were around.

Visitors bring offerings for the gods and payment for the balian: banten (small offerings of palm and flowers), lengths of white cloth, rice, coconuts, coffee, fruit, cookies and some money. Those too poor for elaborate offerings are still welcome. Ketut Rendo says that the goddess helps anyone of good heart—'Christians, Muslims, people from any country. The goddess is the *sakti* (sacred, holy object) with magical powers of Wisnu, the lord of truth; she doesn't care what religion a person follows, she will help give power to reach the people's ancestors if the people make the right offerings and if the feeling is right.' Ketut believes.

Ketut Rendo never neglects the small ceremony and prayer that welcomes the goddess to the compound. It helps connect her with the spirit (much as office workers have to report to their boss):

> *Here, people have come*
> *So please descend*
> *Help give guidance*
> *And sit here for a while.*
> *I have an offering for you.*

Her prayer is simple and direct. 'That's all that is needed; I think it's funny to say things in Kawi, to say things that I don't understand the meaning of. All the power comes from the heart,' she explains.

As for the efficacy of the power from the heart, Puspa, for one, believes in it. The day after visiting the balian, the young woman went to an office adjacent to her home to confront the man who fitted the balian's description of the thief. The boss there told her the man had not come to work for two days though he was meant to pick up several weeks' wages. A colleague said he had seen him carrying 'some stuff' the day he was last seen—the same day Puspa was robbed.

Ketut Rendo has been a balian now for 25 years and though she gained the spirit only in her mid-20s, she says there were early signs that this would be her destiny. 'I was a premature baby, with a lump on my head and a tusk in my nose and out of my ear. My mother was upset, of course, but a balian told her it was a good sign.'

The signs soon disappeared. When she was 16, Ketut earned her living by dancing the arja at the Bali Hotel. At 20 she was married and selling coffee in the market. By the time she was 30, she was often in a trance at home. 'When I felt confused, I'd often go to the river that flows from Batur. Once, I found two stones which I knew I had to take home and put away. Soon, there was an odalan at the dam at Batur. Someone went into a trance, the goddess asked, "Where are the two stones? They belong here." I had not gone because I was nursing my baby and could not enter the temple. But my sister, who knew nothing of the stones, told me about the person in the trance. "I know who has them," I told her. I felt the goddess, it was only like a shadow. I knew I had to be a balian or I would die. Next day, people were waiting outside, as they do now—I had told no one, they just came.'

Sometimes people come seeking black magic. These she firmly turns away. 'I know if someone doesn't have a clear conscience. Sometimes they will become angry and threaten me with black magic, but I don't worry. It's often jealousy that spurs evil here in Bali and those who use black magic are usually greedy and want things others own. They will go to the temple at night, to ask for more power. I don't worry; I'll give the problem to the goddess.'

Monumental Bali

Some of the oldest archaeological remains in Bali, dating back to the tenth and 11th centuries, can be found between two rivers which start on the slopes of Gunung Batur and run parallel courses south to the sea—the Pakerisan River meaning 'keris', and the Petanu River meaning 'cursed'. A J Bernet Kempers in his excellent book *Monumental Bali*, speaks of this as 'The Land between Parallel Rivers', a region, as he puts it, 'preeminently suitable to hewing out rock-cut candis and monasteries. The wells, as springs of fecundity and prosperity for agricultural Bali . . . were long ago transformed into sacred watering places and temple compounds.' According to *Usana Bali* (Balinese history/legend), fearsome demons, giants and evil kings inhabited this land when Hindu priests and nobility came to the island. In fact, the land was probably already occupied by the original Balinese—Buddhists, Hindu ascetics and hermits, long before the Javanese Majapahit gentry made their impact on the island in the 14th century. A day or two may easily be devoted to exploring this older Bali, with its monasteries and sanc-tuaries hewn out of ravine walls. It is best to start early in the day, while the air is still fresh and the tour buses are still waiting in hotel parking lots. Though some of these sites have only been 'discovered' in the past few decades, the speed with which they have become 'destinations' is, in itself, monumental. It is advisable to take a picnic lunch along; the scenery begs for one to stay just a little longer and, although there are some restaurants, none can be heartily recommended.

On the Road to Tampaksiring

The first stop along this road should be Bali's Archaeological Museum, **Parbakala Gedong Arca**, north of Bedulu. It is open from 7 am–2 pm, Monday to Thursday; 7–11 am, Friday; 7 am–1.30 pm, Saturday. It is closed on Sunday. The museum, started earlier this century by the Dutch, is now directed by Made Sutaba, who has asked all farmers in the area to notify him should they find something unusual. In fact, many sites have been discovered by archaeologists and scholars thanks to information from local residents. Dr W F Stutterheim in the 1920s, could never have completed his study (which continues to be the basis of academic research in the area) of the Pejeng region without such unofficial field workers. J C Krijgsman, who headed the Archaeological Service in the 1950s, found the rock-cut candis at Tegal-linggah from local information. The museum's modest displays give a quick overview of prehistoric Bali, with a map of the sites, and neolithic and pa-laeolithic stone picks, adzes, beads and tools. Most interesting of all are the sarcophagi, some dating back to 500 BC. Bali is one of the most productive sites of such prehistoric stone caskets. Some of these caskets are small—

90–120 centimetres (35–47 inches long), others are large enough for the burial of one or more corpses at full length. Each was carved out of a single block of tuff or, in some cases, coral. The lid, and sometimes the lower section, were equipped with knobs carved with rather frightening faces. (Apparently, so a volunteer at the museum said, two heads—one on top, one at the bottom—suggest copulation and so, the beginning anew of life.) Most of the sarcophagi were found after grave robbers had got to them, but some, still untouched when unearthed, held weapons and jewellery along with the corpse.

Tirta Empul

If the morning is still fresh and undisturbed by tour buses, the next stop is ten minutes up the road at Tirta Empul. This is a major tourist site and best avoided during most of the day. According to an ancient text, the site was founded by the holy priest Sang Ratu Candra Bhaya Singha Varmadeva around AD 960. Legend has it that a demon king, Mayadanawa, restrained a holy hermit of Majapahit from making appropriate offerings to the gods because the demon believed himself to be supreme. The gods descended from the mountains and marched with their armies from Besakih Temple to Tirta Empul. During the battle, the evil king's minister created a river of poison: 'Whoever drinks its water dies, whoever bathes in it falls dangerously ill.' The gods' army drank and was wiped out and, try as they might, the gods could not change the river's water into holy water. Faced with this dilemma, the gods created a new watering place to revive their warriors. This was Tirta Empul. From this spring comes the Pakerisan River, along which many holy sites are found. Mayadanawa, seeking escape, changed himself into various forms, finally becoming a huge stone in the poisoned river. The gods' archers were not fooled and shot the stone with their arrows killing Mayadanawa and his minister. Their blood became the cursed river, the **Petanu**. For 1,700 years, until the 1920s when the curse was deemed at an end, the Petanu was not used for irrigation, drinking or bathing.

Although the spring—clear, quick water bubbling out of a sandy bottom—is considered most holy and banjars from all over Gianyar bring their barongs here each year for a blessing, the path leading to Tirta Empul is profane and lined with dozens of hawkers' booths. High above the temple, most of which has been recently built, is the former weekend palace of the late President Sukarno, a noted ladies' man who is said to have liked to watch women bathe in the pools.

Just a short way down the valley is **Mengening**, another spring, less well known on the tourist circuit but quite well known among the Balinese, who come here to bathe their kerises for good luck in the holy water.

Gunung Kawi

A bit further south, in the village of Tampaksiring, is Gunung Kawi, the 'Mountain of the Poets'. A long steep path of stairs leads past the inevitable trinket shops into a beautiful gorge and the impressive, almost forbidding entrance of the **11th-century temple**, hand-hewn deep into the volcanic rock. Immediately to the left of the entrance are the **queen's tombs** and directly across the Pakerisan, the **royal tombs**. These were never literally tombs but simply touted the spiritual grandeur of the royalty before and after death. The candis, or temple façades, are somewhat similar to those found in central Java, and are cut into the rock. Springs, flowing past the king's candis and spouting into a pool, are said to purify those who bathe here. To the left of the king's candis is the main cloister, a powerfully simple cluster of niches and rooms, one carved deep into the rock with windows and a skylight. Still further to the right, reached by a path that winds up a slope past rice fields, is what archaeologists call the '**Tenth Tomb**', which was discovered by the Dutch artist W O J Nieuwenkamp in the 1920s.

The Pejeng Region

The Pejeng region contains the majority of the island's antiquities, with over 40 puras. **Pura Panataran Sasih** in Intaran, houses one of Bali's most important antiquities, a kettledrum cast in one piece of bronze dating back to the early Metal Age, around 300 BC. Although bronze kettledrums, shaped something like an hour glass, have been found elsewhere in Southeast Asia (particularly in Alor, an eastern island in the Indonesian archipelago), the **Pejeng Bulon** meaning 'Pejeng Moon', as it is known, is by far the largest at 186.5 centimetres (73 inches) high and 160 centimetres (63 inches) at its greatest diameter. According to ethnomusicologists, this drum was used to accompany ceremonial dances and funeral rites of kings. Legend has it that, originally, the giant drum was a wheel on the heavenly chariot that carried the moon on its journey across the night sky. On one trip, the shining wheel spun off and landed in a tree at the temple compound of Pura Penataran Sasih. A thief who had crept into the temple, worrying that he would be caught because of the wheel's brilliance, climbed the tree and urinated on it. The wheel lost its shine, but the thief lost his life.

To this day, it is unclear whether the Pejeng Bulon was cast in Bali, as fragments of a mould suggest it was, or whether it was imported from elsewhere in Southeast Asia. Some scholars believe the latter to be the case since the motifs on the drum have nothing to do with designs found elsewhere on the island.

A little to the south is **Pura Kebo Edan**, with its enormous statue called the **Pejeng Giant**. This robust statue which is over three metres (ten feet) tall, is wreathed with snakes and dances on a statue of a human body, while a pair of lesser demons watch.

Close by is **Pura Puser ing Jagat** (Navel of the World) or, as the temple's priest puts it in more modern terms, the 'Centre of the Island'. Dewa Ketut Arta, who lives just outside the temple compound with his wife, is happy to show visitors around the temple, pointing out the ample cockfighting arena in front and the two stone elephant temple guards. The temple gates are new, the old ones toppled during the 1963 eruption of Gunung Agung.

Happily, the eruption didn't destroy the temple's fine statuary, including the **Pejeng Vessel**, a cylindrical stone vessel 75 centimetres (30 inches) tall, that to this day is used for holy water. Its surface carving, a bit worn from the elements, shows snakes and gods in regal costume. *Kinnara* (human-like birds) and *apsaras* (nymphs) fly past a mountain background of trees and rocks, while at the base, fishermen work the sea. The Balinese name for the vessel is 'Naragiri' meaning the 'Mountain of Man' and, according to the priest, it dates back to 1329. Every six months, the priest holds a ceremony in which he places a small silver cup in front of the vessel. He and supplicants pray and, in a quarter of an hour, says Dewa Ketut Arta, the cup is filled: 'Sometimes the water is red and I must throw it away for it means hard times for the village; other times it is yellow; the water is then clean, holy, and the economy will be good.' Festivals here are accompanied by topeng, wayang kulit, legong and dramas.

Another temple mystery the priest is pleased to relate involves a 120-centimetre (47-inch) stone phallus, placed in a small shrine towards the mountains, and a triangular stone carved in the shape of a vulva, lying seawards. If, after ten years of marriage, a couple still has no children, the couple come and pray and take holy water that has been dripped on the stones. In three months, the priest predicts, the woman will be pregnant.

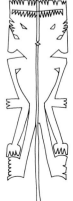

Male good-luck figure

Linear masks decorate the side of the Pejeng Moon

Yeh Pulu

Still further south, just off the road heading towards Ubud, is Yeh Pulu, a place known of only by local Balinese until Nieuwenkamp heard about 'a rock with many and large wayang figures' and decided to investigate in 1925.

Past a small stream, the 'rock' is a long strip of reliefs carved into a solid rock, about 25 metres (82 feet) long and two metres (seven feet) high, which culminates in an excavation that must have once been a hermit's lodge.

The reliefs, rustic scenes which bear little resemblance to traditional Balinese motifs, tell several stories in comic-book style. The first is most likely of Krishna, who has offended the god Indra and tries to safeguard himself and others from the resulting storm by using a mountain as an umbrella. Elsewhere, a high-caste woman is followed by a porter to a hut where an old woman stands behind a half-closed door. Monkeys cavort, pedanda-like characters pray while demons look on. Hunters attack a bear-like creature, a frog does battle with a snake, and a woman holds a horse's tail the better to travel further, faster. All of this culminates in a two-armed ganesha, to which people make offerings. Wayan Kutat, the old pemangku who calls the temple home, lives off the money left at the ganesha's feet and the fish she keeps in the spring. She knows little of the history of the place, but archaeologists date this very unusual set of reliefs to the 14th or 15th century.

Teges

Most visitors have seen **Goa Gajah, the 'Elephant Cave'**, long before they walk down the steps to the huge carved-rock retreat in Teges. The character of Goa Gajah has bulging eyes, pointed ears and fearsome teeth and shows up on T-shirts and ashtrays and even at the Bali Hyatt hotel pool. Along with Tanah Lot, this is the most visited site on the island and some modern-day explorers simply may not have the patience or endurance to put up with the crowds of other tourists and pedlars.

Briefly, the site consists of the Elephant Cave, rediscovered by a Dutch archaeological officer in 1923 who wrote of 'a monster's head with elephant's ears'. The carvings are quite flamboyant, with fantastical scenery populated by monsters, animals and a witch. Yet, for all this, the cave—a T-shaped crevasse thought to have been used by Siwaite monks at the beginning of the 11th century—is not so large. Nearby is a small pool, the remains of which were unearthed in the early 1950s. Buddhist figures can be found in the pavilions in front of the cave and down in the ravine. Fragments of stupas are found further along the Petanu River.

The village of Teges is also famous for its gong kebyar. Stop at one of the banjars and find out when the groups practise playing.

Ancient wooden female mask

Tegallinggah

The lure of undiscovered archaeological treasures enchants scholars. It was only in the 1950s, for instance, that the Archaeological Service excavated a complex at Tegallinggah called **Candi Tebing**, an unfinished rock-cut candis with hermits' quarters down the Pakerisan River. Access to the site is still relatively difficult: a sign on the main road leading to Gianyar, just 100 metres (about 300 feet) or so after the turn off for Peliatan, is all that marks the way. A guide or, if one can speak Indonesian, a local resident, will be needed to lead one through rice fields and down a steep ravine to the site. Perhaps because of its relative inaccessibility, there is a very ancient, otherworldly feeling to this complex carved out of the side of a cliff over-hanging the rushing river. Excavations have revealed that this had been a cloister with a courtyard, candis hewn out of rock, alcoves and a small stairway, and gateways (one of which is still standing, while the other has collapsed). An unfinished cloister—evidence of a roof can be seen—may have been abandoned after an earthquake. Now, however, it is shaded with tall trees and surrounded by steep slopes lush with ferns. Residents suggest the name of the village may be a distortion of *tiga* (three) *lingga* (religious phallic symbol), as there are three linggas cut into the walls. The people consider the site to be very holy and twice a year make their way down the steep slopes before the first morning light for prayer and to cleanse themselves in the holy springs. This is a ceremony called *banyu pinanuh*.

The East

In the feudal period, the remote region of east Bali was home to the land's most powerful kingdoms, a conservative heritage which can be seen in the courts and temples, and the enclaves of artisans who once worked for the royal families here. East Bali is also home to descendants of the island's original inhabitants, the Bali Aga of Tenganan, who live in the hills above the gentle resort of Candi Dasa.

It was East Bali that was devastated in the 1960s by the eruption of Gunung Agung.

Blahbatuh

A casual glance suggests that the village of Blahbatuh is little more than a crossroads, its modern Balinese-style market wallowing in a lake of mud during the rainy season. But if one slows down there are some delights.

One is the **Puri Blahbatuh**, dating back to 1758. After Indonesia attained its independence and the rajas lost what remained of their power, the palace, like so many others in Bali, faced hard times. How, without the revenues formerly generated by taxes, could the 25,000-square-metre (30,000-square-yard) palace be maintained? I Gusti Ngurah Kesiman, a doctor and grandson of the last king of Gianyar, came upon an answer through his hobby: orchids.

Today, the Puri Blahbatuh, otherwise known as the **Puri Anggrek** (Orchid Palace), has more than 50,000 plants under cultivation. Seven kinds of orchid stretch in long potted rows in the palace's inner court. These include *dendrobium*, the small cherry-red blooms that sprout at night on pillows at first-class hotels, and the ethereal *phalaenopsis amabilis*, called *bulan* (moon) orchids, whose white faces are tinged with pink or gold, like the moon blushing with the sun's last rays.

The best months to visit the compound are April and October, when the most orchids are in bloom. Between 6 am and 4 pm every day, walk through courtyards where floral butterflies of every shape and hue dance on slender stalks. Buy cut orchids here, seeds, or a potted plant for an Indonesian friend. The doctor has no certification for export.

Nearby the Orchid Palace is the **Pura Gaduh**. According to local legend, the original Pura Gaduh, destroyed by a great earthquake in 1917, was first built by the giant Kebo Yuwo, who lived in Bali during the first half of the 14th century. A large stone head—its bold style atypical of Hindu-Javanese carvings—is said to be a bust of the magical giant and is kept in the temple, as are bronze statuettes.

Two famous smiths live in Blahbatuh, Made Gableran and Wayan Sukarta, who forge the keys and kettledrums for many of Bali's gamelans. It is well worthwhile taking a look at their work.

Bona

On the small road heading east past the palace lies the village of Bona, long known for its kecak dance and more recently for its large bamboo furniture. These are copies of a design by Linda Garland, who has her showroom in Sanur. Though the prices in Bona are considerably lower, word is that the number of wood-devouring insects in the bamboo is considerably higher. Caveat emptor.

On the Road to Gianyar

The road through Bona, like the road heading south of the palace, is considerably less travelled than the main road heading towards Gianyar, and both will lead—albeit at a slower and bumpier pace—through tiny villages to the town's palace. A short trip down past the coastal village of **Lebih**, near the mouth of the Pakerisan River, leads to the deserted beaches of **Saba** and **Masceti**, with their wild surf; fine spots for quiet picnics.

Gianyar

The town, as well as the regency, has long been known for its weaving of fine endek, Balinese ikat in which the weft (lengthwise) threads are tied and dyed to create a pattern before the cloth is woven. The road leading into the town is dotted with shops selling textiles from nearby weaving factories. One of the better known is **Anoman**, which recently opened a shop in the tiny village of **Buruan** nearby. Stop in to see a display of weaving, or better yet, get directions from the manager to the factory in the hills above the Gianyar Palace. Here over 100 people are at work, tying the complex patterns, dyeing the threads and then weaving them on foot-pedal-powered looms.

Though the Dutch left this part of Bali long ago, their influence is still discernible in Gianyar's many Dutch-style buildings that now house Indonesian government offices.

Gianyar was one of the most recent of Bali's kingdoms, formed only in the latter part of the 18th century by the first Dewa Manggis under rather dubious circumstances. Dr R Friederick, who travelled and studied in Bali in the mid-19th century, wrote that the Dewa Manggis, the local raja, forged his kingdom through 'deceit, violence and poison . . . On account of his infamous deeds, his poisoning, etc., . . . he is said to have changed after death into a serpent, which was kept for a long time in the palace at Gianyar, but disappeared in the last few years.'

Decades of constant battle with neighbouring states followed. Eventually, in 1898, Dewa Gde Raka negotiated with the Dutch resident to accept the region as a protectorate and a Dutch controller actually moved into the puri.

The impressive red-brick **palace**, rebuilt after the 1917 earthquake destroyed the original building, stands in the centre of Gianyar, just across

from a large playing field. Still the private residence of the former royal family, the palace—under Ide Anak Agung Ngurah Agung, the last raja of Bali—was the site of one of the most splendid courts on the island, attracting talented dancers and sculptors, painters and weavers. Lavish entertainment took place here, enjoyed by Balinese and foreigners alike, including Charlie Chaplin who visited Bali before the Second World War. The old king, according to Willard Hanna in his book *Bali Profile*, was among the last of 'Balinese royalty who lived in the grand manner of Balinese feudalism—autocratic, eccentric, extravagant . . . but also far-sighted and shrewd . . .'

A short distance east of Gianyar, a road leads north to Bangli, approximately 13 kilometres (eight miles) away (see pages 145–6).

Klungkung

About 13 kilometres (eight miles) east of Gianyar lies Klungkung, another palace town. Gajah Mada, the great Javanese general, annexed Bali to the Majapahit Empire in the late 14th century, and established the court of the first Dewa Agung in the nearby village of **Samprangan**. With the collapse of the empire at the turn of the 16th century, thousands of Hindus—including priests, nobles, warriors and artisans—fled Java and pledged their allegiance to the Dewa Agung, then ensconced in Gelgel.

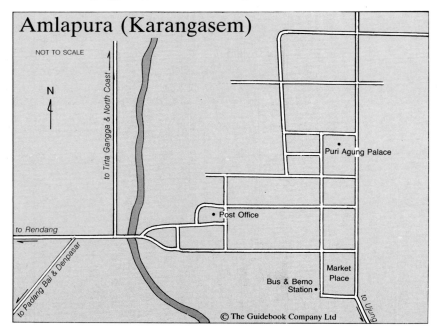

Amlapura (Karangasem)

NOT TO SCALE

N

to Tirta Gangga & North Coast

to Rendang

to Padang Bai & Denpasar

Puri Agung Palace

• Post Office

Market Place

Bus & Bemo Station •

to Ujung

© The Guidebook Company Ltd

In the 16th century, such was the power of the royal court that the Dewa Agung managed to conquer and colonize both Lombok and Sumbawa, but two generations later, the colonies were lost and the power over Bali's other kingdoms dissipated. Finally, believing that Gelgel Palace was under a curse, the entire court moved to Klungkung.

For more than 500 years, Klungkung played a major role in the politics of the island, its influence extending into diplomacy and the arts. Tracing its ancestry back to lords of the great Javanese Majapahit Empire, the royal house of Klungkung was considered 'innermost' of all the courts of Hindu Bali.

Today, little of this glory is seen by the casual visitor. The Dutch, in their push for control over the island, bombarded the city in 1908, levelling what was perhaps the island's most glorious palace.

At the main intersection of the town stands a **Dutch-style clock tower**, where a road heads north to Besakih. Here, too, are the **Kerta Gosa**, the Royal Court of Justice, and the **Bale Kambang**, the Floating Pavilion. Built in the 18th century and restored in 1960, the two bales are noted for their **ceiling murals**, ferocious and sublime depictions of retribution for miscreants and rewards for honest men and women. They are painted in the red, gold, amber and black hues traditional to the area.

Three pedandas presided over hearings in the Kerta Gosa, assisted by *kancas* (lawyers) and a scribe. Defendants would walk up the steep stairs to the open bale. Here, listening to the claims and counter-claims, the judges sat in great gilded chairs, staring up at the panels for guidance on what penalties to impose. And what penalties: in one panel, giants burn the offending parts of an unfaithful woman; in another, a man gets similar treatment. Witches sit under trees, the leaves of which have turned to daggers. Other sinners are boiled alive in giant pots. Above, the gods welcome those who have led more fruitful lives.

Wayang-style murals are also found in the Floating Pavilion. The bale 'floats' in a moat surrounded by stone figures from the *Mahabharata,* good characters to the right, bad characters to the left. Two jovial-looking seated figures, carved to represent moustached and top-hatted Dutchmen, flank the entryway. Sometimes, self-appointed local historians will attempt to tell visitors the stories behind these paintings for a little pocket money; a few know what they're talking about.

Just beyond the pavilion is the gate to the former palace. Royal descendants now live in nearby compounds, where the women weave some of Bali's most prized *songket*, a rich brocade-like cloth of silk with golden threads in geometric and floral patterns.

Stroll awhile in Klungkung. With the exception of the trinket hawkers guarding the gates to the Kerta Gosa, Klungkung has been little touched by tourism. In the **market** peasant women sell poultry and vegetables, others sell

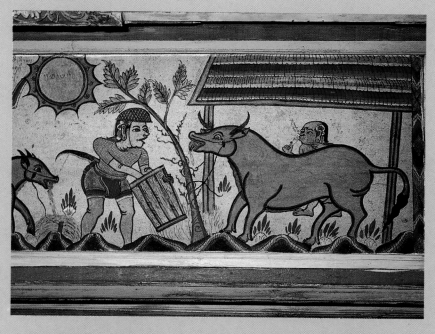

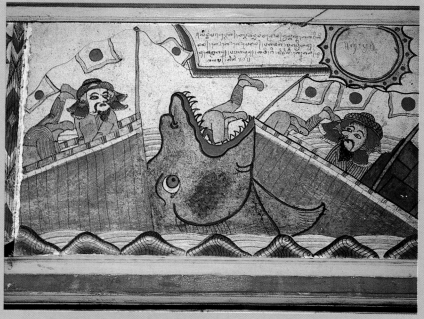

brightly coloured sarongs of endek and songket. On Jalan Diponegoro, music-blasting tape stores sit cheek-by-jowl with shops selling foot-operated sewing machines and colour televisions. Hidden among them, east of the market, is a row of four small **antique shops** specializing in Kamasan paintings.

Kamasan

To see the village where the **wayang-style paintings** come from, just head south a few kilometres to Kamasan, a small village which claims over 100 artists and about 20 designers. Traditionally, the highly stylized works were drawn in natural dyes with a sharp quill pen made from the sugar-palm leaf. They would use bamboo brushes, most often on handwoven cotton from Nusa Penida, but occasionally on paper and wood. More recent works are painted in acrylics on canvas with standard brushes, the ink lines drawn with steel pens. Of late, the 'single-artist syndrome' has hit Kamasan, thanks to the pressure, primarily from Western buyers, for 'name' artists. Among these are Mangku Mure, an old priest who now heads an entire family of painters in **banjar Siku**, and in **banjar Sangging**, Ketut Rabeg (who originally attracted the notice of Walter Spies), and the younger Nyoman Mandra. Mandra, in addition to working on his own paintings, started a school in 1973 and since then has taught hundreds of young boys and girls in the village the rigorous Kamasan style. Visitors are welcome to drop in at the bale. Students' works, which have won prizes in exhibits as far away as North America, are for sale here. They feature battle scenes from the *Mahabharata* and the adventures of Rama, Sita and Laksmana from the *Ramayana*. Balinese calendars, called *wariga*, are also widely available.

Most works are still communal affairs. The master draughtsman plans the theme and layout of the painting, directs and corrects his apprentices, who colour in the figures, and finally outlines the painting with Chinese ink, highlighting certain details with white or gold paint.

Tihingan

Northwest of Klungkung is Tihingan, a traditional centre for gamelan smiths. Here, a look around the workshops can be interesting. A painstaking description of the place is given in Geertz's *Negara: The Theater State in 19th Century Bali.*

On the Road to Candi Dasa

On the eastern limits of Gianyar, a bridge crosses over a wide gorge and the **Unda River**. In the late afternoon, this is possibly Bali's largest *mandi* (bath). Literally hundreds of Balinese come to wash themselves in the river, the men, as always, upstream, while the women, children, washing, livestock and cars are downstream. In the slanting afternoon sun, the scene takes on the quality of a naive painting, a Balinese Grandma Moses, with bathers and the large volcanic boulders which are scattered along the river painted in sunset hues of orange, pink and gold.

A few kilometres east, the road takes a sharp bend to the right at **Pakse-bali**. There are about a half dozen shops here that sell temple umbrellas and gold-painted streamers called *prade*. A small road to the north, just before the sign for Sampalan, leads to **Sideman** and **Iseh** (see page 143).

From the main road, the sharp green hills of east Bali stand out clearly now, covered with webs of cow paths and ancient terraces. Only occasionally are they hidden by the low white-washed walls of small, dusty villages that hug the road. Life is quiet here, though judging from the number of roosters standing sentinel in their bamboo cages, cockfights are a favourite pastime.

As the sea comes into view, the road passes **Gunaksa**. Here, in small palm-roofed huts, villagers harvest salt from the sea in an elaborate process which involves evaporating seawater on the black volcanic sand.

In **Kusamba**, the flow of lava that devastated the region in 1963 is still evident. You can sail to **Nusa Penida** and **Nusa Lembongan**, do it on the cheap on a local boat, or splash out on a hotel excursion (see page 195).

The road traces the shore, passing **Goa Lawah**, the 'Bat Cave'. It is rather a wretched site now, for it is home not only to thousands of squeaking bats, but to almost as many hawkers who fly towards tourist cars and vans. Nonetheless, it is considered a very holy place by the Balinese. According to local lore, the cave extends up to Pura Goa, a small temple in Besakih. The temple guarding the entrance is thought to have been founded in 1007 by Empu Kuturan (see page 97).

After passing the huts of salt makers in **Antiga**, the road weaves through a green cathedral of coconut palms and banana plants. In small villages like **Manggis**, men hollow small boats out of huge logs cut in nearby jungles.

Padang Bai

Men also build and sail jukungs in Padang Bai, Bali's easternmost port. It was here that Cornelis de Houtman, one of the earliest Dutch explorers, landed in 1597 and christened the island Jonck Holland (Young Holland).

Even with the shamble of small buildings crowding the harbour, one can understand his enthusiasm. Green hills rim the crescent-shaped bay, brightly coloured jukungs line the beach or skim across the waves past the rocky headland. Large luxury cruisers sometimes weigh anchor here as do some smaller cruisers from Australia and Singapore, as well as the occasional Bugis trading prahu. The ferry to Lombok departs from the pier every day at 10 am, 2 pm and 5 pm. The passage takes three hours and costs $4 for a round-trip, second-class ticket. First-class seats are available on the morning and late afternoon crossings for $6 a round trip.

Sailing with the Gods
Wayan Sukarta, Fisherman

Ask anyone in Padang Bai who is the most courageous, some might say craziest, sailor and most probably the answer will be Wayan Sukarta.

People love to tell of a wild and stormy day when the captain of a passenger ferry crossing from Lombok to this small port was astounded to see a single jukung set out to sea. No other fishermen had ventured out as the seas, whipped by the southeast monsoon, were too rough and the captain was sure the sailor would soon turn back.

As the hours passed, the captain's surprise turned into amazement as the five-metre (16-foot) craft of wood and bamboo ran with the howling wind, keeping pace with the large ferry until, at the end of the 43-nautical-mile passage, it shot past the ship and made it first to port.

Wayan Sukarta, a compact, powerfully built sailor explains: 'I was in Lombok, I wanted to get home, I wanted to see how fast I could go—why not try?' Top speed, he figures, was ten nautical miles an hour.

Late in 1988, the same sense of adventure took him on a 1,600-kilometre (1,000-mile) race to Darwin—a long distance in any sailboat, but in one of the open, dugout sailing canoes that line Bali's beaches, it was an expedition in the full sense of the word. He won, 'too easily', he sighs.

Wayan is a man apart, especially in Bali, where most of the population traditionally looks at the sea as a place of demons, a place to shun. 'That's what the mountain people believe,' shrugs Wayan, adding that the sea is the home of good gods, such as Baruna. 'For Balinese who live near the beach, the sea is a holy place. Me, I love the sea; I don't like the mountains.'

Wayan, like virtually all of the men in the 100 or so families who live in Padang Bai, is a fisherman, just as his father and his father's father were before him. Born in 1955, Wayan first went sailing with his father at the age of 14, and by the time he was 21, had his own boat. He goes out twice a day, from two to eight in the morning and again from noon until six in the evening. He says he never considered doing anything else, but he hopes his son will find some other occupation, as every year the catch is smaller, the sea over fished by the local fishermen and the huge Japanese factory-like trawlers that prowl these waters.

Sometimes Wayan sails on larger fishing boats with engines up to Ujung Padang in Sulawesi and to Lampung in Sumatra. But most of all, he likes to sail his jukung. According to Bob Hobman, an Australian sailor–adventurer who has made his home in the hills overlooking Padang Bai, these trim craft have not changed significantly for 7,000 years.

'The design hasn't changed because no one has been able to improve upon it,' said Hobman. 'The jukung was, and is, made without metal; none is needed, there's no keel. The materials, wood and bamboo, flex with the waves; the oceanic lateen sail, with the triangle starting at the bottom, keeps the working part of the sail low down, so the boat doesn't turn over. Change one thing, and you've lost the perfect balance.'

Wayan believes that there are other important aspects to the success of the Balinese jukung. According to him, the trees, which grow in the nearby hills of Slumbung and Manggis, must be cut on a propitious day. The woodcutter must pray, giving thanks to the gods and the tree spirits for the use of the tree, explaining that it will be used for a prahu so that people can catch fish and eat. And he must promise to plant another tree. 'All of this must be done so that the wood will be strong and so that it will not be eaten by worms,' Wayan says. He also adds that those who do not follow the customs soon have nothing but a wreck of a jukung.

In Padang Bai, one of the seven boat builders then hollows out the hull from a single log with an axe and adze. The bow is carved to resemble an elephant fish. Pontoons of giant bamboo are attached to the dugout by graceful arches of wood. Once everything is finished, the boat is painted in bright colours, with great bulging eyes peering ahead 'so that the jukung will be able to see where the fish are,' Wayan explains.

Before launching, a holy man blesses the boat, and makes sacrifices of chickens and ducks. 'But never pigs,' Wayan says. 'If you do, the prahu will act like a pig, it will roll around in the water and capsize.'

During the fishing season, Wayan continues to make offerings of a black chicken three times every six months.

'Some 15, 20 years ago, the entire village would make offerings to the gods: black lambs, black ducks, so that the catch would be good,' he says. 'Now, people don't do this, they don't work together. Everyone thinks of himself.'

Nonetheless, there is still camaraderie at sea. Once, Wayan was quite sure that he would die. The wind and the rain were so fierce that he did not see land for two days. The pontoons broke off his boat. Just when he had given up hope, a fisherman from Lombok found him and took him to his home across the Lombok Strait. Here Wayan worked for three days repairing his jukung.

He sailed to Padang Bai to find no one at home. 'Finally my father came back; everyone had been out looking for me, worried that I was dead,' Wayan recounts. 'My father walked into the house and looked at me, stunned. "How did you get here?" he asked, and then gave thanks to the gods. Now the man who saved me is considered part of my family. Just as I am part of the family of a man I saved. That's the way it is here.'

Plans are being launched, rumour has it, for an exclusive hotel at the top of the cliff, but until such time, accommodation is basic and food simple. Those who like the slightly gritty feel of a tiny, working fishing village, well away from most Western tourists, should try two losmen at the eastern end of the beach (see page 211).

A climb up the cliffs above the port leads to **Pura Silayukti**, said to have been built on the site of the former hermitage of Empu Kuturan, the great Javanese Hindu priest who arrived here in the 11th century and devised the philosophical geometry of the microcosm and macrocosm of Balinese society and its beliefs, symbolized by a turtle wreathed with two dragons, supporting the earth and the heavens. Empu Kuturan was also Bali's most famous architect. He designed complex building laws based on body measurements, ratio and ceremony, that were meant to assure harmony among the builder, the user and the structure. The laws, inscribed on lontar palm leaves, have been passed from generation to generation and are still used as references today in the construction of traditional buildings. Empu Kuturan also introduced the meru, the graceful tower of receding black palm-fiber roofs.

Candi Dasa

In the 1980s, Candi Dasa grew from a sleepy fishing village to a tiny resort, a reminder of what Kuta used to be like. The beaches are not as broad as those of Kuta, nor the waves so big. Also missing are the beach hawkers and the motorcycle jockeys. If one must communicate with the outside world, post and telephone offices are located near the eastern end of the main road. There are now more than 30 beach-side bungalow-style losmen, and even a few luxury hotels with air conditioning and swimming pools. Can tennis courts and over development be far behind?

In the meantime, however, there are quiet beauties to enjoy—the elegantly curving corniche to the south, the palm-fringed lagoon that would look perfect on a Hollywood set, and days snorkelling or diving around the coral reef. Candi Dasa is also a fine base from which to explore the rest of eastern Bali.

Tenganan

Northwest of Candi Dasa, nestled against steep hills, lies Tenganan, once an isolated village of the Bali Aga—supposedly the first Balinese—that is now connected to the rest of civilization by a well-maintained asphalt road. Some of the fascinating facts about the village, that Corvarrubias describes in *Island of Bali*, still hold true such as the ritual war. In this, village men, fortified by *tuak* (wine), fight each other armed with rattan shields and fists full of razor-edged *pandanus* leaves. But the custom of banishing villagers for marrying 'outsiders' no longer takes place, and they can now stay if their

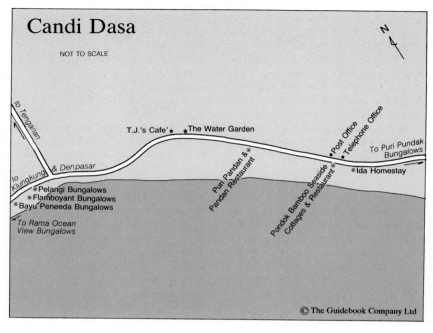

Candi Dasa

NOT TO SCALE

N

to Tenganan

T.J.'s Cafe' ★ ★The Water Garden

& Denpasar

to Klungkung

Puri Pandan &
Pandan Restaurant

Pondok Bamboo Seaside
Cottages & Restaurant

Post Office

Telephone Office

To Puri Pundak
Bungalows

★Ida Homestay

★Pelangi Bungalows
★Flamboyant Bungalows
★Bayu Peneeda Bungalows

To Rama Ocean
View Bungalows

© The Guidebook Company Ltd

spouse goes through a ritual cremation after which they are 'brought back' in a new life as a native Tengananian.

While the eccentricities of Tenganan's society and ritual may be beyond the grasp of the casual visitor, the strikingly different architecture of the village can be immediately appreciated. Longhouses and granaries parade down long, terraced avenues that look like old village greens, each terrace dropping off steeply to the next in a ramp of cobblestones. Of late, a number of the austere, elegant mud-brick compound walls have given way to more elaborate 'with-it' brick-and-paras versions popular in the south. Well to the north of the village, shaded by a giant bringin tree, is the temple of origins, the **pura puseh**, a simple grouping of shrines, lacking the elaborately carved temple gates and towering merus associated with other Balinese temples.

On festival days, revellers fill the broad avenues. Basic wooden foot-powered 'ferris wheels' are erected, the longhouse-style bales are transformed into grandstands for onlookers and bandstands for the village's sacred **gong selonding**. One of only a dozen such gamelans in Bali, Tenganan's gong selonding consists of nine instruments made unusually of metal, rather than bronze. Mentioned in lontar manuscripts dating back to the 12th century, the seven-tone gamelan has a repertoire of sacred music that is used only in this village. Young women, dressed in headdresses of gold flowers and sarongs of the village's double ikat, or *gerinsing*, dance in tight formation.

In the afternoon, men come out to chat and fondle their pet roosters. Some ultra-trendy fighting cocks sport feathers dyed in DayGlo colours of hot pink and chartreuse. This 'makes them stronger in fighting' according to one owner.

The afternoon is also often filled with the sound of young boys and men practising gamelan or tingklik in the **home of Nyoman Gunawan**, who heads the village gamelan and who is also the village headman. His home, about midway up the central avenue, is open to visitors, who may sit and listen. A cassette of the selonding *The Best of Gamelan/Selonding 1 Tenganan*, recorded by the World Centre for Music, is available here, as well as in tape shops in south Bali.

The village is prosperous, as Balinese villages go, largely due to the vast lands it controls. These lands, according to legend, were the bequest of one of the ancient kings of Bedulu who, upset over the loss of his favourite horse, sent men out to search for it. The ancestors of the Tenganan villagers eventually found the corpse of the horse and, as a reward, the king deeded them all the land covered by the smell of the rotting corpse. The wily Tenganan chief accompanied the raja's man for days and everywhere they walked, the smell followed. Finally, the king deeded the entire valley to the village. After the king's man left, the village chief removed a rotting piece of meat from under his sarong. According to villagers, the penis of the horse turned to stone and rests on a hilltop above the village.

Only a few women still make gerinsing, which is endowed with mystical powers and created in what must be the most difficult dyeing procedure yet devised. Both weft and warp threads are dyed in the pattern, through elaborate tying procedures, before the fabric is woven. For the pattern to be at all clear, the threads must align perfectly. Women may take several years completing a gerinsing sarong, so not surprisingly they are considered heirlooms important to the village rituals and are not for sale. There are, nonetheless, seemingly endless numbers of vendors selling 'gerinsing' cloth, some of which has nothing to do with double ikat and much of which is poor quality. Best simply to look at the family heirlooms which the villagers are proud to show if they detect a true interest. Consider the endless hours that went into the crafting of the subtle designs of red, buff and indigo—all colours from dyes of roots and leaves.

Another cottage industry in Tenganan is the inscription of lontars, the traditional books of the Balinese in which Kawi (Bali's ancient language) and miniature pictures are inscribed with a stylus onto palm leaves, then rubbed with a black compound. There are whole forests' worth of old, shredded lontars for sale and an office full of scribes making new ones. One, Wayan Muditadnana, sits on his high porch, working away at tales of the *Ramayana*, mostly ordered by foreigners. His prices are not cheap, nor should they be: a

'book'—a long, Venetian-blind-like series of leaves—takes at least a month
to complete. On holy days, this elderly man can be found intoning passages
from the lontars in the temple. On other days, his voice rises above the
crowing of roosters and yapping of village dogs, as he gives a short reading
on special request.

On the Road to Amlapura

East out of Candi Dasa, the road heads up sharply to curve through forests
and past terraced mountains. At the top of the climb are two small Dutch-
style viewing pavilions, overlooking rice fields and the small village of
Bugbug. Above all this looms the great volcano, Gunung Agung. The valleys
bear dark traces of the lava flow that killed so many in the 1963 eruption and
the villages here are lined with low walls of black volcanic rock, unlike most
areas of Bali.

Karangasem (Amlapura)

Some traces of the devasting lava flows that brought death and destruction to
so many in 1963 can also be seen as one drives into Amlapura. It was
previously known as Karangasem, but the town fathers decided to change the
name. This was an attempt to trick the gods into thinking it was elsewhere,
so that they would not engulf the town in lava again.

Karangasem was home of one of Bali's mightiest kingdoms. According to
some historical accounts, the region broke with Klungkung in the mid-18th
century when the raja of Klungkung ordered the raja of Karangasem killed,
purely out of aesthetic dislike. Predictably, the murdered raja's sons sought
vengeance and after a brief military sortie, rejected Klungkung's authority.

The town rose to prominence at the turn of the 19th century when the
king, Gusti Gede Ngurah Karangasem, managed to re-establish Balinese
control over the nearby island of Lombok and the Balinese states of Buleleng
and Jembrana. After he died, the family split up over a series of land disputes.
One ruler committed such hideous crimes, including incest and cannibalism,
that he had to abandon his throne in Bali and seek shelter in Lombok, where
he established himself as raja.

In 1849, the raja of Karangasem joined forces with the celebrated Prince
Djilantik of Buleleng, and met the Dutch hostilities with cleverness and
determination. Upon hearing of the devastation of nearby Kusamba and the
insurrection in Lombok which was also Dutch inspired, the raja killed
himself, his children and his wives.

Subsequent rulers, however, maintained friendly relations with the Dutch.
As a result, the Dutch allowed the kings of Karangasem, like those of
Gianyar, to retain autocratic, if partial, rule over their subjects. Karangasem,
like other palace towns, was the site of a thriving opium trade in the 19th and

early 20th centuries, controlled by the Dutch who made a handsome profit out of the ugly business.

Puri Gede, an austere, red-brick palace, which may still be visited, was the headquarters for the royal family from the 17th century until **Puri Kanginan** was built in the mid-19th century. It was here, in a crazy quilt of Balinese, Chinese and European architectural styles, that the last raja was born. The royal taste was quite eclectic: the reception hall was named **Bale Amsterdam**, another compound **Madura** and a third **Ehrlangga**—the Balinese for 'England'. **Bale London** was so named because the furniture bears a royal crest the ruler thought looked English. It was, perhaps, here that Anak Agung Bagus Djelantik received his inspiration for architectural fantasy. Whatever the source, Karangasem's last king spent much of his life, and a great deal of the royal income, building water palaces.

The Water Palaces

Ujung, the first water palace, was built in the period 1920–4. It still stands, at least in part, near the shores of Ujung, about three kilometres (two miles) outside Karangasem. All sorts of architectural elements combine to make the floating palace—Balinese, Graeco-Roman, European—and yet the king had no formal training and there was little Western influence in Karangasem then. And there were certainly no films, though the site and the style are very much 1920s Hollywood Grandiose. Building, as one of his sons puts it, 'was just his passion'.

In the palace's heyday, terraces lined with sculptures rippled down to the main lotus pond and band shells perched ear and eye distance away from the main pavilions, so that the royal company could sit comfortably, listening to the gamelan play and watching the dancers. The scale of the water palace was absolutely grand as the raja intended; he said he wanted former Karangasem subjects across the straits in Lombok to be able to see the shining lights of the palace. But nature intervened: the water palace was destroyed twice by earthquakes, once in 1963, after which it was rebuilt by a Dutch Australian who lived there until 1981, when another quake rocked the buildings off their foundations.

The royal family of Karangasem is negotiating with some foreign developers to restore the site, in exchange for permission to build some deluxe bungalows. Until that happens, visitors may satisfy their curiosity by talking with one of the groundsmen who have a photo of the palace taken shortly before the last earthquake. Those visitors at the site during a heavy rainstorm should look back up the steep cliffs, where water cascades from three giant stonecarvings of an elephant, a lion and a bull. No doubt these are more examples of the raja's playful humour.

Djelantik's second water palace, **Tirta Gangga**, six kilometres (four miles) north on the road to Culik, was completed in 1948. The raja built the

gardens for everyone to enjoy. A rococo mixture of styles, this elaborate labyrinth of pools and statuary is now a public bath and a rather neglected one at that. It is, nonetheless, a salute to an imagination that can only be described as Walt Disneyesque. Stop for a simple meal at a warung overlooking the pools. General entrance to the palace plus swimming is about 25 cents.

On the Road from Karangasem

One of the most beautiful drives in Bali skirts the southern base of Gunung Agung. The road veers north just out of Karangasem at a fork presided over by a rather gaudy statue of two soldiers and a chariot pulled by two horses.

In **Sibetan**, the rice fields are wrapped in woven palm-leaf fences and the mountains are dusted with flowering teak trees. Squat dark *salak* trees, which produce some of the island's best 'snake-skin fruit', encroach upon the road, while higher up the mountain's slopes are planted with aromatic clove trees.

In the tiny village of **Telega**, which clings to the hillside, there is a big morning market and just beyond, a stunning view of the valley below. Ferns flow down the cliffs like emerald waterfalls. At **Selat**, one may choose to veer south again, down a valley to the sea or to continue to **Rendang**, and head up to **Besakih Temple** from there.

On the Road to Iseh

To head south is to travel down one of the most beautiful valleys of Bali. Following the **Yehunda River**, waves of rice fields flow to the sea. Purple cat's whiskers and white star flowers track the small irrigation ditches and streams that turn this valley into a Shangri-la. The mountains are studded with bamboo, clove and coffee trees. The onion-shaped metal dome of a small mosque pokes up incongruously against a backdrop of palms.

Iseh

At the visually perfect confluence of mountains and terraced rice fields is Iseh. It is here that the German artist Walter Spies set up his haven from Ubud. This home on a knoll rising in the middle of the rice fields, was later adopted by the Swiss painter Theo Meier.

Meier also often stayed at the home of Dewa Ayu Putu, who now has a small homestay in **Sideman**. Spend a while here, or at least take a walk up the steep stone stairs for an awe-inspiring view that stretches all the way down to the coastal resort of Sanur and the sea beyond.

Sideman is also a good spot to buy endek and to watch it being dyed and woven. There are several **weaving factories** here. To find them, just walk through the village and listen for the sound of the wooden looms. One, a stone's throw from the homestay, is **Pelangi**, run by Dewa Ketut Alit.

Further down the road in **Lebu Gede**, the **banjar of Babakan**, a gaudy wooden ferris wheel, in turquoise and yellow paint, sits motionless until the Galungan and Kuningan holidays when children stand in line for their spin. It's a few more kilometres to the main road, just east of Klungkung.

Besakih

An alternative to heading south is to continue driving west, along the road to Rendang. Turn north at the town and travel seven kilometres (four miles) up the road to reach the temple complex of Besakih, a third of the way up the towering volcano, Gunung Agung.

For centuries, Besakih has been the supreme holy place of the Balinese. It may be older than Bali's Hindu–Buddhist civilization, and date back to times when the god of the volcano was worshipped in an ancient megalithic terraced sanctuary. If this were the case, this sanctuary was probably appropriated by the Hindu kings of Gelgel as their ancestral shrine in the 14th century when they became rulers of Bali.

The **temple complex**, nearly 1,000 metres (3,048 feet) above sea level, is massive, with forests of black thatched merus scraping against the brutal backdrop of the volcano. A broad paved road leads up to the terraced temple, which encompasses some 170 shrines and sub-temples for each of the eight regencies (now known as kabupaten) as well as 18 separate sanctuaries belonging to various groups.

A trip to Besakih when no festival is going on can be a bit daunting: there are so many parking attendants, hawkers and would-be guides. But when a ceremony is taking place (the annual cycle has about 55 events) the austere atmosphere is enlivened with throngs of temple-goers carrying elegantly prepared offerings. It is also here that Eka Dasa Rudra, Bali's most important religious ceremony, meant to occur every 100 years or so, takes place. According to some Balinese, Gunung Agung erupted in 1963 because the priests of Bali, pressed by President Sukarno who wanted to show off the island to a convention of travel agents, scheduled the ceremony too early. The offended gods, they say, devastated the countryside but spared Besakih. The Balinese placated the gods by celebrating Eka Desa Rudra again in 1979, at the correct time.

On the Road to Klungkung

The steep and winding road passes several good vantage points of south Bali.

On the Road to Bangli

Bangli may be reached via a road to the west, just below Rendang, which curves its way through dense woods and forests of fern. On the way, trays of pink and white rice cakes dry in the sun. The road from Rendang ends at **Cempaga** and a turn to the south leads into the town of Bangli.

Bangli

Slow-paced and dusty, Bangli is the former capital of a kingdom which evolved in the 18th century. Now the area hardly resembles an administrative seat, but takes its character instead from the food stalls, bemo stands and the smells of its busy produce **market**. This assembles every three days and rotates between Kayuambua and Kintamani.

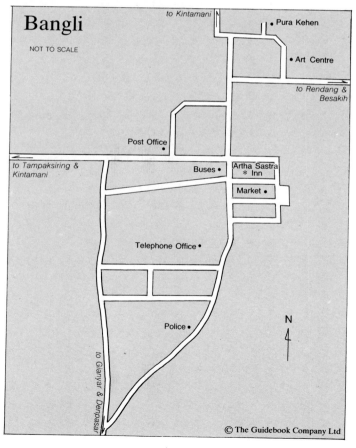

In the centre of town, facing the market, is the **former royal palace**, built about 150 years ago and maintained now by the daughter of the last king, who has converted the inner court to an inn.

Bangli's major attraction, other than the psychiatric hospital, is the **Pura Kehen**. Dating from the 11th century, the Pura Kehen is Bali's second-largest temple and was the original state temple of Bangli. Surviving documents detail a major feast that was held here in 1204 and include travel instructions for guests from far-away villages. Now, to gain access to the temple, one must do battle with a throng of film/temple-sash/postcard vendors. There are three terraces and two stone elephants flanking the base of the central stairs, the split gate is mirrored on a smaller scale on both left and right. Small rose bushes add colour. Steep steps lead up past stone statues of characters from the wayang stories. A great banyan tree dominates the first courtyard and an array of Chinese porcelain plates decorates the stone walls. In the inner courtyard is a handsome 11-roofed meru.

To the southeast is the **Susana Budaya**, where art exhibits and performances by local gamelan and dance groups are presented. It is closed on Sunday.

South of Bangli's market square, on the road towards Gianyar, is the **Pura Dalem Penuggekan**. Its outer walls are decorated with stone friezes of sinners suffering in the afterlife for their crimes in this life—a woman is impaled as her head is sliced open, others hang by their feet over flames, a demon wields a saw and a woeful man is castrated.

Visitors yearning for exercise might make a trip to the **Bukit Demulih**, approximately three kilometres (two miles) west of town on the Tampaksiring road. A turn-off on the left indicates a narrow road to **Desa Demulih**. Near a village banjar, a dirt road called Jalan Tamansari leads up the hill past a house which, somewhat incongruously, has 'Bronx' written on it. At the top is a simple stone temple and a view of south Bali, on a clear day, all the way to the Hotel Bali Beach.

Is There a Doctor in the Palace?

Djelantik, Doctor and Prince

The first time Anak Agung Made Djelantik went outside the walls of his family compound everyone he met fell to the ground.

'I was a bit surprised,' recalls the elderly doctor.

Such was the custom in the Karangasem of the 1920s when commoners came face to face with a prince, even if he was only five years old. Times, of course, have changed. Indonesia won her independence from the Dutch and feudal states and colonialism were replaced with a republic. The young prince has become an internationally recognized doctor, as enthusiastic about his country's continuing progress towards democracy as he is knowledgeable about his family's illustrious, and sometimes infamous, history.

'Equality was very quickly recognized as a good value after the war,' he observes. 'Every Balinese knows his place in society. Now, however, the place is not defined by heritage, but by achievement.'

At his home and medical office on the outskirts of Denpasar, there is little to suggest that, from the 14th century, Djelantik's family led one of Bali's strongest kingdoms. Walls are lined with books in English, Indonesian, Dutch and Balinese, tapes of classical Western and Balinese music and paintings by children, grandchildren and friends. A chapter of an unfinished autobiography lies under an outline for an aesthetics course Djelantik teaches at the College of Indonesian Arts. A copy of a book he wrote on Balinese paintings acts as a paperweight for a flurry of papers—plans for an upcoming arts festival.

A smile, surprisingly winsome for a man of his accomplishments, plays across Djelantik's face as he reviews his life. 'Life,' he beams, 'is filled with all sorts of adventures and surprises.'

Despite his noble birth, Dr Djelantik's own childhood was not particularly easy. His mother died while he was still an infant. Without a strong supporter in the palace, the third son of Raja Anak Agung Bagus Djelantik soon became what he describes as a 'second-class citizen', expected to wait on his elder half-brother.

The raja had seven wives and ten children—not many, Dr Djelantik reflects, compared to the king of Klungkung, who had more than 100 wives. 'Father would come to a temple celebration, where of course the most beautiful girls would act as his servants, each trying to attract the attention of the ruler. It was an honour to live in the palace. And, of course, the villagers wanted the girls to be chosen, so the village would gain prestige.'

Though Dr Djelantik's childhood was not particularly happy, it was not as constrained as his sister's. 'She, too, was like a second-class citizen,' he recalls. 'Unlike me, she was only allowed to study at the local Malay school—it was simply not common for girls to be highly educated. That's how they ended up doing so much weaving.'

There was very little Western influence in eastern Bali at the time. Karangasem was a semi-autonomous region and the raja was educated solely in Balinese customs. So young Djelantik was sent to school, first in Denpasar and later in Jogyakarta in Java, where he decided to become a doctor after reading inspiring accounts of Albert Schweitzer. But he ran into opposition from his father. 'The Dutch officials in Bali discouraged father from sending me to Holland for medical school. Why? Because Indonesians who went to Holland saw that the Dutch were quite common people; there was no discrimination as there was here in Indonesia. Once Indonesians were in Holland they formed groups; it was in the air, the fervour of nationalism,' he explains.

Determined to get to Holland, Djelantik offered to act as a manservant to a Dutch teacher who was returning on home leave. When the raja heard of this, he fired off a letter to his son: 'Don't put your father to shame'. Included were 1,000 guilders to pay for a first-class ticket.

Djelantik bought a fourth-class ticket, pocketed the rest of the money for future use and sailed for Holland. 'Though I had no plans, no place to stay—I was so sure I would succeed,' he says.

At medical school, Djelantik joined a debating club, the Amsterdam Student Corps, where the young Balinese was faced with exciting questions never dreamed of at home: 'Why is there a god? Why are you Hindu, not Muslim?' recalls Djelantik.

As the Second World War engulfed Europe, Djelantik, like other students in Amsterdam, went underground, working on farms, cutting firewood. Even in these hard times, Djelantik found happiness and excitement. At one point, he was asked to take some cherries to a sick nurse, the friend of some friends. 'I walked in, and at first sight, I was completely gone,' he says. Astri, the Dutch nurse, became his wife and in 1948 they moved to Indonesia, where the couple worked as a doctor–nurse team. They went to dozens of sites on the islands of Buru, Sumbawa, and the Celebes (now Sulawesi). The doctor remembers those days fondly: 'In Buru, 30 bearers had to carry the medical supplies and when we came to a river, we would have to cut bamboo and make a raft. I was like a pathfinder. I liked it, I miss it . . . '

'I don't know how many hospitals we started up,' he says, adding that each presented its own difficulties. 'It was like Providence: everywhere I came there was trouble.'

In north Celebes, the doctor arrived with his wife and children just as the People's Army had deposed the local raja and set up headquarters in what was to have been the doctor's house. 'I was carrying a letter of safe conduct from the raja, not the right man that day, and so we were captured and put in a room guarded by 20 trigger-happy soldiers with guns and bayonets.' After ten days, the captors went off to loot some local gold mines.

'I told my wife, "We must take our opportunity. I want to occupy that house." And that's what we did. The men came back furious and told us to get out. "No, I belong here," I said. "If you want to shoot, go ahead." They went away and came back with kerosene. "Go ahead, burn the house, but I will stay here." Nothing happened. They drove off, and I stayed. I was the idol of the population, we worked there for five years. You'll still see the portrait of our family in some of the older houses,' he says.

By the late 1950s, Dr Djelantik had returned to Bali as chief of the health service. He worked with traditional healers, explaining what he could do and what he couldn't. 'Most balians are very sincere in their desire to heal, and in the end, they often would refer patients to me,' he says. He helped teach the people that leprosy—still prevalent in the islands then—was a disease, not a curse of the gods, by moving into a house near the leprosy hospital and inviting leprosy patients into his kitchen.

In 1963, he worked in his native Karangasem, where 1,600 people were killed during the volcanic eruptions of Gunung Agung and another 500 died from starvation, malnutrition and burns. Later years were spent in the Philippines, Somalia and Afghanistan with the World Health Organisation. In 1979, Djelantik returned to Bali.

'I got back and ran into an old student, Made Bandem. When he saw me, he said "You must help with ASTI," ' says Djelantik, and he obliged.

Just as the young prince faced questions in Holland he never before imagined, so Bali, awash with tourists and visions of the outside world via television and films, faces questions and choices never imagined in the 1920s court of Karangasem. Some observers worry that Bali's unique culture will be overwhelmed; not Djelantik. 'I am optimistic,' he says, with a bold smile. 'We don't want Bali to become a dead museum. As anything with life, it will change. It's up to the Balinese to determine whether the change will be for the better or the worse. I believe it will become better. The enjoyment of beauty will become more conscious, because people read; it will grow, because beauty will be approached more critically.'

Religion, he is sure, will gain in strength: 'It will become more consciously believed. The Balinese now are no longer afraid to take in knowledge of other religions. They can do that with more self confidence.'

Self confidence, believes Dr Djelantik—who took off for Holland knowing only that he would succeed—can lead to many exciting and marvellous discoveries. It also can lead, as in Dr Djelantik's case, back to Bali.

The Central Mountains

From Gunung Agung in the east to Gunung Batukau in the west, Bali's volcanic mountains dominate the spiritual and physical life of the island. They are the home of gods and the source of Bali's rivers which, fed by rain-bearing clouds caught in the high peaks, course down the terraced mountainsides to the sea.

Gunung Bratan
On the Road to Bedugul

The 48-kilometre (30-mile) drive north of Denpasar through Mengwi leads past rice fields, in the lower country, to more elevated areas where onions, cabbages and even strawberries are cultivated. The countryside is rich and fertile, well irrigated by rivers running down from the mineral-laden volcanic slopes. The banks by the side of the road are lush with ferns and elephant grass, and the houses are sturdily built of bricks and tiles to withstand the heavy rains.

Bedugul

Sir Stamford Raffles, founder of Singapore and one-time British governor of Java, once observed that the climate of the tropical mountains was the most delightful in the world. Bedugul is a case in point. At 1,500 metres (4,921 feet) above sea level, the small village is deliciously cool and often enveloped in a thick white mist. A road on its southern edge drops down to Lake Bratan, in the crater of the ancient volcano Gunung Bratan. Dark-green forests reach right down to the lake, where a small area has been cleared for swimming.

There is a small tourist centre with two restaurants and a hotel. Some of the water sports available are water-skiing and parasailing. (Until recently, parasailing was forbidden, for fear that the height of the parachute and passenger would offend the gods.)

Bukit Mungsu

Back on the main road, the **Bukit Mungsu market** soon appears and is well worth a stop. Stalls, open daily during daylight hours, offer a cornucopia of carefully arranged displays of passion fruit, unusually large pineapples, green beans, oranges, broccoli, strawberries and more. Behind the produce is an even more resplendent display of wild orchids from the nearby forests.

A **botanical garden**, formerly the Lila Graha Orchid Plantation, lies at the southern end of the market. A few hours can be spent wandering through the fields and dells and chatting with the gardeners, who take great pride in their mountain garden.

Candikuning

Continuing north, past the village of Candikuning, Lake Bratan reappears to the east. Along this stretch of road is the **Pura Ulu Danu**. The temple honours Dewi Danu, the goddess of the lake, and is the sacred water temple for north, south and east Bali. It is also strikingly pretty: manicured lawns surround the bales of the inner court and an 11-roofed meru projects up at the lakeside. Upside-down creamy trumpet flowers, oversized yellow day lilies, bold red bilu-bilu stalks and a clump of golden bamboo make a colourful explosion against the misty green-and-blue backdrop of the crater.

Pancasari, a five-minute drive north, is a treat for golf lovers as it is the site of the **Bali Handara Kosaido Country Club**, an 18-hole championship golf course.

On the Road to Seririt

To the east, a narrow road winds past **lakes Buyan and Tamblingan**. Some important archaeological digs are going on along this route. According to a copperplate inscription recently found in **Gobleg**, there was a mountain kingdom in the **Gobleg–Munduk** area as far back as the year AD 900.

On the Road to Singaraja

The main road winds sharply through a forest of monkeys and cool mists that gives way to rice fields, topped by electrical wires and brightened by bougainvillea and blue trumpet vines. An hour's drive and suddenly, it's hot. Banana plants grow out of the clay-coloured ground and houses perch high above the road. Just past **Beratan**, Buleleng region's silver centre, Dutch-style stone houses along Jalan Iman Banjol announce the beginning of the former colonial capital, Singaraja (see pages 164–5).

On the Road to Gunung Batur

Much of central Bali is dominated by the charcoal grey, 1,717-metre (5,635-foot) peak of Gunung Batur, Bali's second most revered volcano. A number of roads lead up to the **caldera**: the regularly travelled road past the pre-Hindu sites of Pejeng; the serene route that briefly follows the course of the Ayung River past Kedewatan; and another charming route out of Ubud which cuts through **Petulu** and **Tegalalang**. All along the way, wooden banana trees, flowers, garudas, and even dinosaurs, peek out of villagers' houses, there for the buying, if one pleases.

From east Bali, it is easiest to go through **Bangli**. The area is rich in cottage industries, whose craftspeople are more than happy to invite visitors in to view their work. Slightly north of the centre of Bangli (see pages 145–6), on Jalan Nusantara at **banjar Pande**, is the **Toko Mawar silver shop**, where simple jewellery and ornate ceremonial bowls for temple

offerings are crafted and sold by the family of Nyoman Geloh. A short drive
further north leads past tiny towns where the main 'industries' are woven
mats, known as *gedeg*, baskets and bamboo furniture. Occasionally, one
passes a tree laden with spiky durian fruits, ripe from late September to
December. Within a half-hour drive, shiny leaved umbrella trees crowd the
forest and red and green 'good-luck' plants line the road.

Gunung Batur

All these roads lead to Gunung Batur, the sleeping volcano that awoke in
1917 and again in 1927. Life here is rough and isolated. No rice farming is
possible; instead, farmers grow sweet potatoes, peanuts, vanilla, cloves,
coffee and cabbages.

Penelokan

On the crater rim at Penelokan, 22 kilometres (14 miles) north of Bangli,
swarms of vendors—selling the usual carved garudas, temple-sashes and
oranges—are particularly unpleasant. But one should stop, if only briefly. By
midday, Gunung Batur, black and bald, and the caldera of the crater, Lake
Batur, are under a heavy coat of mist. The crater is 11 kilometres (seven
miles) in diameter and 183-metres (600-foot) deep. From Penelokan, it is still
possible to see the black ridges of lava on Batur's slope. **Gunung Abang**, at
2,153 metres (7,064 feet), dominates the horizon to the east.

Penelokan starts to look and feel like a big tourist trap after a few minutes.
Unless one is planning a climb, best stop only for lunch, enjoy the view and
move along.

Lake Batur

East of Penelokan, a road skirts the crater to the town of **Kedisan**, from
where you can drive down to the lake to rent boats or embark on a long hike
up Gunung Batur; the path from **Purajati** is a two-hour ascent; from **Toya
Bungkah**, it is about three hours. Another road curves its way along the lava-
blackened western side of the volcano to the *air panas*, the **hot springs**, of
Toya Bungkah. These bubbling medicinal waters, fed by volcanic mineral
springs, are said to be the domain of Dewi Danu, the goddess of the lake and
provider of irrigation. They are also the village's natural launderette.
Trekkers who come here after a long day's climb should not be surprised to
find a circle of old women washing their families' clothes, the lake's surface
frothy with soap suds. There are a few losmen and an art centre with resident
orchestra and dance troupe in the vicinity of the hot springs.

Trunyan

Motorized canoes at Kedisan and Toya Bungkah cross the lake to the
formerly isolated village of Trunyan, home of other Bali Aga people. Fares
should be payed at the end of your round trip as there are many tales of
boatmen refusing to return passengers until extortionate fees are paid.
According to legend, the village was founded at the spot where a *taru
menyan* tree grew, emitting an incense-like perfume which lured the goddess
Dewi Danu from the heavens. The art and customs of Trunyan are believed to
date from pre-Hindu Bali and the villagers' social codes are unique on the
island; cremation, for example, is not permitted and the dead are left to
disintegrate in a fenced-off outdoor area. Villagers, unable to grow rice, have
traditionally had to beg for it from other parts of the island; now they beg,
quite aggressively, from tourists. Trunyan's culture centres around its temple,
the **Pura Pancering Jagat**, or 'Temple of the Navel of the World'. Hidden in
a meru is a statue of the guardian of the village, **Dewa Ratu Gede Pancering
Jagat**, the 'God who is the Centre of the World'. This place is worth a visit
only if one is interested in Bali's pre-Hindu past.

Batur

Less than ten kilometres (six miles) north of Penelokan is the village of
Batur, rebuilt on the high, safe ridge after the eruption of 1927. That disaster
covered the original village at the base of the mountain in hot lava, but its
inhabitants managed to escape with their sacred temple relics and some
belongings. (In 1917 they had been luckier: the gods saw to it that the
burning lava halted its path right at the temple door.) Construction of the
Pura Ulu Danu began immediately after the 1927 eruption, but most of its
285 planned shrines are, as yet, unfinished. The temple's stark rows of tall
meru towers are easily visible from the main road in Batur. It contains a bell
of solid gold, which is said to have been presented to the temple by a king of
Singaraja in retribution for having once insulted the gods.

Kintamani

Just a few minutes' drive leads to Kintamani, 1,500 metres (4,921 feet) above
sea level. Tenth-century lontar and stone inscriptions date the traditions of
this village to pre-Majapahit times. Now, Kintamani is a market town, where
produce-vendors assemble on Monday and Thursday. This is also the home
of Gede, probably Bali's most popular mountain guide, who manages to play
his flute while other members of his hiking party are gasping for breath.
Since he is much in demand, it is best to make arrangements with him well in
advance. Hotels can usually manage to reach him somehow. Tjampuhan
Hotel, outside of Ubud, regularly schedules treks with him. Plan to stay in the
area the night before the ascent, or get up very early. But be warned, climbing
on black volcanic rock at high noon is tough work.

Balinese Animal Depictions

On the Road from Batur

The road winds north, surrounded on most days by thick white mist. Tiny, grim towns of houses with rough wood walls and tin roofs seem suspended in the clouds. Shops selling spare car parts and old appliances are brightened only by the stacks of small oranges sold at warungs. Casuarina, mango and coffee trees dot the landscape. At **Serai** is a fine view over the foothills far to the west.

Gunung Penulisan

An enormous split gate announces the temple of **Pura Tegeh Koripan**. Perched on an adjacent hill, the Permutel Stasiun Radio Microwave receiver, which picks up programmes relayed from Jakarta, strikes a bizarre contrast to one of Bali's oldest temples.

At 1,745 metres (5,725 feet) above sea level on Gunung Penulisan, the Pura Tegeh Koripan is Bali's highest temple. It is believed to date back to the 11th century and was the mountain sanctuary of rulers of the Pejeng kingdom. The pura is actually a series of temples, built at different levels and separated by hundreds of steep steps. The steps are modern, but their arrangement imitates the terraced style of ancient Indonesian sanctuaries. A simple enclosed courtyard above all the terraces contains bales which hold sculpted stone statues of Balinese rulers and deities. According to the archaeologist A J Bernet Kempers, some of these still bear visible inscriptions identifying the subjects or sculptors and date from the tenth to 12th centuries.

On the Road to Singaraja

The hills thicken with orange and clove trees, and coffee beans ripen in the sun on this stretch of road. At the town of **Dausa**, the sea for the first time comes into view as an extraordinary and unexpected backdrop of blues. One hour later, the air warms up for good and palm and banana groves are once again the common greenery. The road meets the ocean at **Kubutambahan**, 47 kilometres (29 miles) north of Penulisan. Singaraja is 16 kilometres (ten miles) to the west.

The North

After the lush rice fields of the south and the dark-green forests of the central mountains, the northern coast of Bali is a startling contrast, with its tawny-red earth, silver and yellow-green foliage of grapevines and citrus trees and black sand beaches. In the dry season, the soil cracks and the grass shrivels. Oxen, which seem to be sunburned under their white coats, are seen bathing more often than grazing. A number of houses date back to colonial days, with columns and courtyards that must once have been formal gardens. Shining silver domes of mosques reflect the sun, and the Muslim call to prayer, broadcast over loudspeakers, is jarring to an ear grown accustomed to the gamelan.

The Buleleng regency, settled long before the influx of Majapahit princes, rose to prominence during the 17th century when the reigning king, Gusti Pandji Sakti, extended his control over Karangasem to the east and Jembrana to the west. An association with Mengwi further strengthened the kingdom until the end of the 18th century, when warring princes in Karangasem established their dominance.

Until earlier this century, when paved roads cut through the mountains to the south, Buleleng was geographically isolated from the rest of Bali, and, lying on the Java Sea, was more exposed to foreign influence. Bugis traders from Sulawesi frequented the port, and Chinese and Muslim traders made it their home. The Dutch came too, and after two bloody campaigns, conquered the kingdom of Buleleng on a third expedition in 1849. It was here that Gusti Ketut Djilantik, the proud prince who had denied Dutch sovereignty in 1844, assembled Balinese forces. Holding their jewelled kerises and dressed like mythical warriors in bright-red sarongs and white head cloths, Djilantik and his brother, the raja of Buleleng, walked out of the palace to meet the invaders. An equally ceremonious crowd of high priests and warriors accompanied them. The Dutch pressed for concessions, but the Balinese refused to negotiate. Tired of the stalemate, the Dutch attacked. The raja and Djilantik managed to escape with some troops to Karangasem, but thousands of others were killed and the Dutch gained their first foothold on Bali. Djilantik, caught in the mountains, took poison; the raja was later killed in battle at Lombok.

Although a royal family member continued as regent, a Dutch controller held the reigns over him and his kingdom. Singaraja became the administrative centre of Dutch rule over both Buleleng and Jembrana, as well as the eastern islands. This meant that the people were subject to Western influences 60 years earlier than were the rest of the island's inhabitants. Women in Buleleng were the first in Bali to cover their breasts with the Malay kebaya, possibly at the request of the lust-fearing Dutch. Others say women took cover after Independence, when the more conservative Javanese suggested that Balinese bare breasts were not a sign of a modern nation.

Dutch control also meant that Buleleng was the first area to prohibit slavery and its villagers were also the first to receive vaccinations against smallpox. A few Christian missionaries even ventured upon the northern shores, but for the most part failed to convert the Balinese. However, the Reverend de Vroom did make one 'convert', who unfortunately was made so miserable by the purgatory of straddling two faiths that he arranged for the death of his Christian teacher.

The arts, also, were influenced by Western ideas. The jazzy gong kebyar originated here at the turn of the century and, to this day, the area's joged dancers are the island's most suggestive, some of them actually grasp at male partners' balls.

Singaraja

The Dutch government buildings, used by the Japanese during their Second World War occupation of Bali, still dominate much of Singaraja's streetscape. The imposing former office of the Dutch governor, on Jalan Veteran, exists in its present incarnation as a government tourist office.

The diminutive **Gedung Kertya lontar museum** next door was established by the Dutch in 1928 and, for the time being, contains about 3,000

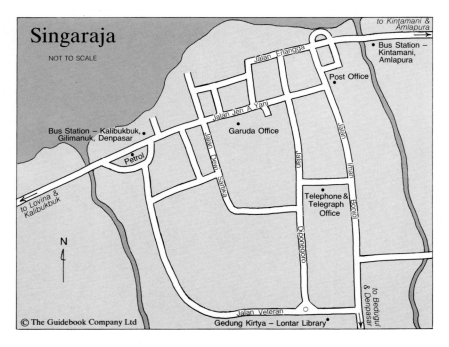

lontar books (there is talk of bringing them to a yet-to-be-built reference centre in Denpasar). Written on lontar palm-leaf strips and bound between two narrow pieces of wood, lontars were first used as books in Bali in the 13th century, and can last at least 100 years, much longer than paper, which is quickly ruined by the damp air and insects. Among the museum's collection of original lontars are mantras, folk tales, poems and documents on mysticism, medicine, ethics and geneaology. There is no lending service, but photocopies can be made of typewritten manuscripts. A glass case displays a small collection of *prasastis*, metal strips of copper and bronze chiselled with royal edicts, which date as far back as the tenth century. Mila, the curator, speaks English well and is a great source of information. Opening times are from 7 am–1 pm, Sunday to Thursday; 7–11 am, Friday; 7 am–noon, Saturday.

Until the opening of the Ngurah Rai Airport, Singaraja was the main port of entry into Bali, with steamships dropping off Western tourists. Though the passenger ships are gone, the docks are still busy. Not far from the warehouses, on a small street off Jalan Jen Achmad Yani just east of Jalan Dewi Sartika, women sift and sort coffee beans. South, on Jalan Dewi Sartika, the smell of vanilla wafts out from the Nusa Indah processing plant.

By following Jalan Iman Bonjol a short distance south of the town to **Beratan**, one arrives at the region's gold- and silverwork centre. Ask villagers for directions to the smiths. A good place to start, right on the main road, is a small shop marked **Gemler**, where ceremonial silver pieces are made and sold. Nearby, women weave songket cloth with gold thread.

Singaraja is a hot, dusty place to stay, with a handful of losmens. It is better to travel 14 kilometres (nine miles) west to the area's small beach resorts.

Lovina Beach

The road from Singaraja, lined with handsome tamarind trees planted by the Dutch, runs between the beach and a narrow strip of tobacco fields and corn patches that give out at the red foothills of the mountains.

The eight-kilometre (five-mile) stretch of beach, losmen and restaurants, commonly referred to as Lovina Beach, is actually made up of three small villages, beginning at the east they are: **Anturan**, followed by **Kalibukbuk** and then **Lovina**. A decade ago, there were five losmen on the strip; now, there are nearly 30, with more on the way. Nevertheless, the area still retains the feel of a quiet fishing village.

The black sand beaches are uncrowded and unspoiled. A well-spoken child may offer to sell you a pineapple, but no one will try to plait your hair, or saddle you with yet another pair of sunglasses. It is easy to charter a jukung and to rent equipment for snorkelling off the coral reef. Longer trips can be made for dolphin spotting; prices must be negotiated with the sailors.

Of Rice and Men

Wayan Runtun, Irrigation Cooperative Representative

Despite the fact that it was Sunday, Wayan Runtun and his wife, Wayan Suri, were in their fields with their two children, pulling weeds out of the thick mud and hoeing back the steep dykes. They were four well-worn straw hats, bobbing in a sea of green rice plants.

A wiry man in his mid-40s, Runtun is an important figure in his community. He heads Subak Bena Gangsang, one of three groups that make up the Subak Bena, the irrigation cooperative responsible for the area from the paved road above Marga to the Sungi River, some of Bali's most fertile land.

Runtun and elected representatives from other cooperatives meet to decide, with the help of priests, the distribution of the water that flows from Lake Bratan and irrigates all the fields in this part of Bali. Like officials of all Bali's 1,200 subaks, they oversee the maintenance of dams and weirs that divide the water, select the types of seed to plant and fertilizer to use and resolve conflicts that arise among neighbours.

Perhaps most important of all is the determination of when to plant and when to harvest, a decision controlled by 1,000-year-old religious traditions. Some years back, farmers followed a government decree and everyone planted at the same time: fields at the tops of the mountains had too much water, those below not enough; plagues of locusts and mice ate what little rice did grow. Disgruntled with the harvest brought about by scientists and bureaucrats, farmers returned to their religion for guidance.

In 1987, Runtun's subak came in second in an island-wide competition, with an average of 120 kilos (265 pounds) of rice per ara (100 square metres; 120 square yards) in five months, just behind Rijasa, also in the Tabanan regency. For their efforts, the 250 family members of the subak were praised by President Suharto and given 20 head of cattle to plough with and numerous spades, hoes and shovels.

This year, Runtun hopes to come in first. 'We've planted new rice, Kruing Aceh, which has a higher yield and better taste than IR36,' he says, referring to one of the 'miracle rices' developed as part of the Green Revolution. Taste has become an issue with the introduction of the new rices. Balinese prefer the taste of Beras Bali, the old-style rice. 'It was beautiful to see in the fields, the heavy heads nodding,' says Wayan. 'But you can only get one harvest a year, as opposed to two with the new rice, plus some months for other crops. It's 40 kilos [88 pounds] an ara, just not enough.'

Another modern advance that has recently sputtered onto Bali's rice terraces is the 'Japanese cow', a small, motorized plough. 'It's easier and faster than using a Balinese cow, but the real cow leaves the earth softer, richer. So we alternate,' says the farmer.

Runtun studies all the latest information on fertilizers, insecticides and seeds. He also fervently believes that the success of his subak is rooted in following the proper religious ceremonies. 'First planting on an auspicious day, then 42 days later a cleansing ceremony. A day of no work and, two months after planting, a day to celebrate the conception of the rice, "morning sickness". When the rice turns yellow, we must make a penjor and then we may harvest, after a small rice figure, Dewa dari padi [representing the goddess of rice] is put at the head of the field. The women chant then.'

Runtun's wife, Wayan Suri, sang the invitation to the rice goddess:

> *Here's an offering,*
> *Dewi Sri, and all attend.*
> *Please come to feast on this,*
> *So we may eat little, but feel full.*

With the increased number of harvests each year (two and sometimes three), Runtun says the farmers have not changed the way they worship the gods of planting and harvest, just the frequency: 'We try to stick to the old timing, and add new dates. For example, the sacrifice of a cow, it used to be once every three harvests, or once every three years. Now, once a year, we go up to Bratan to sink the cow into the lake. If there are troubles, we go to the temple, we wash sacred objects and then later sprinkle the objects in the rice fields. It still works. And once a year, the head of the subak goes to Besakih to ask the gods for water for the sawah.'

Sometimes, farmers will put up a *pindekan* (wind-driven bamboo propeller) in the field, just for the fun of it; other times, the subak will get together and beat sticks to chase away birds: although Runtun says that for years, they have not been bothered by birds: 'We don't have to worry about birds like other areas because we've made the right ceremonies. Still, sometimes we just go out in the fields and make noise anyway, just because we want to.'

According to government statistics, Bali is now self-sufficient in rice and is exporting to other islands. But for all the hard work, Runtun says that the Balinese farmer is usually broke. 'The Balinese work hard, but if all the land were divided equally, each person would only have 15 ara, not enough.' As it is, Runtun's family works 50 ara owned by the local palace whereby the profits are divided equally, and 15 ara of his own.

'From the fields, we make enough for eating and for festivals, not enough for the children to go to school. That comes from raising chickens and cows and ducks,' he explains. 'It's important that the children go to school, maybe they can be something else, or maybe just a farmer. It is good enough to be healthy; they can be happy farming. Everyone now wants to be a government worker, and maybe that isn't the way. But I want my children to go to school so that they can understand what is going on, so that they won't be cheated, so they won't cheat others, so they get knowledge. Later, they can decide what to do with it.'

Perhaps to its credit, Lovina has little by way of regular tourist activities, the only scheduled performances now are legong dances, performed free of charge at 8 pm on Saturday night at Aditya Bungalows. The area is, nonetheless, an excellent base for exploring some of the natural and architectural sights of the north coast.

Communications

Telephones are available only at the larger hotels (see pages 213–4), postal services are available at the Perama Beach Inn on the main road. Opening times are from 8 am–2 pm.

Labuanhaji

To the west, past a series of vineyards, is the village of Labuanhaji and **Singsing Air Terjun**, a waterfall. The springs drain into two pools, cool and deep enough for swimming, except at the end of the dry season.

Dencarik

Approximately eight kilometres (five miles) west of Lovina, in Dencarik, is the Buddhist monastery of **Brahma Vihara**, a tranquil spot, where visitors may stop and wander about a bit without seeing anyone at all. To reach it, turn left at the sign just before the market in the town of Banjar. A small road leads south and uphill through a hot, red, dusty town. At the top of the hill is the pink and white stone monastery, with three terraced courtyards that are eerily quiet and empty. Two painted wood Buddhas sit on the second terrace, and on the third is a huge stupa.

Air Panas

Back down in Banjar, drive west through the market and turn south at the sign 'Air Panas' (Hot Springs). Just a short distance inland, a sulphur spring gushes down a slope, drains through a metal pipe and is spat out of several stone dragons' mouths, arriving finally in a tepid, greenish swimming pool. The pool's stone deck might be more attractive if it were not embellished with a Beck's Beer umbrella, the brainchild of an Australian tour director. Changing rooms and an outdoor shower are provided. Admission is about 20 cents for adults and ten cents for children. A bale-style restaurant has been built into the hill.

Pulau Menjagan

Lovina is just an hour's drive from the **Taman Nasional Bali Barat**, the West Bali National Park, and 15 minutes more from Teluk Terima, where boats cross to **Pulau Menjagan** (Deer Island), and what are perhaps the most beautiful undersea coral gardens in Bali. To enter the park, stop first at the small parks office (PPA) and pay about the equivalent of 30 cents for a

Temple decoration of dancers

permit. Motorized boats can be rented on the beach. Be on the lookout for the tiny deer which give the rocky island its name. It is best to bring a picnic lunch along; there's nothing on the island and the small warungs on the mainland are quite basic.

Gilimanuk

A small and very basic cottage near the park ranger's post at **Teluk Terima** may be rented, but to get running water and electricity, head for Gilimanuk, on the westernmost tip of Bali, where there are a number of losmen offering cheap, basic accommodation and a few Chinese and Padang restaurants. There is not much to do in the evenings but ride the horse carts and, for the fun of it, take a quick ferry ride to Java for about 30 cents one way, or pay $2.75 for a car. **Gunung Merapi** (Fire Mountain) is 2,800 metres (9,000 feet) high and still smoking, looms over all.

On the Road East

East of Singaraja lie the historic villages where Buleleng's fighters made their last stand against the Dutch. The road runs past banana groves, tobacco and corn fields, and shady grape arbours. Thatch-roofed houses and tall piles of lumber are set back from the road; horses plod slowly in front of dokars and cows pull low wide wagons.

Sangsit

Seven kilometres (four miles) east of Singaraja, the odd sight of cacti greets the eye. In the centre of town, a dirt road leads to the market to the south. To the north, through a pink stone split gate, is **Pura Beji**, an outstanding example of the flamboyant, baroque style of northern Balinese temple architecture. Built in the 15th century, the Pura Beji is a *subak* (irrigation cooperative) temple, dedicated to Dewi Sri, goddess of rice. Its split gates are carved of soft pink sandstone, with snakes, beasts and demons keeping evil spirits away while benevolent-looking bearded men extend a welcome. The stone vegetation continues in the inner court, which is brightened by a large frangipani tree.

Kubutambahan

Just beyond the Pura Beji, a turn is marked for **Jagaraga**, about eight kilometres (five miles) to the south. In Jagaraga, cornered by the invading Dutch in 1849, the wife of Prince Djilantik and a small crowd of other noble women committed puputan by walking directly into the enemy gunfire, rather than surrendering. In the soft sandstone of Jagaraga's central **pura dalem**, artistic defiance of Dutch power lives on today in a series of bas-reliefs that cover the temple's outer walls. In one, two big-nosed, morose-looking Dutchmen glower from a Model 'T' Ford, which is driven by a servant and menaced by bandits. In another, sea monsters rise up against Dutch steamships. Elsewhere, aeroplanes flounder above Bali's seas. Jagaraga also has one of the most famous gong groups and an excellent legong troupe.

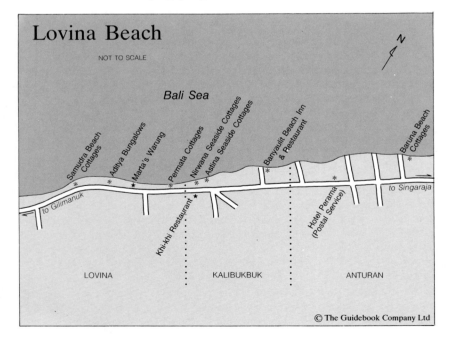

Sawan

A few kilometres up from Jagaraga is Sawan, where gamelans are made for north Bali. Villagers direct curious guests to the foundries.

Just off the main road in Kubutambahan is **Pura Madrwe Karang**, honouring the sun and Mother Earth, the forces ruling the harvests of fruit, coffee and corn from the area's unirrigated lands. One carving depicts a Westerner riding a bicycle. This is W O J Nieuwenkamp, the Dutch painter who carried out his archaeological explorations in the early 20th century, often seen riding his bike.

Air Sanih

To cool off after these hot archaeological excursions, visit two freshwater pools overlooking the beach at the springs of Air Sanih, about eight kilometres (five miles) east of Sangsit. The pools, one large enough to swim in, the other shallower and better for children, are fed by an underground spring which, according to local lore, is said to drain down from Lake Batur. The site is considered a holy place by villagers, who visit it 15 days after the full moon. Admission is ten cents for adults and about seven cents for children. There is a small restaurant serving standard fare adjacent to the pool and some less touristic warungs serving cheap food across the street. A comfortable, moderately priced hotel has been built on the beach, just past the swimming area.

On the Road to Karangasem

About 35 kilometres (22 miles) east of Singaraja, in **Tejakula**, are the royal horse baths, once used for the mounts of rajas and their entourages. Many of the villages along this stretch of road were devastated by the 1963 eruption of Gunung Agung, which towers above them; most of the villagers get by on fishing and subsistence farming.

Tulemben

Arid, hot and about as deserted a place as one can find in Bali, Tulemben is the jumping-off point for divers who wish to explore an American Liberty ship that was torpedoed by the Japanese in 1942. There is also a coral reef with shoals of fish, (although much of the coral has been dynamited). A small losmen, Paradise Palm Beach Bungalows, rents out gear and boats. There is also a small restaurant and four simple rooms with no electricity.

The West

With the exception of the tiny sea temple of Tanah Lot, the western part of Bali, encompassing most of the regency of Tabanan and, further west, Jembrana, is little known to tourists. The region, however, contains some of the most spectacular scenery to be found anywhere on the island. This is Bali's Rice Bowl. Torrents stream down steep hills to quiet pools where the Balinese bathe at sunset; rice terraces form complex puzzles in hues of jade, emerald and gold; huge waves crash on deserted beaches of black sand. In Jembrana, huge orchestras make musical thunder and bulls race, quite literally, down country lanes.

On the Road to Tabanan

A heavily travelled road leads from Denpasar to the city of Tabanan. With no stops, it is about a 45-minute drive. About ten minutes' outside the capital, one passes in quick succession the towns of **Sempidi**—centre for woven bamboo panels called gedeg—and **Luk Luk**, with its roadside collection of cement reproduction Roman columns.

This is one area of Bali in which Christianity took a hold. Gradug, a carver who first worked with the Dutch artist Willem Hofker, has his studio here. Gradug specializes in carvings from the Bible and has done many of the bas-reliefs and altars found in Catholic churches in the area, curious and delightful combinations of Christian myth and Balinese vision. Such contextualization is evident in many churches where communion rails are similar to gates in Balinese temples, angels in sarongs bear a definite likeness to the carvings of Balinese spirits that traditionally guard baby's cradles, and ceremonial umbrellas shade sculptures of the saints and the Virgin Mary (the features of both often Balinese).

Kapal

Kapal, the next village on the road, is the kitsch capital of the island, where house shrines of cast cement are sold by the lot, their wooden compartments with black palm roofs looking like mophead dolls. There are also garden statues of gnomes, tigers and zebras. A well-marked turn seawards leads to **Pura Sada**, a dynastic sanctuary of the Mengwi kingdom, believed to date back to the 12th century. Certainly the giant *waringin* tree just outside the temple gates suggests this is an ancient holy site. Much of the pura was destroyed in a 1917 earthquake and later rebuilt in 1950 by the people of Kapal, some of whom remembered what the original pura looked like. The candi bentar is truly old, but the meru inside is not. Made of brick rather than thatch roofs, the meru looks much like those erected in Java during the Majapahit reign. A testament to the capabilities of the villagers, this is a lovely temple; everything is in miniature, including whimsical stone animals and a curious grouping of 58 stone 'seats' that the temple pemangku says are devoted to ancestors who committed suttee.

Mengwi

At **Bringkit**, where there is a morning auction of cattle, a road to the north heads towards Bedugul and Singaraja. **Pura Taman Ayun** is in Mengwi. A serene temple surrounded by a lake-like moat, the Taman Ayun was built in 1634 as the main state temple of Mengwi. Mengwi, one of Bali's original seven kingdoms, was defeated when the rajas of Tabanan and Badung joined forces in 1891. The temple, renovated in 1937, has been well cared for and is one of the most elegant examples of the Balinese ability to combine site, materials and water. A quiet place, still off the 'See-Bali-in-a-day' circuit.

Sangeh

To the northeast of Mengwi is **Bukit Sari**, the monkey forest, where an impressive stand of tall nutmeg trees is home to hundreds of monkeys. A myth tells how the forest, part of a mountain being carried by the white flying monkey Hanuman, broke off and fell to earth with its army of monkeys.

On the Road to Marga

The road north of Mengwi is lined with temple umbrellas, the work of several families who have supplied the temple for years. At **Denkayu**, a small road to the west and to Marga passes Belayu. The **Geriya Taman Belayu**, home to

Rice barns

the village's Brahman family, is a centre for songket weaving. Gusti Sari and her daughter-in-law, Gusti Ayu, weave silk-and-gold sarongs on backstrap looms and are pleased to give a demonstration for anyone who is interested.

Marga

At **Baha**, a road cuts west to Marga, a Brahman village and site of a modern-day puputan. In 1946, Colonel Ngurah Rai warned the Dutch: 'Bali has become a boiling pot and the people are suffering . . . We want you out, or we fight.' It was *Merdeka atau mati* (Freedom or death)!

The Dutch did not leave and the officer led 96 men against the superior Dutch forces in Bali's most famous battle in the Indonesian war for independence. The Balinese were killed to the last man, almost every family in the village lost a relative. A memorial commemorating the Colonel's brave words and heroic attack lies up a hill in **Margarana**, past Marga's market, and every year ceremonies are held here and in Denpasar.

There is also a sacred spring, just above Marga, called **Yeh Bubuh**. According to local history, during a fight between Marga and Mengwi in the 17th century, the warriors of Marga found themselves trapped on the wrong side of the river. All prayed to be saved and suddenly, a huge tree appeared bridging the water. The men from Marga ran across the bridge, but before their enemies could follow, the tree turned into a giant eel, killing all the invading soldiers. The villagers of Marga all vowed never to eat eel and, whenever they wish for protection, visit Yeh Bubuh to feed eggs to the eels that live here. The site of the spring is quite spectacular, as it is one-quarter of the way down the steep ravine. It is also virtually impossible to find without a local guide. Ask in the market for one of the boys to show the way. From the turn-off on the road to Marga, the walk is about two hours round trip.

Alas Kedaton

Continuing a short distance from Belayu to Kukuh, a turn west will lead to the **monkey forest** of Alas Kedaton. This is on the tourist circuit, with T-shirt vendors, tour buses and an admission charge of about six cents. But the friendly Kra monkeys, somewhat better behaved than their more brazen relations at the monkey forest of Sangeh, are worth a visit. More than 700 of them, divided into three major families, inhabit the forest. The strongest group resides in the holy temple, the 400-year-old **Kayanan Kedaton**. Past the temple and down a path to the right, bats with a one-metre (three-foot) wingspan hang from the trees.

Tanah Lot

South of **Kediri** lies the coastal temple of Tanah Lot, ten kilometres (six miles) off the main road. The 15th-century temple, perched precariously

above the sea on an outcrop of rock, is one of the most holy spots in Bali. It is also, unhappily, one of the most commercialized. Its image shows up on everything from T-shirts to give-away calendars and, as one of the island's favourite tourist institutions, it is plagued with trinket pushers. Officials are bandying-about the idea of connecting the tiny islet, which is scarcely a stone's throw from the shore, to the mainland by bridge or cable car. Bali's growing corps of social cartoonists have taken up the battle cry against such crass and misguided Disneyization, but whether the pen will be mightier than the tourist's dollar, only the gods know. In the meantime, go early in the day to avoid the sunset-viewing rush hour. Legend has it that Danghyang Nirartha, the itinerant priest who founded Bali's Brahman caste, giving them their roles as priests and holy-water makers, persuaded villagers to build a temple to celebrate the spot's beauty.

In recent decades, Tanah Lot has also attracted some Balinese artists who have set up studios. Gusti Nyoman Nodya paints vivid, surrealistic scenes. Wayan Teher creates highly symbolic paintings based on traditional Balinese philosophy.

In **Pejatan**, near Tanah Lot, the villagers earn their living from *tanah air* (earth and water), as potters. At the **Ceramics Project** at banjar Pamesan, young villagers run a well-equipped studio with a sophisticated kiln, combining Western designs with Balinese styles sold in an adjacent shop.

Tabanan

Tabanan is a busy commercial town, with streets of retail stores, export companies and government offices, consequently there are no tourist hangouts here. The area's wealth is mirrored in a two-level shopping mall now under construction, in the Bali-*moderne* style. More traditional are the produce and night markets located in the centre of town.

Though not as well known as the Ubud area for its arts, Tabanan has produced a number of talented dancers and musicians. The kebyar *duduk*, a dance uniting the movements of the heroic baris dance with those of the graceful legong, was created by a dancer from Tabanan named Mario. One of Bali's most famous dancers, in the 1920s and 1930s Mario impressed such Westerners as Miguel Corvarrubias, Beryl de Zoete and Walter Spies with his grace and agility which were emphasized by the confines of the dance, performed in a sitting position.

Tabanan is also the home of the respected **Rama Dewa dance group**, which first won notice in Dutch-sponsored dance competitions during the late 1920s. The group still dances locally and at some hotels around the island. South of Tabanan, at **Abiantuwung**, in **Kediri**, the **Wrhatnala Dance School** teaches traditional Balinese dance to elementary school children. Classes are held all day Sunday and visitors are welcome to watch or to take lessons. Contact **Pak Suratha**, the head of the school, or **Nyoman Sumandi**, an instructor who speaks English. On a wide open-air stage at the **Sudana Budaya Centre**, a few kilometres south of the city, secondary-school students practise classical dances from 7.30–9.30 am and 2–4.30 pm, Tuesday and Wednesday; 7.30–9.30 am and 1.30–4 pm, Saturday.

The regency of Tabanan was one of the original seven fiefdoms granted shortly after the first Majapahit princes came to Bali to establish a Hindu

Woven-palm cili

kingdom in Gelgel, near Klungkung. Although the other kingdoms fought often among themselves, Tabanan engaged, at least in the early days, in few wars. 'The men of Tabanan understand the art of war much less than other Balinese,' wrote Friederick, the 19th-century visitor. 'Two men of Tabanan are calculated to be no more than a match for one of Mengwi and the people of Badung add to this that one man in Badung is equal to two of Mengwi.'

At peace, Tabanan flourished, fuelled by its abundant production of rice. But feudal power suffered a blow in 1903, when Raja Ngurah Agung died, and two of the king's widows made preparations to perform suttee at his cremation. The Dutch resident, alarmed by the political impact such an act might have back home in the Netherlands, demanded that suttee was not to be performed. The prince of Tabanan, trying to appease, assured the resident that this would be the last such act. The wives jumped onto the king's funeral pyre, while Dutch warships cruised menacingly off the coast. The resident had been right: citizens in Holland were outraged and in 1904 Dutch officials forced the Balinese to sign a contract prohibiting suttee.

A subsequent gesture of defiance by the king of Tabanan intensified Dutch rage and caused the downfall of the house of Tabanan. In 1906, the king of Tabanan ordered his subjects, along with the men of Denpasar, to pillage a ship wrecked off of their coast. The Dutch ordered the king and crown prince of Tabanan to report to Denpasar, where they were to be detained overnight, then exiled to Lombok. Learning of the Dutch plans, the king and crown prince committed suicide. The Dutch subsequently marched on Tabanan and razed the palace, effectively destroying the kingdom. A central square in the town of Tabanan marks the place where the king's palace once stood.

Today, the inheritors of the noble titles here and elsewhere on Bali have no official titles or powers, but they are still influential in civil agencies, local government offices and banks. Anak Agung Ngurah Agung, the man who would have been king, is venerated by the local people—in part because of the popularity of his late father, the last king of Tabanan, Cokorda Ngurah Gede. One story tells of a time when the rice crop was failing and a local subak requested the king to bring his holy keris to their aid. Borne high on a carved-wood chair by his attendants, the king visited the rice fields, wielded his keris and sprinkled the *padi* (rice) with holy water. The venture was so successful that, in subsequent years, it became a standard remedy for poor crops. As proof of the late ruler's power, people say, the heavens split with sudden, unseasonably heavy rains at his cremation.

Subak Museum

A few kilometres south of Tabanan town centre, on a small drive veering southwest off the main road, is the Subak Museum which attempts to show the way in which Bali's farmers work together communally to produce rice.

Kerambitan

The descendants of the region's kings still inhabit three palaces in Kerambitan near Tabanan. These are the **Puri Gede**, completed in the mid-18th century, the **Puri Gambe**, which is part of the Puri Gede, and the more recent **Puri Anyar**.

To reach Kerambitan, follow the main road from Tabanan past the market, then turn left onto Jalan Putau Balem, after a bridge. About four kilometres (two miles) down the road, a sign announces Desa Baturiti; the Puri Anyar is on the left. Go straight on until the road ends, then turn left to the Puri Gede.

Puri Gede

The royal family of Kerambitan is distantly related to that of Tabanan and was under its influence through the 19th century, although it functioned independently and had its own king in the Puri Gede.

There are a few conflicting accounts as to how the dynasty at Kerambitan came to be founded. One scholarly version states that, in the early 18th century, the founder of Kerambitan separated from his lower status half-brothers, the founders of Badung and Tabanan, and settled in Kerambitan because he liked the scenery.

Anak Agung Ngurah Agung, who prefers to be called Rai Girigunadhi, tells it differently. In the 17th century, he explains, the king of Tabanan,

frustrated because none of his wives had given birth to a son, promised a common woman that if she bore him a son he would make him king. The woman had a baby boy, and the king named him heir. Soon after, one of the king's high-caste wives also gave birth to a son. Years later, this high-caste, titleless son, overwhelmed by his unlucky fate, withdrew to meditate with a priest. When the prince refused to return home, the priest suggested that he head through the mountains and forests and build a palace at a spot where smoke came out of the earth. Kerambitan was that place. His father, the king, tried to persuade the prince to return to Tabanan. The young man refused and remained in Kerambitan, where he built the Puri Gede, to the same plan as the palace at Tabanan.

Puri Anyar

Much of the Puri Gede is closed to the public, but visitors may still explore the Puri Anyar. Across from the split gate is a similar entryway, leading into what once was the home of one of the king's common wives and her family. Today, there are as many as 500 related families in Kerambitan. Diagonally across the street from the palace, a building contains the royal family's impressive collection of musical instruments which are played at special ceremonies. A whimsical array of plates adorns the brick exterior.

Puri Agung

In the first court, which is used for dance and gamelan performances, there is a *cempaka putih* tree which, according to the family, emits cooking smells and good spirits during festivals. In the second court are the bales for family ceremonies, such as weddings and tooth filings. The family receives visitors in the third court. Five *sarens* (clusters of small buildings), beyond the third court, are the family's living quarters and there is also an ancestral temple. Traditionally, the palace was the centre for the arts and it is still a place to hear lontar readings and see village dancers and musicians perform. With Mr Girigunadhi's help, visitors may arrange to study dance, and *pancak silat*—a dance-like fighting technique—in the palace grounds. Visitors may also stay at the Puri Agung Wisata (see page 214).

Western Beaches

Tabanan's black sand beaches are believed by villagers to help those with rheumatism. Curative or not, they are wide and breezy, good for fishing and, in some areas, for swimming. Most of all—for now, at least—they are empty of tourists.

Down the road to the southwest of the Puri Gede, three kilometres (two miles) away, is **Kelating Beach**, with views on a clear day to Benoa Harbour.

Slightly further west, at the mouth of the Ho River, is **Pasut Beach**. To

Tabanan Mountain Drives

The mountains of Tabanan are some of Bali's most spectacular, and recent improvements in the roads mean that travellers can tour areas that still follow traditional ways of life. Each drive outlined below can take a day with stops, though some vistors spend days walking the area's trails and exploring its beaches.

Gunung Batukau Drive

The first drive starts in the centre of Tabanan, on a road that heads up towards Penebel. About 15 kilometres (nine miles) along the road is **Mengesta**. Here seven hot springs are blessed by their proximity to Gunung Batukau, which is called 'Coconut-shell Mountain' because of its odd shape.

Gunung Batukau, Bali's second-highest peak at 2,276 metres (7,467 feet), dominates Tabanan physically and spiritually. It is the source of the rivers that water the rice fields and it is the site of **Pura Luhur**, the state temple kept by the rajas of Tabanan in bygone days. Because of its distance from any major tourist centre, there are no crowds here or hawkers. Hidden in the jungle, the temple is quite simple with a few sanctuaries scattered on the mountainside. The main temple, directly at the end of the path, has a seven-tiered meru dedicated to the god of the mountain, Mahadewa, and shrines for the three mountain lakes of the region: Bratan, Buyan and Tamblingan. It is to this temple that local farmers come when it is time to plant rice. Just to the right of the main temple is a holy spring and, beyond that, a square lake that virtually disappears during the dry season and which is reminiscent of the moat at Taman Ayun, in Mengwi. To the left, down a jungle path, is a clear mountain stream, which is a lovely site for a picnic, if one ignores the few scrawls of graffiti on some of the huge boulders.

Slightly down the mountain from Pura Luhur, the road leading from Wangayegede to Jatiluih is potholed and winding, but well worth the trip. Along the way are villages where farmers still store their rice the old-fashioned way in *lumbungs* (bow-roofed rice barns) that stand high on stilts to keep the grain dry and out of the path of mice. Notice the carved wooden ornamentations that work as shields to keep out the unwanted four-legged visitors.

Jatiluih, which means 'beautiful view', was once a favourite spot of Dutch colonialists seeking to escape the coastal heat. If you get here early enough in the morning and the clouds have not come in off the sea, you can see all the way to the coast, up to Kuta and the Bukit and out west towards Jembrana. There are no homestays here, so an early morning start is required. Adventurous, hardy souls may try an overnight stay in one of the village homes; the village head may be able to arrange this.

A little further east of Jatiluih is **Apuan**, a very special place once a year when barongs from all over the island come to celebrate the odalan at the village temple. Because so many barong masks are made from trees from this region, this is considered the magical creatures' home. In the days before the odalan, dozens of these huge lion-like beasts, along with all the people from their respective village or banjar, can be seen walking along the road or piled into bemos and trucks. The festival itself goes on for three days, sometimes more, and each barong has its turn at dancing and being blessed. To see all of the great, furry creatures lying in wait in bales inside the temple's innermost courtyard, with all their different faces, is to witness a menagerie of Balinese imagination and faith.

Further north, the road eventually leads to Bedugul and Lake Bratan (see pages 152, 200). To the south is Mengwi.

Pupuan Drive

To take full advantage of Tabanan's beauty, take the 50-kilometre (31-mile) drive from the city north to Pupuan and come back by way of the shore. The road is well paved and well marked all the way and affords one of the most beautiful drives on the island. The Denpasar–Gilimanuk road heads west out of Tabanan, running along the steep, palm-lined valley of the rocky Ho River. High bilu-bilu flowers, bright red on their thick stalks, dot the roadside. Rice fields, scalloped to hug the land, are bordered by palms.

At **Antosari**, turn north and enjoy the view of Gunung Batukau in the distance. A 45-minute-drive brings one to **Belimbing**. Past a school and a playing field a small stone shrine on the right marks the entrance to the **Makori Temple**. Take a short walk back along the grassy path to a grove of tall trees with high, flaring roots. A small stone shrine and two bales for offerings form the simple temple.

About nine kilometres (six miles) north is Pupuan. A good place to stop for lunch is at one of the warungs that line the main road. Most of the regions' coffee plantations are nearby.

From Pupuan, one may head on to the north coast, which is a grand drive, particularly during Galungan when the towns are beautifully decorated.

To return south via a different route, continue west to **Pelukan**, then bear south to return about 19 kilometres (12 miles) to the coast. Coffee beans dry on mats by the side of the road. Gradually, the landscape changes, and coffee plantations begin to mix with banana plants and palm groves and the sea glimmers beyond the high trees. The scent of cloves fills the air at Asah Duren. At **Pekutanan**, turn left to head back to Tabanan or turn right towards Negara.

Tabanan Hikes

Tabanan is an excellent place for hiking. Some of these suggestions require a driver to drop you off and pick you up at certain destinations.

An easy walk starts at Antosari, just before the main turn-off to Soka Beach, along a small road heading south. Follow this to the beach road, which passes fishermen's shacks and great stretches of beach. A leisurely walk down and back takes about three hours.

A two-hour hike begins at **Ampadan** where a small road leads off the Antosari–Pupuan road up at the top of a rice field. Follow it to the left of the field and walk down to **Antagana**.

Take the small paved road from **Wangayagede**, the last village before Pura Batukau, until it is met by another heading south to **Penebal**. Follow this to complete a three-hour walk.

reach it, follow the same road away from Puri Gede, but take a fork north-west, rather than straight to Kelating. Jukungs line the upper dunes of the beach, protected by bamboo shelters.

West of Tabanan, turn south off the main road at Antosari and a glorious 20-kilometre (12-mile) drive leads to **Soka Beach** where the rice terraces extend to the beach. Here the seas are wild, just right for skilled surfers who, because of the hour-and-a-half drive from Kuta, like to stay at the nearby village of **Lalang Linggah**. Even for non-surfers, a stop for lunch at the Balian Beach Club, a modest complex of bungalows at the mouth of the Balian River, about ten kilometres (six miles) west of Antosari is desirable.

The Jembrana Region

The coastal road out of Soka Beach winds into Bali's least populous regency, Jembrana, a 'place of dense jungles'—the island's wild west. Small villages teeter on the edge of the West Bali National Park. Only recently has the region been connected with the rest of Bali. Because of the rugged terrain, as recently as the 1960s, it still took three days to make the trip from Jembrana's capital of Negara to Denpasar. The road now is very good, but there is still a feeling of remoteness. Indeed, much of the history of the place is cut off from the rest of Bali. In the 17th century, a Bugis prince from the island now known as Sulawesi set himself up as ruler of Jembrana. Later, at the turn of the 19th century, the raja of Karangasem, fresh from victories in Buleleng and the island of Lombok, captured the region. In 1847, the raja of Jembrana relinquished his power to the Dutch. Throughout the years,

Javanese Muslims crossed the nearby narrow straits and set up communities. This influence can be seen in the architecture of the small mosques and the wood-and-concrete houses, and the scarcity of compounds.

Today, the kabupaten of Jembrana is quite successful. It produces rice for export every year and residents are pleased to tell visitors that it won the president's award for the cleanest spot in Indonesia, something that is a welcome relief after some of the trash dumps of south Bali.

Pura Luhur

Near Yeh Buah, a small road runs down to the sea to **Rambut Siwi** and the Pura Luhur Temple. According to legend, the priest Danghyang Nirartha stopped in a village here during his travels and cured the people of a plague by using holy water. He gave them a hair from his head which he promised would protect them from further disaster thus the name of the temple, which means 'Siwa's hair'. To this day, truck drivers and motorists stop to receive a blessing from a pemangku standing at the roadside, sprinkling holy water on all who pass.

Bull Races

So proud are the people of their bulls—big, strong, sunburned-looking beasts, so unlike the doe-like cows of southern Bali—that they hold bull-racing contests during the dry season, testing teams against each other. Every Sunday morning from about 6.30 until 9.30 or so, these wild meets, known as *makapung*, are held in the small villages—such as Delodbrawa and Dauhwaru—around Jembrana, places that aren't even on the map. Villagers are happy to help visitors find their way.

Gamelan Museum

In **Sankaragung**, about three kilometres (two miles) east of Negara, just off the main road near **Pangintukadaya**, is a new private museum devoted to gamelans of the region. Ketut Suwentra, a musician–dancer–composer, uses the money he makes as a tour guide to the Japanese to buy the instruments. By far the best way to experience the music is to have him give a perform- ance, complete with musicians and dancers. To make arrangements either call Ketut Suwentra or his wife at their city house in Denpasar (tel. 27330) or write to them at Jalan Sandat, Gang III–IV, Denpasar. It's worth a quick visit just to see the instruments, particularly the jegog ensemble which consists of xylophones of oversized bamboo. After the turn-off, ask for Ketut Suwentra. If he's not at the museum, someone else will be there. Donations to help buy more gamelan sets in other styles are much appreciated.

Dewi Saraswati riding her sacred goose

Perencak

On the coast is Perencak, so named for the ancient temple, **Pura Ancak,**
where Danghyang Nirartha, the great wandering priest, is said to have arrived
from Java at the turn of the 16th century. Here, too, at the confluence of the
rivers that water the region, are swamps and waterways alive with all sorts of
wildlife, including Bali's few remaining crocodiles. Local residents hold
canoe races on the river to celebrate the Kuningan holiday.

Negara

Negara is the seat of the kabupaten, with government offices, banks, a few
Chinese restaurants and stores to service the small villages. There are losmen
here which are cheap and basic. All in all, not much to see. Drives through
the surrounding mountains, however, can be worthwhile.

About 40 kilometres (25 miles) into the craggy mountains that tower
above Negara are the huge clove plantations surrounding **Asah Duren.** The
production of cloves is new to Bali. Traditionally, the Maluku islands and
northern Sulawesi have been the chief clove producers, but the sweet-
smelling buds are now being collected here with as much care and are
reaping considerable profit.

Candi Kesuma Beach

About 15 kilometres (nine miles) west of Negara is Candi Kesuma Beach, well away from the European tourist rush and scattered with a few simple losmen. **Madewi** is nearby and its fine waves, simple bungalows and restaurants make it a good place for surfing.

Palasari and Belimbingsari

Many of the people living in the district are transmigrants, poor Balinese peasants from Bali's populous east and south who, in 1939 and 1940, were given uncultivated land by the government in hopes of increasing agricultural production and easing overpopulation. The experiment, unlike some other attempts at transmigration, was hugely successful—so much so that Palasari, which means the 'garden of nutmeg trees' was described by Indonesia's minister of social affairs as a 'model village of transmigration'. The area is also the site of Bali's largest Christian communities.

To the west, the main road leads to Gilimanuk and the ferry to Java (see page 171).

Thundering Bamboo
Ketut Suwentra, Gamelan Leader

Rain spits from dark clouds, thunder threatens in the distance. As if in reply, music rumbles through the courtyard, the first chords rolling low, followed by an explosion of notes. In a bale, 15 men hammer away at huge bamboo tubes of the xylophone-like instruments, riding tall wood benches like cowboys on horseback, chasing some unseen quarry.

Sweat glistens on bare chests, mallet heads strike the bamboo so fast, so hard that some mallet heads break and others go flying into the darkness. A wall of sound breaks out of huge bamboo tubes, some of them 43 centimetres (17 inches) in diameter and four metres (13 feet) long, and reverberates through the night. The Suar Agung, the giant jegog orchestra of Jembrana, is at practice.

The leader of the group, Ketut Suwentra, sits in the thick of the music, beating out a tune so fast, so deep, so intensely jazzy it is hard to imagine the musicians keeping up the pace one minute more, and yet they do, on and on into the night until the thunder of the heavens and the jegog merge into one apocalyptic roar.

The set finished, the musicians towel themselves off and sit smoking kreteks and drinking the sweet dark coffee women bring from the kitchen. At the first bright, shimmering notes of the gong kebyar, the men scurry through the rain to an adjacent bale to watch as a joged dancer starts her rounds, tapping first the one responsible for all this, Suwentra, who immediately jumps up, his movements as fresh and lithe and, to the delight of all the onlookers, as insinuating as the young woman's.

A man of irrepressible energy and enthusiasm, Suwentra is Bali's, producer–director–choreographer–dancer and musician extraordinaire. The first person from Jembrana to go to university, he has worked for the last two decades to keep the musical tradition of dance alive in his and other villages and, since the early 1980s, to establish a gamelan museum. His group of 32 musician–farmers, who play the jegog and the gong kebyar, and 24 dancers, have achieved some fame. They have made trips to Japan and the Philippines, played at the president's palace in Jakarta and appeared on Indonesian television and at Bali's Arts Festival. Equally important, he says, are the smaller groups in out-of-the-way villages, where every week rudimentary gamelans and dance groups gather eagerly for instruction from him. Schools and universities may teach the elements of dance and music and push the boundaries of the arts, but it is the villages that give life to Bali's music and dance.

'I learned from my grandfather and father,' Suwentra explains. 'Life in the village was relaxed. In the morning, I'd go to school, then come home and put on a *kain* [cloth] and work in the rice fields. After dinner, everyone would get together and practise music. We did it for the good feeling; there was no television or radio in those days, actually television only came in 1984 to our village, and so we made our own entertainment.'

The elders passed down art and culture; it didn't fade. The village is an old one, and so many types of music were to be found.

Jembrana area is best known for the jegog, which quite simply means 'big', no exaggeration, considering that the largest instrument requires two men to play and weighs 150 kilos (337 pounds).

'The idea came from our village, starting from the kulkul and the tingklik, though the tuning is different,' says Suwentra. 'The material was easy to come by, the large bamboo grew close by and there was plenty of wood. Then, there was an exposition in Klungkung for a meeting of rajas. A group from Istanbul came and on the way back, stopped here and told my grandfather what they saw,' he says. On the road from east and central Bali to Java, the musicians and dancers of Jembrana came into contact with Europeans and Chinese, as well as palace troupes going to play for sultans in Java. 'Our village became a sort of transfer site for the arts,' Suwentra proudly declares.

Not all foreign influence was constructive, however. 'After the Second World War, the jegog was almost finished, the Japanese were like a bulldozer,' explains Suwentra, who worked with his father in the 1960s and 1970s to create a special jegog troupe of musicians and dancers. He even purchased land to assure that there would be a healthy supply of giant bamboo for the jegog.

'I had meetings with musicians; in older houses there were a few people who remembered and in Walter Spies' book there were photos dating back to the year 1937. I made the dance from the photos and from what the older people told me, from our history and from the daily life in the fields.'

One of the most popular dances of Suwentra's jegog group is the bull race, a lively bit of choreography inspired by the bull races that are held almost every Sunday morning on the small, unpaved roads around Jembrana. In fact, some of the musicians in the group have their own teams of bulls.

'It combines sport and art, something like *Ben Hur*,' says Suwentra, who doesn't seem to be afraid of what might strike others as odd combinations. Recently, he was commissioned by the leaders of the Catholic and Protestant churches in the area to create a sendratari, a kind of dance-drama, for Christmas, backed by the gamelan.

'It is very exciting, combining the new and the old, working in the villages,' says Suwentra. 'The music is in the adat and the religion. The people know how to make music, because we start with the tunes from God, from the pedanda, from the chanting of the priest. There isn't a priest without a bell, there must be sound. Music is so basic to Balinese life, everyone knows it.'

At Sea

With over 600 kilometres (373 miles) of sand and coral coastline, Bali offers excellent opportunities for snorkelling, scuba diving and sailing, as well as some of the best surfing in the world.

Surfing

At Ngurah Rai Airport, the luggage belts are crowded with surfboards wrapped in their brilliantly coloured bags. Surfers from Australia, Hawaii, California, and, of late, Japan hang out at the Dwipa Bali Hotel, nursing feet cut by coral and talking about the five-metre- (16-feet-) high waves at Uluwatu. In the evening, along Jalan Padma and Jalan Pura Bagus Turna, losmen courtyards are lined with surfboards, and in the morning, the young surfies can be seen roaring off on motorcycles, boards tucked under one arm, in search of the perfect wave.

The best places to get information on conditions are at surf shops, such as **Lilii's Surf Shop**, on the north side of Jalan Legian in Kuta, near Midnight Oil. There are plenty of boards to rent, which are less expensive than those for rent on the beach—the selection is greater too. To buy, the prices can be quite reasonable when an Aussie has to sell his board for a ticket home. Owner, Gede Narmada, is one of Bali's best surfers and is generous with suggestions, when he's not out surfing himself.

One big event here is the Bali International Surfing Pro-Am, held in Kuta every year. The surfing conditions and judges' decisions are discussed in bars and warungs for weeks after.

There are waves for every level of surfer, most within easy reach of the southern resorts. **Kuta**, **Legian** and **Seminyak**, with their two-and-a-half-metre (seven-foot) beach breaks, are ideal for beginners.

Intermediate surfers head for **Bingin**, with a left-hand surf break, south of **Airport Reef** in Kuta. About a half an hour west of Legian on a hauntingly striking rocky coast, **Canggu** has easy one-to-two-metre (three-to-seven-foot) left-hand and right-hand reef breaks. Further west are **Lalang Linggah** and **Medewi**, with two-and-a-half-metre (seven-foot) reef breaks. Both places are about two hours away from Kuta.

There is a wide selection of spots for experts. In Kuta, **Kuta Reef**, accessible only by fisherman's boat available for $3 in front of the Sunset Club, has a left-hand reef break with three-metre (ten-foot) waves and there is also **Airport Reef**, to the south. In **Sanur**, the reef that wrecked so many ships is a challenge to surfers, with some of the world's best right-breaking waves. Take a jukung lift to get there. By far the most celebrated spot is **Uluwatu**, near the temple at the southernmost tip of the peninsula. Surfers ride six-to-eight-metre (20-to-26-foot) waves that are left-hand reef breaks, dwarfed by the cliffs that shoot straight up from the rocky beach. Nearby, and equally challenging, is **Padang Padang**, with waves of up to six metres (20 feet). Nearer the Nusa Dua Complex are **Ngn Ngn**, with two-to-three-metre (seven-to-ten-foot) waves, and **Nusa Dua**, a right-hand reef break where the waves can be higher than three metres (ten feet).

Experienced surfers who want to get away from it all head for **Nusa Lembongan**. Boats sail from Sanur, just east of the Hotel Bali Beach, every morning and the crossing to the island takes about two hours. The water is colder here and the life much quieter. Riding the three-to-four-metre (ten-to-13-foot) waves that break just off the reef is the main attraction.

At another surfer's mecca, **Grajagan Bay** or 'G-Land' on Java's west coast, full days are devoted to the legendary giant waves. Surfers live in isolation in a camp of bamboo bungalows in **Plenkung** surrounded by a national park. Trips are organized by Bobby at Lilii's Surf Shop and cost $170 a week, including transportation, room and board.

Sailing and Cruising

Sailing through the Indonesian archipelago can be one of the most fascinating voyages in the world. The Bugis, the famed 'pirate' (their piracy depending on who was talking!) sailors so feared by early Western explorers, still sail these waters in great wooden boats, loaded with produce, cattle, motorcycles and passengers. There are literally thousands of islands to explore. However, lack of marinas and bureaucratic red-tape have discouraged many modern-day pleasure sailors. Probably the easiest way to sail in Indonesia is to charter a boat in Bali. The captains have all the necessary permits and know the waters, which can be dangerous. Most recreational boating facilities on Bali are found at **Benoa Harbour** and trips range from half-day to weeks-long adventures. The day trips generally head out to the island of **Nusa Penida**. The island is so dry, that villagers have to climb down to a spring at the base of steep cliffs for water, then scale the cliffs via bamboo catwalks. Snorkelling in the clear-water coves and lagoons of the island is excellent.

The **Bali International Yacht Club** is at Jalan Pantai Karang 5, Sanur (tel. 88391; telex 47319 FINASIA). The club is planning to build a modern 50-berth marina in Benoa. For the time being, the clubhouse will assist sailors in obtaining the documentation required to sail Indonesian waters, including the essential security clearance valid for three to six months. The club also has five ships available for charter. Some of the tours available are on a 13-metre (43-foot) jet boat with a capacity of 20 passengers which makes day trips to Nusa Penida for snorkelling and sight-seeing—$56 includes lunch, refreshments and snorkelling equipment, as well as transportation to and from Benoa. You can also take the **MS *Raden Mas***, an 18-metre (59-foot) air-conditioned motor yacht, which makes journeys to various islands between July and October. A five-day tour around **Komodo Island** departing from the

port of **Bima** on the island of **Sumbawa** costs $690 per person, airfare to and from Sumbawa not included. Another boat is the **MV *Putri Bali***, a 13-metre (43-foot) motor yacht which also makes day trips to Nusa Penida—$50 per person, including a buffet lunch. These, and other ships including a 17-metre (56-foot) ketch rig yacht, a 14-metre (46-foot) dive boat, an 18-metre (59-foot) gaff rig, a two-mast ketch rig tall ship, a ten-metre (33-foot) two mast tall ship, and a turtle boat can be chartered with crew, by the day or week.

The *Sri Noa-Noa*, a 14-metre (46-foot) teak schooner, is available for charter from Naomi and Philippe Petiniaud, Jalan Lantang Hidung 2, Sanur Kauh (tel. 88639). It has two cabins and a convertible dining room and can accommodate five passengers on short trips and three on long trips. It is equipped with a windsurfer, a dinghy and a bathroom with hot and cold water. Charters are available from three days to a month at $350 per day, including food, crew and fuel.

The Bali Hyatt has two power boats for hire as well as three speedboats. The *Bali Hyatt One* is a nine-metre (30-foot) power boat which can accommodate eight passengers. A $375 full-day trip includes snorkelling and fishing equipment with a crew of two, a half-day trip costs $275. The *Bali Hyatt Two* is a six-metre (20-foot) power boat which can accommodate four guests and two crew members. A full-day charter is $275 and a half-day trip costs $175.

Certainly the most luxurious way to see the islands is aboard the *Island Explorer* or *Lumba Lumba*, which makes journeys to **Komodo**, **Sulawesi**, the eastern **Lesser Sundas** and beyond. There are only 36 passengers in 12 staterooms and six suites, and almost as many crew members. Gourmet meals are served aboard ship and well-planned trips lead the visitor to the places few other ships can go to as the diesel catamaran has a shallow draft of two metres (seven feet). More information can be obtained from the *Island Explorer* office at Benoa Harbour (tel. 34822; fax 31137), or from Jack Daniels, MT Jakarta Pusat, at PO Box 98 (tel. 593401; telex 46683). Bookings can also be made through Salen Lindblad Cruising, 133 East 55 Street, New York, N Y 10022 (tel. 212 751 2300 or 800 233 5688). Prices start at about $200 per person a day for the shorter cruises and $300 a day for the longer trips. Discounts may be available for cruises that are not fully booked. But this can only be done through the Jakarta office.

Baruna Water Sports is at Jalan Bypass Ngurah Rai, Tuban (tel. 51223; fax 52779). It has branches at Hotel Bali Beach, Bali Hyatt, Bali Sol, Putri Bali and Bali Intan Village. Baruna Water Sports organizes an eight-day trip from **Benoa** to **Flores** via **Lombok**, **Sumbawa** and **Komodo** on a 30-metre (98-foot), 17-cabin cruiser. A double cabin costs $700 and includes full board, water sports and land tours. The return airfare from Flores is not included. Baruna also has day trips to Nusa Penida on an outrigger and a diesel-powered motorboat for $35, including lunch.

Diving and Snorkelling

The island has spectacular diving in warm, clear waters. The reefs are home to coral trout, parrot fish with mouths like beaks, the curious clown fish, the humped Napoleon fish and manta rays. Dolphins and flying fish skim the surface of the waters, and stingrays, white-tipped sharks and Boureau whales play in the depths.

Pulau Menjagan, off the northwest coast, is perhaps the best diving and snorkelling site around Bali, with a coral shelf that drops off a 40-metre (131-foot) wall. The small island is a marine reserve and permits for diving must be obtained from the warden in Teluk Terima.

Tulamben, on the northeastern tip of the island, has an artificial reef created by a Liberty ship that sank during the Second World War. This site has a sloping topography and a depth of three to 30 metres (ten–98 feet).

Although there is a **coral reef off Sanur**, much has been destroyed by dynamiting for coral used in the construction of walls of hotels on the beach. Nusa Dua has a sloping and flat sea bed and is ideal for fishing and underwater photography.

Bali Dive Sports Club is run by Ketut Wetha, Br Semawang, on the beach south of the Bali Hyatt, Sanur (tel. 88582, 87692). The club offers a variety of diving and snorkelling trips, including night dives. Baruna Water Sports also has diving trips around the island and provides instruction.

For the true devotee, **Balina Diving** offers bungalow-style accommodation in Manggis Village just outside Candi Dasa (see page 136). There are daily trips to nearby **Blue Lagoon** and **Kambing Island** and longer trips around the island. For information, contact Balipro Batujimbar, Sanur (tel. 88451).

The **Hotel Club Bualu** is at Nusa Dua (tel. 971310). It offers diving instruction and certification. Details upon request.

Windsurfing

Bali's best windsurfing is during July, August and sometimes in September when the trade winds buffet the coasts of Sanur, Nusa Dua and Benoa. When the trade winds change, sailors take their boards to **Jimbaran Bay** and the south end of **Kuta Beach**. Rental sailboards are available at many locations; equipment is good when it is not broken. In Sanur, try the **Bali Dive Sports Club**, south of the Hyatt on the beach, where boards include a Hifly, a Mistral SST and a Cobra. **Jeladi Wilis** at the Sanur Beach Market south of the Hotel Bali Beach, also has some good boards. Boards are also available at **Baruna Water Sports** at Benoa, at the Hotel Bali Beach in Sanur, at the Hotel Putri Bali and at the Bali Sol and Nusa Dua Beach Hotel on Nusa Dua.

Water Skiing and Parasailing

Lake Bratan, nestled in the foothills of the central mountains, has become Bali's water-skiing capital, the site of various water-skiing competitions, including the Asia-Pacific Water Skiing Competition and the Asia Open. Boats, skis and ramps are available at the **Bedugul Hotel and Restaurant** in the arcade along the lake, for $15 per half hour. In **Sanur**, water-skiing is available at **Bali Marine Sports**, on the beach south of the Bali Hyatt, for $10 per 15 minutes and at **Jeladi Wilis**. Parasailing is also available at both sites, as well as in the major hotels of **Nusa Dua**, at $10 for three to five minutes.

Inter-island Travel

The Indonesian state shipping company, Pelni, offers regularly scheduled passenger shipping routes through the archipelago. Their offices are at Benoa Harbour. Write to Pelabuhan Benoa, PO Box 386 (telex 35184). Opening times are from 8 am–3 pm, weekdays. There are four classes on Pelni ships. First-class cabins are double rooms with a television and private bath, second-class accommodation has two bunk beds and a sink and bath, third-class cabins sleep eight and economy-class cabins are vast dormitory-type arrangements. The ships are entirely air-conditioned and trips work out a real bargain. Meals are included in the low prices, but bring along your own deck chair. Overnight from Padang Bai to Ujung Pandang in Sulawesi is $35 first class; $14 economy. Other ships, which do not stop in Bali but do stop in nearby Surabaya on Java, go out to Irian Jaya for six days at $170 for first class; $50 for economy. Tickets can only be purchased at the Pelni office at Benoa or at the central Pelni office in Jakarta. Write to Jalan Angkasa 18 (or tel. (Jakarta) 416262, 417163, 49121, 49360).

Hotels

There are so many hotels in Bali (over 5,000 rooms, with the number doubling and perhaps tripling in the next three years), that to even begin to mention all would be difficult. Instead, what follows is a highly personal list of some of the best places to stay.

The hotels vary in price and style. Some are South Sea palaces, updated versions of the tropical mansions that were backdrops to the tales of Somerset Maugham; others are simply clean, friendly places for the traveller on a low budget. The very cheapest hotels, known as *kelas kambing* (goat class), have not been included; it is best to check them out on one's own.

During July and August, and Christmas and Easter, reservations with deposits are absolutely essential in Sanur, Kuta, Nusa Dua, Ubud and Candi Dasa. Rates per night for a double room have been put into five categories:

$	Under $25
$$	$25–49
$$$	$50–74
$$$$	$75–100
$$$$$	Over $100

In recent years, hotel rates have increased about ten percent every year, with some hotels boosting rates by as much as 30 percent. Consequently, figures quoted can only be used as a general guide. Many hotels raise their prices in high season, but in months when rooms are not filled, the visitor can often get discounts of 15 to 50 percent through good-natured, on-the-spot bargaining. Adding considerably to the bills are government tax and a service charge, usually 15.5 percent, charged at all except the least expensive lodgings.

Hotels are listed in order of preference within the separate headings. **Deluxe** hotels offer recreational facilities, such as tennis courts, swimming pools, travel services, conference rooms, shops, restaurants, bars and nightclubs on the premises. Rooms meet an international standard of modern comfort and amenities. **First-class** hotels are small to medium-sized with high-quality accommodation, attractive grounds and some resort facilities. Rooms almost always have air conditioning, hot and cold water and tub showers in garden bathrooms. Most rooms have radios and telephones. **Moderate** accommodation has comfortable rooms, sometimes with air conditioning, but more typically with fans. Some places have hot water—which is not particularly necessary in Bali's tropical climate—and tub showers; others, out of the main resort areas, have the traditional Balinese mandi (bath), a huge, tiled trough filled with water which is scooped up with a plastic container then thrown over oneself. Phones are usually in the office. **Modest** lodgings, generally known as losmen, are run by Balinese families and are basic, but usually clean. All rooms have electricity and private bathrooms with a mandi or Balinese shower, which drains directly onto the bathroom floor. Though the least expensive, rates usually include breakfast and afternoon tea: typical traits of Indonesian hospitality.

Southern Resorts

Sanur

Deluxe

Bali Hyatt, Jalan Tandjung Sari, PO Box 392, Sanur (tel. 88271; telex 35127, 35527 HYATT DPR IA; fax 87693). 387 rooms, $$$$$ (with high-season supplements). All major credit cards are accepted. The hotel is on a wide, quiet stretch of beach and offers extensive facilities, including two swimming pools, one with a waterfall fashioned after Bali's famed Elephant Cave.

Hotel Bali Beach, Jalan Brigjen Ngurah Rai, PO Box 275, Denpasar 8001 (tel. 88511; telex 35133 HBBDPR IA; fax 87917). 605 units, $$$$–$$$$$. All major credit cards are accepted. Rooms in the awkward nine-storey tower are unremarkable, but separate cottages, tastefully decorated in Balinese-*moderne* style, are set in a beautiful park.

First Class

Tandjung Sari, Jalan Tandjung Sari, PO Box 25, Denpasar (tel. 88441; telex 35157 TANSARI; fax 87930). 29 rooms, $$$$$ (with high-season supplements). All major credit cards are accepted. Grass-roofed bungalows surrounded with coral walls are hidden in gardens of frangipani and bougainvillea. Tandjung Sari was one of Bali's first hotels and continues to be one of its most elegant.

Villa Bebek, corner of Jalan Pengembak and Jalan Mertasari, PO Box 47, Denpasar 8001 (tel. 32507; fax 88886). Three villas, $$$$$. Landscape architect Michael White has nestled three Balinese-style houses around a handsome pool. The distinctive houses and personal service (each house has its own staff) command the high prices.

La Taverna Bali Hotel, Jalan Tandjung Sari, PO Box 40, Denpasar (tel. 88497, 88387; telex 35163 LTVN IA; fax 87126). 34 bungalows, $$$–$$$$$ (with high-season supplements). All major credit cards are accepted. One of the nicest beach-front hotels, with charming semi-detached bungalows and gardens.

Moderate

Santrian Beach Bungalows, Jalan Tandjung Sari, PO Box 55, Denpasar (tel. 88009, 88671; telex 35229). 81 rooms, $$$. All major credit cards are accepted. Brick, tile-roofed bungalows are arranged in a maze of palm trees and winding stone paths that lead to the beach.

Santrian Beach Cottages, Jalan Tandjung Sari, PO Box 55, Denpasar (tel. 8818/1/2/4; telex 35169; fax 88185). 80 rooms, $$$. All major credit cards are accepted. These very pretty single- and two-storey bungalows, modelled after traditional Balinese rice barns, stretch directly down to a wide strip of beach.

Segara Village, Jalan Tandjung Sari, PO Box 91, Denpasar (tel. 88407, 88231; telex 35143 SEGARA DPR). 116 rooms, $$$–$$$$$. All major credit cards are accepted. This beach-front resort retains the feeling of a small inn while offering a wide range of activities. Most rooms are in bungalows styled after Balinese rice barns.

Puri Klapa Garden Cottages, Jalan Segara 1, PO Box 436, Denpasar (tel. 88999; telex 35519 PURIKA IA). 15 bungalows, $$. All major credit cards are accepted. This new hotel, just a short walk from the beach in northern Sanur, has tastefully furnished air-conditioned bungalows.

Modest
Werdhapura, Jalan Tandjung Sari (tel. 88171). 56 rooms, $. No credit cards are accepted. Built in 1969 by the Indonesian Government, this beach-front hotel remains the greatest budget find in Sanur.

Swastika Bungalows, Batu Jimbar, PO Box 8573, Denpasar. 46 rooms, $$. American Express and Visa cards are accepted. Its two-level, tile-roofed cottages have garden patios and white brick interiors, with sparse, but clean and bright furnishings.

Hotel Laghawa Beach Inn, Jalan Tanjung Sari (tel. 88494, 88214). 14 rooms, $–$$. All major credit cards are accepted. Although it is removed from the beach by a short walk and has no swimming pool, the Laghawa is worth a look for travellers on a budget.

Private Houses
There is a small but growing number of houses that may be rented by the month. Typically, they are built near the beach in Balinese style and come fully furnished. Full-time staff cook, clean and tend the grounds; visitors are responsible for paying the grocery and phone bills. Rental rates, which start just under $1,000 per month in high season, vary depending on the size and location of the house. One Balinese who lets several such houses is Rudiana. Write to Banjar Batujimbar, Sanur (tel. 88707).

Kuta and Environs

The Kuta area's myriad types of accommodation vary from paradisical deluxe hotels to spartan rooms on ill-lit alleys. A good number of inexpensive lodgings exist, but their overall quality is generally a bit lower than on the north or east coasts. Just now, the villages of Legian and Seminyak, just up the beach from Kuta, are much quieter and sleepier (plans for large hotels may change all this). Legian and Seminyak can also seem a bit isolated and transport is needed to reach Kuta.

Kuta

First Class
Santika Beach Hotel, Jalan Kartika, PO Box 1008, Tuban (tel. 51267/8; telex 35277 STK DPR; fax 51260). 100 rooms, $$$–$$$$$. All major credit cards are accepted. On a former coconut plantation, this family-oriented hotel sits on a narrow beach at the southern end of Kuta, away from the madding crowds.

Bali Intan Cottages, Jalan Melasti No 1, PO Box 1002, Kuta (tel. 51770, 51469, 52572; telex 35200 BICDPR IA; fax 51891). 146 rooms, $$$–$$$$$. All major credit cards are accepted. Intan Cottages' selling point is its location, right across from the beach, at the border of Kuta and Legian.

Moderate

Poppies, Poppies Gang, PO Box 378, Denpasar (tel. 51059; telex 35516 POPCOT IA). 20 rooms, $$. American Express and Visa cards are accepted. Poppies is probably the best deal in Kuta with small white brick cottages near the beach in central Kuta.

Aneka Beach, Jalan Pantai Kuta, PO Box 337, Denpasar (tel. 52892; telex 35218 PURWA IA). 33 rooms, $$. All major credit cards are accepted. Just off the main strip of beach in Kuta. Good central location.

Modest

Some of Kuta's best losmen are along Poppies Lane and in the small alleyways behind it. All are convenient for the beach, Kuta's best restaurants and Bemo Corner.

Kuta Puri Bungalows, Poppies Lane (tel. 51903). No credit cards are accepted. 14 rooms, $. Perhaps the best of the Poppies Lane budget spots, it is the shortest distance from the beach, among the newest and offers very clean, basic rooms with bamboo furniture and tiled floors.

Mutiara Cottages, Poppies Lane. 29 rooms, $. No credit cards are accepted. Clean, adequately comfortable rooms in divided bungalows just 300 metres (984 feet) from the beach.

Mimpi Bungalows, Poppies Lane, PO Box 41, Kuta (tel. 51848). No credit cards are accepted. Clean, spartan rooms at a minimal price are available here.

Legian and Seminyak

Moderate

Nusa di Nusa Beach Bungalows, Seminyak, PO Box 191, Denpasar (tel. 51414, 53916; telex 35246 DINUSA IA). 23 units, $$–$$$$ (with high-season supplements). All major credit cards are accepted. Stands out for its breezy beach-front location and welcoming feel. A stone path through the grounds leads past a pool to a wide, nearly empty strip of beach. To reach the hotel, turn off Jalan Legian at the 'Gado-Gado' sign, then turn left when the road forks.

Legian Beach Hotel, Jalan Melasti, PO Box 308, Denpasar (tel. 51711/5; telex 35324 LBHTL IA; fax 51715). 132 rooms, $$–$$$. All major credit cards are accepted. Modern and somewhat sterile, this large hotel is situated on the beach bordering north Kuta.

Bali Mandira Cottages, Jalan Padma, Legian, PO Box 1003, Denpasar (tel. 51381/4; telex 35215 MNDIRA IA; fax 52377). 96 rooms, $$. All major credit cards are accepted. With its modern rooms and even rows of cottages, Bali Mandira is almost devoid of colour. It is, however, right on the beach in a secluded part of Legian.

Bali Niksoma Beach Cottages, Jalan Padma, Legian, PO Box 268, Denpasar (tel. 51946; telex 35537 BNK IA). 42 rooms, $–$$. American Express, Visa and Diners Club cards are accepted. Everything—including the hotel, swimming pool and coffee shop—overlooks the beach in central Legian.

Modest

Many of the less expensive places in Legian and Seminyak are scattered along the beach on and between Jalan Padma and Jalan Pura Bagus Taruna. The streets marked as turn-offs for the clubs Gado-Gado and Double 6's off Jalan Legian are also good to explore. Other travellers can often pass on tips about current, inexpensive losmen.

Blue Ocean, Legian Beach, inquiries c/o Yasin Yacob, Jalan Maluku Rt I/34 Denpasar (tel. 28899, 51189, 51190). 29 bungalows, $. No credit cards are accepted. This small, friendly hotel on an isolated strip of beach a brief walk south of Double 6's is one of the best finds available to travellers on limited budgets.

Kerobokan

A leisurely ten-minute drive north of Legian, past rice fields, local banjars and placid cows, leads to the Kuta area's last tourist enclave. Enjoy the isolation while it lasts; more hotels are on the way.

Deluxe

Bali Oberoi, Jalan Kayu Aya, Legian, PO Box 351, Denpasar (tel. 51061; telex 35125 OBHOTL IA; fax 52791). 74 units, $$$$$ (with high-season supplements). All major credit cards are accepted. The Bali Oberoi has been ranked among the world's top five hotels, and the prices match. Some seaside villas rent for as much as $650. The hotel is set in very beautiful grounds.

First Class

Puri Ratih Bali, Jalan Puri Ratih Bali, Kerobokan, PO Box 1114, Tuban (tel. 51546/8; telex 35358 RATIH IA; fax 51549). Eight units, $$$$–$$$$$ (with high-season supplements). All major credit cards are accepted. Bordered by rice fields and the beach, two-storey wantilan-style villas (each with private staff) with two bedrooms can house up to six people. Duplex doubles at the rear of the hotel are much smaller, but pleasant.

Intan Beach Village, Jalan Batubelig Beach, PO Box 1089, Kuta (tel. 52191/2; telex 35532; fax 52193). 50 rooms, $$$$. All major credit cards are accepted. Comfortable rooms are blandly Western, grounds are well tended. There are 200 new rooms planned for 1990.

Jimbaran

Pansea Puri Bali, Jalan Uluwatu, PO Box 1013, Denpasar (tel. 26529; telex 35187 GKRIS IA—ATTN PANSEA BALI; fax 32855). 41 rooms, $$$$ (with high-season supplements). Rates include breakfast and dinner. All major credit cards are accepted. Gloriously isolated on a huge, curving beach only a short distance from busy Kuta and monumental Nusa Dua, the Pansea Puri Bali offers great sunsets, plus the privacy in which to enjoy them.

Nusa Dua

This is an elegant, isolated tourist ghetto. The newest arrivals in a World Bank-sponsored plan for 11 luxury hotels here, include a Hyatt and a Hilton (both scheduled for completion by 1991). A championship golf course is also planned. Visitors should be warned of 'packages', which offer air fare and rooms at reduced prices, the savings are made redundant by the steep charges for food and drink, and the money spent on travelling to other parts of Bali.

Hotel Bali Sol, PO Box 1048, Tuban (tel. 71510; telex 35237; fax 71360). 500 rooms, $$$$$. All major credit cards are accepted. For a hotel of its great size, the Bali Sol is strikingly pretty. Duplex suites are spacious and light; all have terraces.

Club Mediterranean, PO Box 1025, Denpasar (tel. 7152/1/3, 7183/2/4; telex 35216 BHVCM; fax 71831). 350 rooms, rates through booking agents only. Club Med's booking office in Jakarta is in the Hotel Borobudur, ground floor No 8 (tel. 349784; telex 46165 PARIBAIA). Reservations can also be made through Nusa Dua Club Med. The public may use Club Med's impressive sports facilities for a fee of $25, including lunch 11.30 am–4 pm, or 6.30 pm until the disco closes, including entertainment.

Ubud and Environs

The days of dirt-cheap digs are passing fast in Ubud; the era of $100 per night rooms has arrived, with upmarket villas for as much as five times that price! Despite some discomfort, there are still rooms with breathtaking views for $10 or less. A plethora of small homestays is located along Monkey Forest Road; others are found on the small, cobblestone side streets that lead off the main road. Just out of Ubud, another group is scattered on the terraced rice fields just west of the Campuhan River; a third cluster perches on the ridge of the Ayung River around Sayan, several kilometres to the north. Breakfast is included, unless otherwise noted.

Ubud

Moderate

Siti Bungalows, PO Box 227, Denpasar (tel. 28690). Six rooms, $$. Mastercard, Visa and American Express cards are accepted. Just to the east of the Cafe Lotus, a small wooden door and a flight of stone steps lead to brick and stone cottages, laid out like a private family compound. The rooms are comfortable and clean.

Ubud Inn, Monkey Forest Road. 18 rooms, $$. Mastercard, Visa and American Express cards are accepted. The Ubud Inn is set out in a rice field.

Okawati Sunset Bungalows, Monkey Forest Road. 12 rooms, $$. The hotel is divided into two sets of rooms, located on either side of a small rice field and has a marvellous view of the sunset.

Hotel Puri Saren Agung, PO Box 15, Ubud (tel. c/o Hotel Tjampuhan, 28871). 17 rooms, $$. This palace, on Ubud's main street, lacks royal splendour. The rather dark rooms are in small renovated houses where past kings of Ubud used to receive and lodge palace guests.

Campuhan and Penestanan

This area is quieter than Ubud, with marvellous vistas. Visitors will need some transport, or a good pair of legs for the walk into town.

First Class

Hotel Tjampuhan, PO Box 15, Denpasar (tel. 28871, 95137; telex 35428 UBUD IA). 40 rooms, $$–$$$$ (higher rates include full board). Mastercard and Visa cards are accepted. The artist Walter Spies was so enamoured of the lush river ridge just north of the Campuhan River bridge that he built a small house and swimming pool here in 1932. After Spies' death, the former royal family of Ubud, who owned the land, built the hotel around the original house and pool.

Ulun Ubud Cottages, PO Box 333, Denpasar (tel. 26414, 35136; telex 35190 SUNDT IA). 16 rooms, $$$–$$$$. No credit cards are accepted. This peaceful hotel in Sanggingan, off the Ubud–Campuhan road, was built into a slope leading down to the Campuhan River. Terraces belonging to the more expensive rooms have unobstructed views of the rice fields across the ravine.

Moderate

Ananda Cottages, PO Box 205, Denpasar (telex 35428 UBUD IA). 35 rooms, $$. All major credit cards are accepted. Set back off the Campuhan–Sayan road, Ananda sits among rice terraces, with hanging vines and bright purple morning glories.

Murni's Houses, inquiries c/o Murni's Warung, Campuhan. Four units, $$–$$$. American Express cards are accepted. Up an impressive flight of stairs, on the ridge above Murni's Warung and overlooking a rice field are two brick cottages. The room and suites have verandas; the single-unit cottage is large and homely.

Modest

Londo and Pugur Homestays, inquiries c/o Nyoman Londo and Wayan Pugur, Campuhan. Five bungalows, $. No credit cards are accepted. To reach these delightfully simple homestays, climb a steep flight of stairs just north of, and across the street from, the Tjampuhan Hotel. A sharp turn to the left leads up a slope behind the warung to a narrow path between rice terraces. The houses, owned by Londo and Pugur—Young Artists-cum-farmers—are right in the rice fields. Each bungalow has a downstairs bedroom and an upstairs sleeping loft. If Londo and Pugur cottages are full, a good number of other small homestays are scattered along the same pathway.

Sari Homestay, inquiries c/o the Beggars' Bush Restaurant, Campuhan. 14 rooms, $. No credit cards are accepted. This modest hotel's rooms are split between a low building next to the Beggars' Bush restaurant, overlooking the Campuhan bridge, and a compound of bungalows atop a hill across the road.

Arjuna Inn, inquiries c/o the Blanco Art Foundation, Campuhan, (tel. 22809). Ten rooms, $. Clean and spartan accommodation. Great views. Bathrooms with traditional Balinese toilet and mandi.

Sayan and Kedewatan

Some of the nicest cottages in the area, with some of the island's most spectacular views, perch along the Ayung River Ridge in Kedewatan and Sayan.

First Class
Villa Ayu, inquiries c/o PT Amandari, Kedewatan, Ubud (tel. 33336). 30 rooms, $$$$$. Site of Bali's most expensive small hotel. Overlooking the Ayung River Valley, individual wantilan-style bungalows with marble floors and teak interiors are the work of architect, Peter Muller, who designed the Bali Oberoi. The most expensive bungalows, each with a private pool, rent at $500 a night.

Kupu Kupu Barong, Jalan Kecubang 72, Denpasar (tel. 23172, 35663; fax 231 72). Six bungalows, $$$$$. Visa, American Express and Diners Club cards are accepted. Each bungalow has a terrace with superb views. Interiors, however, almost live up to the view: wood-framed glass patio doors lead to rooms with marble-topped antique tables, canopied beds and enormous baths. Still prices are too steep for degree of finish and service.

Moderate
Cahaya Dewata, inquiries c/o I Wayan Munut, Kedewatan, Ubud. 22 rooms, $–$$$. Visa cards are accepted. Just down the road from the Kupu Kupu, also on the ravine's ridge, this multi-level hotel offers some of the most spectacular vistas in Bali. The swimming pool and restaurant jut out nearly to the end of the precipice.

Cahaya Dewata Country Villas, inquiries c/o KCB Tours, PO Box 337, Denpasar (tel. 51094,51517; telex 35218 PURWA IA; fax 51497). Six rooms, $$. This hotel, the original Cahaya Dewata, shares with its southern neighbour a mind-boggling view. Accommodation, in three large houses with no electricity or hot water, is at once spartan and well serviced.

Modest
Sayan Terrace Cottage, PO Box 6, Ubud. Six rooms, $. No credit cards are accepted. These simple, but attractive, two-storey brick cottages are just off the Ayung River

road, and are hidden down a path below a field, behind a warung a few kilometres south of the turn-off for Ubud. **Homestay Ayung River**, a rather inexpensive losmen, is on the same path.

East

Padang Bai

Rai Beach Inn, Jalan Silayukti. Four rooms, $. No credit cards are accepted. Across the road from the beach at its eastern end, where jukungs lie in the sand, the Rai Beach Inn is a pleasure at its low price.

Sedana Kerthi Beach Bungalows, Jalan Silayukti. Seven rooms, $. No credit cards are accepted. Tiny rooms are clean but bare, save for narrow twin beds with scrawny mattresses, but what can one expect for under $4?

Candi Dasa

In 1983, there were four losmen in Candi Dasa; now, there are close to 40. Since all of Candi Dasa's hotels are located on about two kilometres (one mile) of the beach road, it's easy to shop around a bit before settling on a room. At the time of writing, the losmen to the west and east of town are the most peaceful. Unless otherwise noted, hotels in Candi Dasa do not have hot water or telephones. All rates include breakfast unless otherwise noted. Snorkelling, scuba diving and fishing can be arranged at most hotels.

First Class

Rama Ocean View Bungalows, inquiries c/o Ramayana Hotel, PO Box 334, Denpasar (tel. 51864). 30 rooms, $$$ (breakfast not included). All credit cards are accepted. Rama Ocean View is probably the best of a new breed of hotels with Western-style facilities.

Moderate

The Water Garden, c/o T.J.'s, Poppies Lane, Kuta (tel. 35540, 51093). 12 cottages, $$. No credit cards are accepted. Although it is not on the beach, this is by far the most handsome of Candi Dasa's lodgings. Individual white brick cottages, with marble floors and sliding woven split-bamboo doors that open out onto teak verandas, spill down a hillside etched with lily ponds and waterfalls.

Nelayan Village/Balina Beach, Manggis, Karangasem, inquiries c/o Balipro, 129 Jalan Tandjung Sari, Sanur 80227 (tel. 88451). 41 rooms, $–$$$. American Express, Diners Club and Visa cards are accepted. Balina Beach, a few kilometres west of Candi Dasa, is set well away from the road and by itself next to Desa Nelayan, literally the fisherman's village. The site is idyllic: rice fields stretch back to Gunung Agung, while steep hills define the bay. This is the place to come for snorkelling and diving. A diving shop, run by Saniko and Tanti Darwin, arranges outings all over the island, from the nearby Blue Lagoon to the shipwreck at Tulamben.

Puri Pandan, PO Box 6, Amlapura (tel. 169). Ten rooms, $. No credit cards are accepted. Squeezed between two other small hotels, the beach-front Puri Pandan makes the most of its crowded space.

Pondok Bamboo Seaside Cottages, PO Box 5, Amlapura (tel. 169). Ten rooms, $. American Express cards are accepted. Pondok Bamboo's beach-front bungalows stand out for their comfort and pleasant interiors.

Ida Homestay. Six bungalows, $. No credit cards are accepted. Ida Homestay is part of Candi Dasa's old guard, but it has kept up with the times.

Modest

In Candi Dasa, all the cottages in this category rent for $12 or under, except during high season when rates go up a bit.

Puri Pudak Bungalows. Eight rooms, $. No credit cards are accepted. Just as the main road heads to the right out of Candi Dasa towards Amlapura, a small dirt road cuts through a palm plantation to the beach. In the past few years, some simple losmen have been built here. Puri Padak, with its tiny cottages queuing back from the beach, is one of the prettiest and most quiet—and gives one a sense of what the rest of Bali used to be like.

Bayu Peneeda Bungalows. 14 rooms, $. No credit cards are accepted. Bayu Peneeda, on the beach just before the turn-off to Tenganan, is a hidden pleasure with its new white brick and tile-roofed bungalows with comfortable patios and unobstructed views of the water.

Flamboyant Bungalows. Eight rooms, $. No credit cards are accepted. On the beach, just east of Bayu Peneeda, Flamboyant offers clean, thatch-roofed bungalows with large rooms and patios.

Pelangi Bungalows. Nine rooms, $. No credit cards are accepted. Adjacent to Flamboyant, Pelangi's split gate leads to basic bungalows just a few steps from the beach.

Sideman and Iseh

Sideman Homestay, Sideman. Four rooms, $–$$. Guests may stay in the bungalow with its expansive view, or one of the other simple, less expensive cottages. The surroundings are quite idyllic; the food is simple; the service is charmingly gracious.

Bangli

Artha Sastra Inn, Jalan Merdeka 5 (tel. 179). 13 rooms, $. No credit cards are accepted. If the idea of staying in a former royal palace appeals more than the idea of comfort or quiet, try the Artha Sastra Inn, opposite the market in the centre of Bangli. Outside walls are bright with a recent paint job, but rooms are dim and dank.

Central Mountains
Gunung Batur Region

Puri Astina Inn, Kintamani. Four rooms, $. No credit cards are accepted. For a quiet night's rest, where there's nothing to do but stare at the volcano and relax, try the Puri Astina, on the western rim of Batur's caldera. The inn has large rooms with patios that offer views of Gunung Agung on a clear day.

Toya Bungkah Art Centre. $. No credit cards are accepted. This is actually a dance centre, started by a Sumatran poet and painter, that doubles as a conference centre and hotel. Right on the edge of Lake Batur, near the hot springs, it is a good base from which to climb Batur.

Bedugul Area

The air is so cool, and the views are so fine around Bedugul and Lake Bratan, that it's worth a night's stopover to enjoy them.

Bali Handara Kosaido Country Club, Pancasari, PO Box 324, Denpasar (tel. 28866; telex 35222 JANSTAUR DPR). 37 rooms, $$$–$$$$$. Golf rates: $33 green fee (25 percent discount for hotel guests), $3.50 caddy fee. Club rentals available. Bali Handara offers Bali's only 18-hole world-class golf course, plus a driving range and other sports facilities. It has a spectacular view of Lake Bratan.

Bedugul Hotel, Bedugul. 45 rooms, $. All major credit cards are accepted. The bungalows are built high above Lake Bratan and enjoy its cool breezes. Only one, however, has a direct lake view.

Lila Graha Bungalows, Candikuning. 15 rooms, $–$$. No credit cards are accepted. The one room worthy of note here is the suite, which has a view of the lake, two patios—one of which is glass-enclosed with comfortable bamboo sofas, a fireplace and modern bath.

North Coast
Lovina, Kalibukbuk and Anturan

The building boom has hit the north coast, bringing with it an ever-widening choice of accommodation and ever-rising prices. However, most lodgings in the area are simple, inexpensive losmen with minimal comfort, friendly staff and generally contented, unfussy off-the-beaten-track travellers. Hotels dot a stretch of the beach road; all are on or near the black sand beach. Rates include breakfast.

Moderate

Banyaulit Beach Inn, Kalibukbuk, PO Box 17, Singaraja (tel. 41889). 20 rooms, $. No credit cards are accepted. By far the most comfortable and attractive of the area's hotels. The open-air restaurant serves some of the best fish in Lovina. The hotel's owner, Agus Wianto, speaks English well and helpfully provides information.

Nirwana Seaside Cottages, Kalibukbuk (tel. 41288). 37 rooms, $. No credit cards are accepted. Nirwana is tree shaded with a high shrubbery and a path leading to the wide beach. Grass-roofed bungalows with bamboo walls are separated by brick pathways and hedges.

Aditya Bungalows, Lovina Beach, PO Box 35, Singaraja (tel. 41059). 51 rooms, $. American Express cards are accepted. Aditya's highest priced rooms are worth considering for their comfort and quiet location.

Samudra Beach Cottage, Lovina Beach, PO Box 15, Singaraja (tel. 41272). Ten rooms, $. No credit cards are accepted. Samudra, at the quiet western end of Lovina, enjoys a wide and sunny beach-front view.

Modest
Most of the rooms in this category are under $10 for a double.

Baruna Beach Cottages, Kalibukbuk, PO Box 50, Singaraja (tel. 41252). 25 rooms, $. No credit cards are accepted. What makes Baruna Beach appealing is its relatively secluded beach-front location and its extremely friendly staff.

Permata Cottages, Lovina Beach, Jalan Ahmad Yani 99A, Singaraja (tel. 41653). 15 rooms, $ (with additional high-season supplements). No credit cards are accepted. Ignore the grimy inner court and ask to see the tile-roofed cottages: they're right on the beach, clean and pleasant.

Astina Seaside Cottages, Kalibukbuk, PO Box 42, Singaraja. 12 rooms, $. No credit cards are accepted. It's a short walk to the beach from the quiet Astina Cottages, which are shaded by a small palm grove.

Air Sanih Beach

Puri Sanih Bungalows, Air Sanih Beach. 20 rooms, $. No credit cards are accepted. The Puri Sanih sits all by itself on a deserted beach 22 kilometres (14 miles) east of Singaraja.

West

Kerambitan

Puri Agung Wisata, Kerambitan, inquiries c/o Rai Girigunadhi, 3 Jalan Majapahit, Lumintant, Denpasar (tel. 23661), or the office, Jalan Surapati 7, Denpasar (tel. 23399, 23602). 12 rooms, $$–$$$. Visitors at the Puri Agung stay in the family compound and share the communal sitting areas and meals; this is a good chance to experience Balinese life first hand. Rooms vary widely in quality. One impressive room is a former bridal chamber with a carved Balinese bed and garden bath. Request rooms in the Saren Tengah. Lunch, dinner and entertainment can be arranged.

Balian Beach

Balian Beach Club, Lalang Linggah Village, Balian Beach (just east of the Balian River, near Surabrata—a 15-minute drive west from Soka beach, or east from Selabin). Five rooms, $. The better cottages, with rattan walls and small patios, overlook the Balian River. This place is a particular favourite with surfers.

Mask of a manis *(sweet) character*

Restaurants

There is as broad a selection of restaurants as there is of hotels, particularly in the resorts where new dining spots open every month. The restaurants listed below are a few favourites. All serve breakfast, lunch and dinner, unless otherwise noted. Restaurants have been divided into four categories. Prices listed are the average cost for a dinner for two, with appetizer, main course and dessert, but no drinks.

◊	Under $5
◊◊	$5–9
◊◊◊	$10–20
◊◊◊◊	Over $20

At the more expensive restaurants, tax and service of 15.5 percent are added. Tipping, though not required, may be used as a form of thanks for particularly fine service.

Sanur

Ask expatriates in Sanur to recommend a good, nearby place for dinner and they'll probably say 'Kuta'. Still, there are a few restaurants in Sanur which serve fine meals at premium prices in delightful surroundings, and some warungs that prepare tasty, inexpensive meals in friendly and comfortable environments.

One of the former is the luxurious **Hotel Tandjung Sari's restaurant** (◊◊◊◊), off Jalan Tandjung Sari, overlooking the beach. The restaurant serves well-prepared Indonesian and European entrees. On Saturday nights, a rijsttafel is served, following an 8 pm legong performed by some of Bali's best dancers; all this costs $25 per person. For Italian food by the sea, **La Taverna Restaurant** (◊◊◊) off Jalan Tandjung Sari is a local favourite. Pizzas are light and crisp, and calzones more filling. Other Italian dishes include pasta, fish and chicken. **Telaga Naga** (◊◊◊◊), across the street from the Hyatt, is known for good, and sometimes excellent, Singapore-style Chinese cuisine. It is also Bali's prettiest restaurant, with tables scattered among two small bales and a central pavilion with coral walls, all surrounded by a lotus pond. Chilli crabs, fried squid and *kangkung*, a local green, are particularly good. Reservations are recommended. The **Kul Kul Restaurant** (◊◊◊) is a pleasant surprise in a quiet, frangipani-scented garden. Grilled chicken, sea bass, and *ikan pepes* (fish stuffed with Balinese spices) are recommended. The best pizza in Bali, and the loudest acoustic guitar rendition of *Feelings*, is found at **Da Marco** (◊◊◊), a large and breezy restaurant in banjar Semawang. Good steaks, too. Dinner only. A jewel of a place for inexpensive, informal Indonesian and European dining is the **Sanur Beach Market** (◊◊), right on the beach with some tables set in the sand, just to the south at the end of Jalan Segara. Try the fresh grilled fish, and *sate* (kebabs served with peanut sauce) cooked over charcoal.

For real budget dining, try a few of Sanur's better warungs, such as **Wayan's Warung** (◊), set incongruously in the shadow of a big Baygon insect repellent sign on Jalan Tandjung Sari, and the green–blue painted **Warung Pojok** (◊), which is easily spotted on the corner where the Ngurah Rai Bypass intersects the road that becomes Jalan Pantai Sindhu.

Kuta

Dining in Kuta is as much a scene as it is a culinary experience. One chooses a crowd and an atmosphere, along with the food. The following is a small sampling of recommended eateries and drinking places. **Poppies** (◊◊) on Poppies Lane was one of the first tourist restaurants on the island and continues to be one of the most popular, with jungle-like gardens and hearty steaks, grilled chicken and fish. Indonesian dishes, however, are nothing special. Also on Poppies Lane, **T.J.'s** (◊◊), Bali's premier Mexican restaurant, has good food, icy margaritas and great music. A good-natured and efficient staff serve impressive portions of nachos and guacamole, steak kebabs, tacos and tostadas. It's hard to decide which is better at **Made's Warung** (◊◊◊), the food or the atmosphere. All day long, street-side tables are filled with avid people-watchers, drinking some of Kuta's only cappucino and indulging in some of the island's best banana cake. From 9 pm on, the place is packed with a lively combination of expats, *garmentos* (as garment manufacturers and designers are known locally), full-time drifters, part-time tourists and Kuta cowboys. Food is eclectic and satisfying. Tops are: Made's mother's nasi campur special; grilled prawns with fried potatoes and salad; Thai beef salad and Thai shrimp soup; sashimi. It's on Jalan Pantai Kuta.

For breakfast, **Za's Bakery and Deli** (◊) on Jalan Legian is a delight. Fresh juices range from watermelon to strawberry; there are pancakes with mango and coconut, and even bagels, served with locally made cream cheese and Balinese smoked salmon. Lunch and dinner menus feature an extensive salad bar and fresh pasta from Denpasar. In front of **Indah Sari** (◊◊), fish, lobster and crabs are displayed on brightly painted miniature jukungs filled with ice. Patrons make their choice, have it weighed and priced, then walk past the kitchen to a room full of tables. It's on Jalan Legian. Across the street, **Mini** has a similar bill of fare. **The Pub** (◊), with its proud collection of British and Australian flags, is a haven for those homesick for Sydney. There are good hamburgers, sate, the usual jaffles and live music three times a week. Find it on Jalan Buni Sari. **Sawas Dee Thai Cuisine** (◊◊) has batik-covered walls, reggae music, fresh fruit daiquiris, prawn curry, fish in banana leaf and fried noodles with squid. Located on Jalan Pura Bagus Taruna, Legian. Dinner is served only. Across the street is **Marilyn's Warung** (◊◊), a cafe/club that has quickly built a lively following that gathers for late dinners of crepes and Greek salads, breezy gossip and cool jazz. Recently, **Double 6's** (◊◊) has hired a new chef who is very clever with salads, pastas and desserts.

Ubud and Campuhan

Restaurants in Ubud are as much for hanging out in, as for eating. There's no rush here to order, to pay, or to serve. The **Cafe Lotus** (◊◊), on the perimeter of a royal lotus pond, is also a great place to people watch. Some good finds on the menu include *bebek tutu* (traditional Balinese roast duck), whole seasoned fish, and a variety of fresh pastas, and the chocolate cake, which is legendary. **Murni's** (◊◊) has been a favourite since it opened in the mid-70s, with its lush view of the Campuhan Gorge and good food. You can have a full breakfast all day, enjoy a good hamburger with a milkshake, or opt for Indonesian dishes, but save room for dessert. Across the Campuhan bridge is the **Beggars' Bush** (◊◊). The combination plate, with sate, gado-

gado and rice, is a pleasing primer to Indonesian food. **Wayan's** (◊) on Monkey
Forest Road in Ubud has good traditional Balinese food, served in a no-nonsense
manner.

Sayan and Kedewatan

A must is a late lunch or late-afternoon drink overlooking the Agung River Valley at
the **Cahaya Dewata Hotel's restaurant** (◊◊). Never mind the lack-lustre food; drink
in the view. Just north is the **Kupu Kupu Barong Hotel's restaurant** (◊◊◊), with
Westernized Indonesian food and a slightly more sheltered version of the same
spectacular view. Smoked duck is a specialty.

Candi Dasa

Despite a large number of eateries in Candi Dasa, the variety is disappointing; mostly,
nasi goreng, fried chicken and sandwiches, served in open-air restaurants with rickety
chairs. An exception is **T.J.'s Cafe** (◊◊), a branch of T.J.'s in Kuta. With its quiche,
guacamole, roast beef salad and pate, the garden restaurant stands out among its
roadside neighbours for tasty and eclectic food, and a sophisticated selection of soft
jazz and contemporary music. Another good choice is the **Pandan Restaurant** (◊◊), a
fine place to nurse a drink through the sunset, and to stay afterwards for an Indonesian
or Chinese-style fish or vegetarian dinner. Also on the beach, **Pondok Bamboo Restaurant** (◊◊) is worth a visit for sunset drinks and dinner of roast duck, steamed tuna
or Chinese vegetarian dishes.

Central Mountains

Right at the edge of Lake Bratan, under a tin roof, is the **Bratan Restaurant** (◊)
which serves a daily buffet of some 30 Indonesian dishes from 12.30–4 pm. Or
visitors can have à la carte Indonesian meals at **Sindhu Srama Restaurant** (◊◊) and
watch from lakeside tables as water-skiers skim by.

North Coast

Very casual, slow, friendly service leaves plenty of time to swap tales with long-term
travellers. The seafood selection in the local restaurants depends on the day's catch.
Try the restaurant at the **Banyaulit Beach Inn** (◊◊). More lively is **Khi Khi** (◊◊), a bit
west on the main road in Kalibukbuk, serving seafood and vegetarian dishes. A
popular warung is **Marta's** (◊), at the western end of town. The four-table establish-
ment has a long and detailed menu offering many varieties of fried rice, rice pudding,
sandwiches, pancakes and toast. It is best for breakfast or lunch.

Useful Addresses

Tourist Information Offices   Airport Information Centre, Ngurah Rai International Airport, Tuban (tel. 51011 ext. 147). Badung Government Tourism Office, Jalan Surapati 7, Denpasar (tel. 23602, 23349). Bali Government Tourism Office, Jalan Raya Puputan, Renon, Denpasar (tel. 22387). Government Tourist Information Building, Jalan Bakung Sari, Kuta (tel. 51419; telex 35276).

Foreign Consulates and Consular Agents   Australia: Jalan Raya Sanur 146, Tanjung Bungkak, Denpasar (tel. 35092/3). Federal Republic of Germany: Jalan Pantai Karang, Sanur (tel. 88535). Italy: Jalan Padanggalak 3, Sanur (tel. 88777, 88372). Japan: Jalan Moho Yamin 9, Renon, Denpasar (tel. 31308, 34808). Sweden/ Finland: Segara Village Hotel, Jalan Segara, Sanur (tel. 88407). United States: Jalan Segara 5, Sanur (tel. 88478). All other nationalities should contact their embassies in Jakarta.

Doctors   Call the consulates for recommendations.

Modern wood sculpture

Glossary

adat	traditional customs and law
Agama Bali	the Balinese Hindu religion, otherwise known as Tirta Agama, Religion of Holy Water
alang-alang	elephant grass used for roofs
aling-aling	wall just inside entrance to temple's inner courtyard
bade	funeral tower
bale banjar	double-roofed neighbourhood clubhouse
bale	open-air structure, traditionally with grass roof supported by posts
balian	traditional island healer and seer
banjar	neighbourhood association, run by men, to direct local affairs
banten	offerings; *banten tegeh* are metre-high offerings of fruit and cakes
bapak	mister; father
baris	warrior dance
barong	a huge, maned, mystical creature that appears in dances and protects villages
bemo	small public transport van
Bhoma	wild-eyed son of earth who appears atop temple gates and frightens away evil spirits
Brahma	one of the Hindu Trinity, which also includes Wisnu and Siwa
Brahman	the highest caste in Bali, originally the priests
canang	woven-palm offering
candi bentar	split gates leading to temple
cili	small hourglass figure symbolizing Dewi Sri, the rice goddess
dalang	shadow-puppet master
desa	village
dokar	pony cart
endek	Balinese cloth
gamelan	any one of the island's orchestras

gang	alley
gerinsing	double-ikat cloth woven in Tenganan, endowed with magical powers
geriya	Brahman compound
gotong royong	communal work for communal benefit
gunung	mountain
ibu	madam; mother
ikat	handwoven fabric, tied and dyed before weaving
jaba	outside, demarking an area outside the temple; outsiders, either the Bali commoners or foreigners
jalan	street; to walk; *jalan-jalan*, walking
jam karet	rubber time; the operative notion behind scheduling—it's flexible and you should be too
jeroan	inner temple sanctuary
joged	social, flirtatious dance set to the music of the gong kebyar
jukung	small outrigger sailing canoe
kabupaten	one of eight regencies or counties in Bali
Kawi	ancient Sanskrit-based language
kebaya	tight-fitting blouse worn to ceremonies
kepala desa	village chief
kori agung	gate leading to inner courtyard of temple
keris	serpentine sword, often used in ceremonies
Ksatriya	second-highest caste, originally the warriors
kulkul	a split hollow log beaten to call neighbourhood to meet, to sound alarm and so on
legong	one of the island's most graceful dances, performed by three girls
lemak	brightly coloured patchworks of palm
lontar	palm-leaf books
losmen	small hotel; guesthouse
lumbung	bow-roofed rice barn
Majapahit	great Hindu Empire in Java during the 14th century; priests, nobles and artisans fled to Bali after its collapse

mandi	to bathe; a tub from which water is ladled out for bathing
meru	pagoda with black sugar-palm roof (up to 11 tiers), dedicated to high gods
ngaben	funeral
odalan	temple festival
padi	rice growing in field
pantai	beach
paras	soft volcanic tuff used for statues
pasar	market
pedanda	Brahman priest
pemangku	temple priest
pendet	welcoming dance
penjors	arching bamboo decorations with palm-leaf tassels
potong gigit	tooth-filing ceremony
pura	temple
puri	palace
raksasa	giant temple guard
Rangda	witch with wild eyes and pendulous breasts who appears in dances
sawah	field
subak	irrigation cooperative that coordinates planting, harvesting and water-temple festivals
suci	to be clean, holy
Sudra	Bali's commoners
tingklik	small bamboo xylophone
tirta amerta	holy water used in symbolic cleansing
topeng	mask; or mask dance
Triwangsa	Bali's three high castes
wantilan	traditional two-tier roofed meeting hall
wayang kulit	shadow-puppet play
Wesya	third-highest caste, originally the merchants

Food and Drink

arak high-octane distilled palm brandy

ayam chicken (often *goreng*—fried; *bakar*—baked; *panggang*—roasted)

babi guling roast pig

bebek tutu smoked Balinese duck with herbs

Bir Bintang an Indonesian beer

brem sweet rice wine

cap-cay stir-fried vegetables

gado-gado vegetable salad with peanut sauce

ikan fish; *ikan pepes*, fish wrapped in banana leaf with spices

kaki lima pushcart, literally 'five feet', three wheels and the two feet of the vendor

kopi coffee, served like Turkish coffee with small grains and lots of sugar; *kopi susu*, with sweet condensed milk; *kopi pahit*, without sugar

mie goreng fried noodles

nasi cooked rice; *nasi campur*, a miniature rijsttafel of rice with small portions of meat, chicken, vegetables; *nasi bungkus*, a takeout version of nasi campur; *nasi goreng*, fried rice

lawar Balinese slaw of vegetables, and sometimes meat with fresh blood, prepared for celebrations

rijsttafel the Dutch rice table, with a score or more dishes

rumah makan dining hall

soto ayam chicken soup

tuak alcohol made of fermented juice of flowers, coconut, sugar palm, or rice

warung food stall

Useful Indonesian Vocabulary

Many Balinese dealing with travellers speak English and a number of other languages in addition to Balinese, the three-level language of the island, and Bahasa Indonesia, the Malay-based language of the country. Visitors' attempts to speak Indonesian are appreciated, and necessary once in the villages; a good pocket guide to Indonesian is *How to Master Bahasa Indonesia* by A M Almatsier (Penerbit Djambatan); also, *Indonesia Phrasebook* (Lonely Planet Publications). The following are some words and phrases that one comes across frequently in Bali. Pronunciation of Indonesian is relatively easy, but there are differences from English. A few to remember: pronounce *c* as *ch* (as in chart); *j* is often *y* (as in yes); the final *e* is *ay* (as in say); *i* is *ee* (as in see). Thus candi is *chan-dee*; banjar is *ban-yar*; bale is *bah-lay*.

Numbers

1	Satu	11	sebelas
2	dua	12	duabelas
3	tiga	13	tigabelas, etc.
4	empat	20	dua puluh
5	lima	30	tiga puluh, etc.
6	enam	100	seratus
7	tujuh	1,000	seribu
8	delapan	10,000	sepuluh ribu
9	sembilan	1 million	satu juta
10	sepuluh	1.5 million	satu juta setenghah

Greetings and Pleasantries

yes	yer
no	tidak
not yet	belum
good morning	selamat pagi
good afternoon	selamat sian
good afternoon (late)	selamat sore
good night	selamat malam
good-bye (to person leaving)	selamat jalan
thank you	terima kasih

Recommended Reading

Bali, for such a small island, has inspired a large number of books. A short list of some of my favourites follows.

Art, Culture and Anthropology

Bandem, I Made and de Boer, Fredrick Eugene. *Kaja and Kelod: Balinese Dance in Transition* (Kuala Lumpur: Oxford University Press, 1981). A study of Balinese dance by the head of STSI, and by the professor of theatre studies at Wesleyan University, USA.

Belo, Jane. *Balinese Temple Festival* (Seattle: University of Washington Press, 1953). A stroll through one of Bali's most colourful occasions, guided by a perceptive and lively scholar.

Belo, Jane (editor). *Traditional Balinese Culture* (New York: Columbia University Press, 1970). Collection of articles including a look at how children are treated in Bali and a short piece on dance by Colin McPhee.

Corvarrubias, Miguel. *Island of Bali* (Singapore: Oxford University Press, 1972 reprint). New issue of 1938 classic by the Mexican painter who lived and worked in Bali during the 1930s.

de Zoete, Beryl and Spies, Walter. *Dance and Drama in Bali* (Bhratara: Oxford University Press, 1973 reprint). An early and very intelligent look at Balinese dance by the German painter Spies, long-term resident of Bali and originator of the kecak dance, and by the dance expert de Zoete.

Djelantik, A A M. *Balinese Paintings* (Kuala Lumpur: Oxford University Press, 1986). In addition to being a prince and a medical doctor, Djelantik is a fine observer of art.

Eiseman, Fred B Jr. *Bali,Sekala and Nisakala* Vols I, II and III (1985–8: self published). An exhaustive, quirky, informative collection of articles by this former science teacher and long-term student of Bali; it is an encyclopedia on just about everything Balinese. In Volume I is the best description of the Balinese and Tenganan calendars written for the layman. Soon to be published by Periplus Press, Berkely; until then, books may be ordered from the author, 13025 East Mountain View Road, Scottsdale, Arizona 85259, USA.

Geertz, Hildred and Clifford. *Kinship in Bali* (Chicago: University of Chicago Press, 1975). Two eminent anthropologists' study of the intricate social system in Bali.

Holt, Claire. *Art in Indonesia: Continuities and Change* (Ithaca: N Y Cornell University Press, 1967). Still one of the best books on ancient and contemporary Indonesian arts.

Kempers, A J Bernet. *Monumental Bali* (Arnem, Holland: Van Goor Zonen den Haag, 1977). An excellent guide to Balinese archaeology, as well as to walks around the island.

Lansing, J Stephen. *The Three Worlds of Bali* (New York: Praeger Publishers,

1983). An anthropologist's special look at a 'special case' island; it contains a fascinating discussion of water temples and their role in rice cultivation.

McVey, Ruth T (Editor). *Indonesia* (New Haven: Southeast Asia Studies, Yale University Press with HRAF Press, 1967). A thoughtful collection of articles by outstanding scholars, including Mantle Hood on music.

McPhee, Colin. *Music in Bali* (New Haven: Yale University Press, 1966). A definitive study on the Balinese gamelan.

Neka Museum Guide to the Painting Collection (Bali: Yayasan Dharma Seni Museum Neka, 1986). As much a guide to Balinese art as it is to the museum.

Ramseyer, Urs. *The Art and Culture of Bali* (Oxford: Oxford University Press, 1977). Photographs of Balinese art, folk art and everyday objects well keyed to comments on society, religion and philosophy by the head of the Indonesian Collection at the Basle Museum of Ethnology.

Wijaya, Made. *Balinese Architecture: Towards an Encyclopedia*, Vol I and II (Bali: self published, 1980). The most complete and the most humorous look at Balinese architecture to date. Copies are available from the author, care of Tandjung Sari Hotel, Sanur, Bali.

Fiction

Baum, Vicki. *A Tale from Bali* (Singapore: Oxford University Press, 1986 reprint). Written in the 1930s by the author of *Grand Hotel*, it is a gripping, melodramatic novel based on the 1906 puputan of Badung.

The Mahabharata and Ramayana, retold by William Buck (New York: Mentor/New American Library, 1976). Versions of the two Indian classics that are, in the words of Ram Dass, delightful.

Toer, Pramoedya Ananta. *This Earth of Mankind* (Australia: Penguin Books, 1982). One of Indonesia's great novels, written while the author was incarcerated with other political prisoners on Buru. It is the first of a quartet on the liberation of Indonesians from Dutch colonialism. At present the author's books are banned in Indonesia.

History

Friederick, R. *An Account of the Island of Bali*, Vol 8 of the *Journal of the Royal Asiatic Society of Great Britain and Ireland* (London: Trubner and Co., 1876). One of the West's earliest accounts of Bali. Fascinating to see what has and hasn't changed.

Crawford, J. *A History of the Indian Archipelago* Vol II (Edinburgh: Archibald Constable and Co., 1820).

Geertz, Clifford. *Negara: The Theater State in 19th Century Bali* (Princeton, N J: Princeton University Press, 1980). The anthropological jargon can be a bit tedious for the layman, but the vision of Bali as a state of organized spectacle is intriguing.

Hanna, Willard A. *Bali Profile: People, Events, Circumstances (1001–1976)* (New York: American Universities Field Staffs, 1976). A very readable and vivid account of Balinese history.

Natural Sciences

Wallace, Alfred Russel. *The Malay Archipelago: The Land of the Orang-utan and the Bird of Paradise* (Singapore: Graham Brash (Pte) Ltd, 1983 reprint; first published 1869). In the mid-19th century, Wallace headed out from England to explore what is now Indonesia. Eight years later, he returned with a collection of 125,000 specimens (including, by his own count, 3,000 bird skins, 20,000 beetles and butterflies) and a 'weak state of health'. In between, he covered more than 14,000 miles by foot and canoe. The book of his travels is dedicated to his friend and contemporary, Charles Darwin.

Et Cetera

Almatsier, A M. *How to Master Bahasa Indonesia* (Penerbit Djambatan).

Bali Apa Map (Federal Republic of West Germany: Nelles Verlag). The most thorough and up-to-date road map available.

Dalton, Bill. *Indonesia Handbook* (Chico, Calif.: Moon Publications, fourth edition, 1988). Dalton has written what he calls 'a gypsy's manual for the cheapest places to eat and sleep'. A lively book, filled with odd bits of information and personal asides. Banned in Indonesia, because of some political comments.

Lueras, Leonard and Lloyd, Ian. *Bali: The Ultimate Island* (Singapore: Times Editions, 1987). The ultimate coffee-table book, with photos by the photographer of this guidebook.

Neinhold, Margit. *Indonesia Phrasebook* (Australia: Lonely Planet Publications, 1986).

Newson, Sarita J. *Indonesia Bali Plus* (Bali: Bali Tourism Promotion Board, 1987). An informative book with all Bali's hotels, restaurants and guides. May be ordered from Taksu Inc., PO Box 385, Denpasar, Bali.

Owen, Sri. *Indonesian Food and Cookery* (Jakarta: P T Indira, 1983 reprint) The basics of Indonesian cooking.

Santasa, Silvio. *Bali Path Finder* (Bina Wistra Tourist Office).

Skrobanek, Detlef, and Charlé, Suzanne. *The New Art of Indonesian Cooking* (Singapore: Times Editions, 1988). Traditional spices and modern cooking techniques. Glossary of ingredients is most useful, even if I do say so myself!

Index